Pattern Changes

Rose Assier Parvin

Also by Rose Parvin:

Pattern Change Programing
Creating Your Own Destiny

Answer to Humanity

Power Balance Therapy

Programing Excellence

Humanity Held Hostage

Preventive Family Therapy

Beyond Patterns

Self-Programer

Upcoming books by the author:

Love Patterns

Family Patterns of Excellence

Patterns of Leadership

Patterns of Creativity

Pattern Changes

Universal Laws
of Success and Spiritual Excellence

Rose Assier Parvin

Universal Publishing Company
California

Library of Congress Catalog-in-publication Data
Parvin, Rose Assier,1950
Pattern Changes : the universal laws of success and spiritual excellence / Rose Assier Parvin.
P.   Cm.
ISBN   1-885917-08-2
1. Success.   2. Spiritual life   I. Title.
BJ1611.P276   1995
248.4--dc20   95-130
                                                    CIP

Printed in USA

I would like to specially thank my children, Ellie and Shaun whose love has inspired me to reach beyond reality. They are the shareholders of my joy, my pain, my experiences, my personhood, my vision, my mission, and my success and spirituality. They are the power balance within me, beside me and most often, beyond me. Special thanks to: Cari Hoyt who In 1985, when I gave her a sketch of my logo in pencil, materialized what has been representing my life mission Pattern Change, Preventive Care and Peace creation. Mark Jenkins who has religiously filmed my seminars, Figge Family who have photographed all my activities for the past fifteen years including all the book covers. Marlo Brooke, the precious editor. And I thank my clients and interns and the treasure of experience and trust they have given me. And my friends, who dare to share power.

Contents

About the Author

Rose A. Parvin, *author of nine groundbreaking books in one year, is on a lifetime mission to create patterns of health success and spiritual excellence in family and the society with revolutionary methods and vision beyond psychology. Mother of two children of 21 and 17, international consultant, speaker, guide, marital and family counselor, is psychotherapist and the founder and director of Parvin Center for Patterns of Excellence in Newport Beach and Beverly Hills for thirteen years. Graduate of Chapman and California State Long Beach Universities, Rose believes that being a person is more than being someone's daughter or wife, or belonging to a piece of land. Home, to Rose, is where there is peace, compassion, dignity and universal laws of Pattern Change and Power Balance beyond any predetermined labels that mold the multidimensional patterns of humanity.*

A Mind-Body-Spirit Evo-revolution

My life experiences have led me constantly to question and seek the truth to create balance within mySelf and with the people I love. I have watched many compromise the truth of their Self for societal awards, or live in poverty of mind and action and at the mercy of others all of their lives. Only because they were told that success was evil. And the result was the choice of corruption of the soul in some, and despair and decay of the mind in others. I believe there should be neither. There is no reason to compromise the Self in any life dimensions. Only when we have all the options are our choices truly sincere. I believe, success is the prerequisite of excellence and a universal spiritual freedom. We live in a history making time when the lack of recognition of the power of Self and the intentional efforts to oppress its knowledge will cost us far more than our jobs, our relationships or our accumulated wealth. We live in a time when we must know who we are and question where are we going and where have we been. Or else others will lead us to their own destination. Throughout my life, I felt a universal connection: a commonalty of natural laws and the swing of their pendulum with that of my inner being and others. As the day and night need Power Balance and equal existence, as the universe goes through its own crisis of trial and turbulence to calmness and greatness and a spiritual excellence, we follow its footprints. To learn, to nurture and to respect our Universal Laws is the path to success and spirituality that lacks limitations to Self Ignorance, addiction to religion and commitment to corruption.

I will share with you the Life Patterns which I call the Universal Laws; the Power Balance of Patterns that embrace the Collective of Success and Spiritual Excellence; a process and a path where we can begin but never end; a process that clears the clouds of self-doubt and lack of strength; where we no longer need to live by the societal pressure of competitive rivalry, nor by its critical labels that keep us as objects who, in order to operate, need a permit. I will introduce to you different laws, inner laws that you will learn to respect. I will guide you towards a different path and a different pattern of life and living where you no longer feel compeled to rebel. You can become whole and within your own wholeness you can become a part of everything that is near. I don't like to alphabetize things to underestimate your intelligence. We have been given far too much fast food in this society and that is one of our biggest problems. But I would like to make you think, question, analyze and make your mind work, followed by your body so that they can comfortably embrace your precious soul. From my own mind into my body, my soul and my emotion, I process guiding you to getting closer to yours. In my journey I may seem philosophical, societal, spiritual, scientific or just use plain common sense. We are all multidimensional and we have been looked at and treated as flat and one dimensional for too long and that is one of the reasons we never reach true solutions. Our inner Self is the only place where lack of boundary and openness means wholeness. I trust and hope that you will read me and will not feel intimidated by the differentness of my presentation as I try in my own humble existence to close the gap between us, and present patterns of life where we can all equally live in success, prosperity and universal spiritual excellence.

My mission and intent, is to guide you to your purpose. There is a misunderstanding, a myth that Spirituality means giving up Self and all that matters. There is even a bigger misunderstanding that Success can always be achieved on top of the tower that we have made from the bodies that we have walked upon without regret. Simply put, *Success is not a sin; it is the prerequisite of spiritual excellence.* I believe that you can have it all right here on earth, and there is no such a thing as "some can and some can't." It is a sad truth that not all of us are born in the same prosperous land or in the same luxurious homes or of the same popular color, race or gender. But we are all inherently born with the same power and capacity for pattern of freedom-responsibility and right to equal opportunity. And if we have been raised with life patterns that allow us to blossom with all of our Self, we can change; that is a Universal Law that governs me. We all change; it is the *direction* of our change that we choose consciously, or unconsciously. That is why we must be aware.

Success and Spiritual Excellence

My mission is a global one, without bias or prejudice against one land or another, one race or another, one gender or another, or one belief system or another. Many may take that as a sign of a lack of compassion. On the contrary; it takes true compassion to create Universal Patterns that embrace all whom there are to love, not just a selected few, and to have loyalty to humanity globally, and to the universe that holds us all within, not just to a piece of land. By challenging our sensationalized addictive attachments we can develop Patterns of Excellence and arrive at true Universal Spirituality and success. I believe that not even the most justified beliefs are spiritually true if claiming them includes the harmful process of discriminating against certain people. I would like to believe that by seeing the larger picture of a global unity that advocates peace, harmony and excellence in the path of humanity, we can begin to make the changes necessary within Self, essential to making any changes in a larger capacity.

You can have it all: Success and Excellence. I would like to share with you the belief that we can truly have it all in this world. There should not be exaggerated sacrifices for happiness, in this life or after. In fact, the principles are one and the same. Once we step inside, within Self, we become even more capable of stepping outside of Self and connecting fully with others. Once we can step outside of ourselves and engage in a larger purpose, a mission or an intent to serve society or humanity in one way or another, then our own personal purpose and intent blossoms right before our eyes, bringing us the fruits that we were once taught would be impossible to bear simply because we lacked *then*, the vision we have learned *now*, and the desire to look further. Having a purpose outside of exclusive profit-and-loss sheet of existence not only brings us closer to our true Self (for we must step within in order to see a clear path to getting out of ourselves); it brings us closer to our goals, with more consistent and powerful Life Patterns of Joy and Mastery, leaving us no time for preoccupation with corruption or despair. The existence of Self as a whole will enable us to create the power within in order to transcend a non-selective compassion and thus develop a sense of oneness, a unity, a universally spiritual connection, of becoming Part of a Whole, universal grace, and of its parental wisdom and nurturance. Psycho-Universal Spirituality will not only strengthen the Power of Self and move us away from the traditional image of Self as powerless, sick, dependent, worthless, guilty, shameful, and thus envious, prejudiced, and hateful, but will also move us towards health, societal success, and power, universal compassion, inner peace, prosperity and thus excellence within Self and in humanity. The dimensions of Self have always been introduced separate from one another. One has either been able to have an independent clarity of the mind and assertive claim of the body, or an options for spirituality which has meant a focus outside of Self, relying upon an external entity. I believe in Power Balance within all dimensions of existence; a whole Self versus a divided Self; connected with others and creating abundance and prosperity, connected with Self and the Universal Power embracing us all, creating internal and universal peace and harmony.

One

My Self, Your Self

The Knowledge of Being

Our Self is the most significant, precious, powerful and capable tool we need in life in order to succeed beyond our wildest dreams and to excel beyond our destined path. To search within the inner Self and to nurture and master this complex, mysterious, unclaimed land, we must become curious and search, question, analyze, and take notes of the possibilities and patterns of being and doing. We truly have an exclusive Gem of life in our own bare hands, although we look restlessly outside of our Self for the tools to fulfill our life wishes and fantasies. To search ourSelf is the only way we can find another, intimately; to touch ourSelf is the only way we can touch another, softly; to capture ourSelf is the only step to reaching out and forging life at its best, joyfully, successfully and spiritually.

Is there anything in life that does not involve you and your Self? Do you have a business or relationship or family where you can keep your Self out of it and feel that you are being fulfilled? There is no such a thing. Anything in life that goes on within you and around you directly affects Self; your inner being with all your dimensions. So if you don't want to hear about your Self, then you are telling me that you don't want to feel life, nor be engaged in it. But nonetheless, you will still feel life and be engaged in it, only instead of you initiating your Self and utilizing your inner dimensions for life success and spiritual excellence, *others* will initiate your Self for their own personal gains. That is why most people, no matter how intelligent, spend almost all of their lives in despair. Their inner Self, their entire system within, is actually working for others via the programing and influence of others. This is not because they are not capable of power and success and excellence; they were simply told that it is selfish to have a Self. They were told so by others who had enough of a Self to preach to them and to benefit by their feelings of selflessness and shame and guilt.

Have you ever known anyone to succeed at a business they knew nothing about? They succeed only once they learn all the back alleys leading to the sources that give them the clarity about their business. After selective search, brief analysis and use of deductive reasoning to arrive at the right answers, and once they have explored all the possibilities, anyone can reap the fruits of their labor successfully. Most people begin from the bottom and work up to the top. They start from the company mailman to the CEO to companies merging with other companies. But all along they have known one thing clearly: they are special beings and no matter what they do, they will succeed. And they have gone through life giving it all with joy, at every moment of living.

The key to success is building strong foundations based on not only the *Knowledge of doing*, but also the *Knowledge of being.* Our entire lives are based on doing: doing the right things, saying the right things, going to the right places and presenting ourselves with the right tools. Our *being:* who we are and how we relate to our Self, suffers beneath all the doing. In fact, most of us become experts at teaching others *how to be* by *doing* magical things and saying magical phrases. But when it comes to *being*, we fall short for our Self and others. This is the problem today with our society where no one is truly responsible for their *being*, so what they are *doing* has no substance or value in essence. We have learned that we can even tell machines to do whatever we want them to do. We know their being consists of a bunch of wires that at any moment we can pull out or unplug.

The wealth we hold within, in our Inner Being. By the same token, when we reward and praise people for *doing*, we are neglecting and ignoring them for their *being*. Most often, especially as parents, we punish and reward the acts of our children as if their actions are their entire Self, leaving their true being unnourished and unloved inside. And we do the same thing with ourselves. We expect from ourSelf to do everything perfectly and to present a perfect picture to the world while neglecting and starving our guest of honor, our precious Inner Being: our Self. Our inherent, equally deserving and worthy Self is our true wealth and to discover it, we must consistently dig within. But we don't have to be content with just that if we don't want to. We can accumulate wealth the way we are accustomed to or the way we wish and the way that gives us financial and societal security, stability and flexibility. But in all aspects of life where we seek success, the prerequisite to accumulating societal recognition and power involves digging into the wealth of our Inner Being.

Societal Success: prerequisite for Spiritual Excellence. In the process of Pattern Change, which is my therapeutic tool for providing Societal Success and Spiritual Excellence, Societal Success is a prerequisite for achieving higher, more solid and powerful Patterns of Living and Spiritual Excellence in our everyday lives and in humanity: a life where we can have it all, right here in our inner heaven on earth and in the land of freedom and opportunity. The process of achieving material success teaches us dimensions of our Self unknown to many. The choices we make in life after many things we have dreamed of have been made available to us are choices of our true Self. What we learn about Self in interaction with others when our benefit or loss is at stake is a statement of our integrity. What we are willing to do when a great deal of our effort and the fruits of our labor are at stake determines our true substance and capacity.

Patterns of Self

Self Patterns are patterns we learn as children. There are many Self Patterns we adopt or later on choose. Our Self is capable of many patterns, shades and dimensions. We can be anything we want to be and we can always change our patterns to whatever dimensions we focus on expanding. As long as we are aware of the Self within us and embrace our Self with knowledge, we can change any pattern to our chosen direction, and we can create our own destiny. If we live in a dark whirlpool of ignorance and our Self Knowledge is *blocked*, we live at the mercy of those who program our lives and we lose control of our destiny. Life is a playground as well as a testing and trial of Self Dimensions. We polish our Self as we experience life. But if we blindly accept the patterns given to us as children by role modeling and societal and parental expectations, we sacrifice our Self to blind loyalty and we become stagnant. Self-sacrifice is not a virtue, it is ignorance. We don't have to sacrifice ourSelf in order to be helpful to humanity, nor do we become saints as we allow others to use us as objects.

We need not victimize ourSelf in order to be good; there is no such thing as turning the other cheek. That is a misinterpretation of wisdom, and an outdated demonstration of goodness, as is the abuse of power by intimidation and control and creation of fear and distance. Besides, I don't see many of those who advocate the interpretation to be turning their own cheeks at present. My professional and personal experience has been that many people who seem kind on the surface and willing to Self-sacrifice have been detrimental to the welfare of many people's lives and happiness. They have far too much anger inside, from being victimized to be healthy or constructive to anyone. There is also a great deal of payoff and investment in being a victim: far more of an investment than in being a responsible person. The victim will ultimately become the bully and get even, and while acting as victim, never has to make an effort in being responsible. Furthermore, the victim feels like a winner inside while acting like a loser just to punish others. Many people kill themselves to get even with those who have hurt them. This imbalanced and round-about way of winning is a pattern of those who would do anything not to get caught being imperfect. They are terrified of risking approval and would rather die than not be liked, while hanging on to those who are risking, taking responsibility for being who they are, and ultimately succeeding. They have also been taught that by being a victim they can get their way more easily.

We will talk about the Patterns of Self in this book and what they will bring, in detail. I think we all have gone on with our lives neglecting the Self within. Now it is time to stop the past programing. Enough is enough and we are much too smart to leave our precious Self for the whims of those who want to use us as objects and keep us barefoot, Selfless, helpless, powerless and shamed. It is a dangerous time we live in. Every Tom, Dick and Harry has learned to cleverly manipulate us to their way and to use their toxic influences to manipulate the rest of the universe. If not for our own sake, for the sake of our children we cannot go on silently, neglecting our own inherent power within. So we will explore our Self and we will explore the dimensions of Self and the unlimited cast of characters we have existing within us, waiting to be nurtured, recognized and discovered. Honesty and Transparency of Self are patterns that may seem uncomfortable initially. We have all learned the game of being politically correct and societally flat and single-dimensional so that we don't get stamped, judged and axed out automatically. Some have been so oppressed that as soon as they come out they become obnoxious, fulfilling their nightmares and our fears. But to be transparent and honest in a wise and compassionate pattern to ourSelf as well as to others makes us safe for our Self and others. Honesty comes from reaping the fruits of our labor, asserting our rights to what we deserve, appreciating the hard work and the rights of others. Because only when we have worked hard towards our own success can we appreciate that of others and focus more on reaping our own fruit instead of waiting to be fed by others.

The Chosen Self

Patterns of Success are the chosen patterns of the individual. These patterns are directly related to Cognitive-Emotional Power Balance and to the level of clarity of the cognitive vision of success that is created by the individual. There is no conflict between patterns of success and those of spiritual Excellence. In fact, they are all part of a linear process of Excellence. Success is prerequisite for true excellence, for choice creates true clarity of the mind.

We must learn about the victimized Self within us. We must change the patterns of this neglected child of innocence to that of love, nurturance and power balance in order to polish our robbed and silenced abilities and utilize them towards ultimate success and excellence. I will not work with you towards a fast answer of shallow success, but instead towards that which possesses the depth of the sea and the boundary of the universe. This definition of success can carry you throughout your life in all dimensions and is not just a presentation that will leave you lonely and empty on one side while giving you the pretense of success on the other.

In my book entitled *Answer to Humanity* I explore my vision of an excelled society and the tools of achieving it. For any individual who grows enough to care about their Self, the first thing they will recognize and want is a healthier, more excelling environment for their children and for their Self. Those who fight people who try to clean up the air are just as ignorant in the art of raising their children with love and caring about their Self. No one would argue about the basics of life necessary for the flowers of life to blossom happily and healthily except those who are blind to the nurturance and compassion to their own Self as well as the children of humanity. True success does not lie upon making millions of dollars on top of our children's victimized souls and bodies. It lies upon wanting to be empowered and to empower those around us, equally and simultaneously.

We deserve a society that breathes excellence and heightened spirituality, leaving us free to focus our inner power to learn about the life of abundance and patterns of humanity. This, my friend, is not an idealistic vision. It is a tested remedy as an answer to end individual and universal crisis, pain and suffering. The governor of a home and a state and a country all have one thing in common; they are put in a position of responsibility for the people who trust them, and they had better like children. I have been there and have helped others govern their estates and countries with compassion and kindness, yet with firmness and strength. If you think power struggle at home can destroy spirits, just watch C-Span and you can find the same patterns and principles that exist in every little home. Those who care about people embrace the life of every living entity with words of compassion. Those who don't try to oppress and control every breath or, if not careful, make Freudian slips that uncover inner imbalance, lack of Self, pain and confusion.

A Universal Law of Success. It is the same pattern of connection in both a little house and in Congress; those without a Self cannot accept others, and those with a Self embrace all life and its different shades. The process of obtaining Self needs willingness to trust: not trust in me, but trust in your Self. Through Self search, exploration and analysis of all dimensions of our inner world we can heal, sow, and ultimately reap the fruit of a chosen, not predestined, life of abundance. For that we must focus on ourSelf. True success of anyone depends directly on how she or he is perceived and nurtured by the environment that embraces the person. And vice-versa, the success of any society depends heavily upon the wholeness of the individual Self of its members. The feelings of *wholeness within each part* is just as significant as the *togetherness and connection*. This is one of the

Universal Laws of Success and Spiritual Excellence that I have found from my professional and personal life experience.

The Feared Self

Fear by itself may seem harmless to others and at times to ourSelf. But fear can become the most toxic pattern we hold within. Fear is a multidimensional pattern of a victimized Self: a Self that has been controlled and used and abused and neglected. It is a Self that instead of empowerment and nurturance, has been treated with manipulations of power and has been kept in degrees of ignorance. It is a Self who is afraid of Self and a Self who has been criticized against the Self. The victimized Self has no free time to attend to success and spiritual excellence because it is filled within with patterns of jealousy, hatred, envy, bigotry and prejudice.

Fear is the most devastating pattern blocking all success and prosperity. Fear motivates us against Self-Knowledge, creativity, exploration, curiosity, questioning and a clear life path of joy and mastery. I have had to fight fear ever so consciously on every level of my growth and Self Search. There are times when our fear is so strong and powerful that we choose not to give ourSelf the chance at being. We go on pretending and walking like zombies and clones of society. But once we taste the sweetness of the bitter fruit of our Self-Knowledge, once we see and feel far more than ever, we will not want to save the bridge of returning. We will burn it with all the evils of ignorance behind us that want to grab us and throw us into the hole we were living in and leave us at the mercy of ruthless misinterpretations and perceptions of how we should be living.

But it all had a positive and worthwhile purpose up to the moment of our life when we no longer need to hang on to the cause once that affected us. Pain and suffering is always a mystical and magical pattern offered by the universal wisdom and nurturance that watches over us like a good parent of love and compassion in order for us to see the difference between good and evil so that we want and choose to move towards the light. Thus, pain and suffering *is* healing, except when we panic and want to shortcut the pain without exploring and questioning. I have had much pain and suffering throughout my life. When I look back I have much reason to complain. But how can anyone complain about the causes of her inner richness and clarity and all that has brought her freedom and liberty? All that I could hang on to as a reason to feel victimized has already been proven to me as life patterns that have made me more resilient and more flexible as the playful and unpredictable swings of the universe approach me. I feel the balance of powers of strength-flexibility, vulnerability-firmness in harmony with each other working together within me, enabling me to change the adopted patterns of my upbringing; they have given my Self back to me. The imbalances of my past within me had to be overshadowed by the patterns of cognitive, emotional and spiritual strength and self-discipline: patterns I have consciously chosen that will remain with me for the rest of my life, embracing me with multidimensionality as a clear and universal being, guiding me through a path of life: a constant process of joy and mastery. That is why I respect the strength embedded within each and every individual, as well as nurture the fragility that folds them within its thin shell, leaving them open and vulnerable to toxic victimization. I have learned theories and tools that have served me and many others whom I have guided through a path of coming out of the painful victimization of lack of Knowledge of Self, of gaining a universal Self and power balance: traveling through the path of excellence in spirituality.

The Victim Self

I will share with you the common patterns of success and failure briefly here, and I will explore them in detail throughout the book. The common patterns of failure and success both lie within a person. In fact, sometimes one is the other side of the coin of the other and are collectively gathered within one single toxic pattern of Self perception.

Self perception. We have been taught to see our Self as either beautiful, powerful and strong, or as unworthy, shameful and helpless. The latter phrases are ingrained within many of us through religion. Even now, when they sell us religion as freedom and transformation, they are still saying we don't matter and our feelings and rights don't count. I am not talking about faith or spiritual beliefs. I am talking about being fed the kind of language and perception that keeps us down so that others can collect. When we are innocent children and others are already building empires on top of our bodies and planning their properties as the number of bodies increases, we grow up without a true Self, without recognizing and acknowledging that we are powerful and worthy beings and we have a right to be in charge of our own destiny. As children, before we are old enough and tall enough and wise enough to know about our being, they have already planned for us the business of our doing. In so many ways we end up carrying the cross for humanity. Nobody truly knows how to teach us about our Self worth, so instead of getting angry at themselves for being ignorant they blame us by calling us sinful and unworthy. We, as children, are also the only ones sensitive enough to feel the pain of injustice: a sensitivity for which we are also to blame. But we also carry the cross because we reap the fruit of ignorance of others; we live in the midst of the toxicity they create.

The Adopted Self

The Adopted Self consists of all patterns of influences of our past: religion, parents, teachers, society and all the patterns that do not belong to us; it is the Self who is supposed to *do* it right, without even having the slightest notion of what is truly right. The more the forgotten Self wants, the less the adopted Self recognizes and acknowledges her presence. The Adopted Self is the collective of all the critical patterns programed within the critical entity, the institution that takes its own life and begins to live inside of each and every person, demanding obedience, and pushing the free spirit of the person into rebellion; the institution that is modeled after the old and outdated institution of religion.

The best guides are those who respect the individual's choice of path for themselves once they connect with their own Universal Self. A Universal Self is what parents must obtain in order to be healthy parents for their children and prevent their *critical pattern adoption*. Parents are not to blame. The rigid rules and influential expectations of their dogma distorts their vision of parenthood. They end up putting their own children on the cross as a result of obedience and blind loyalty to authority. Consequently they lose their children; they rebel. The pattern of rebelling against their Self long after they leave home, is the burden when they carry when they live with an adopted Self.

The Institution of Self

For just a moment, put the societal controversy on a back-shelf in your mind and begin to feel that you are a whole person that does not belong to any slogan or institution except the reformed institution of Self within you: almost the only institution that you can be sure any money or time or attention you give to it will be utilized with unconditional compassion. The institution of Self is reformed. It is now the most worthy cause and the most legitimate source of focus and effort. Without Self there is nothing else. All the external causes we worship and spend our lifetime to pacify will not do a thing for us if we don't adhere to the person we are told to hold prisoner inside, with us acting as guard. We have been taught to become the most ruthless guard of all in the precious being of our Self: a pattern that must be deleted from our life file.

Pattern Inventory for Self Search. I must exaggerate in order to awaken you from your deep sleep as a selfless individual. If you think the following is valid, spend a few moments, grab a note pad and take inventory.

When was the last time you nurtured your Self? Or do you know what Self-Nurturance means?

When was the last time you took a look at yourSelf in the mirror and said "I love you and I am truly proud of you"?

When was the last time you postponed significant demands of your authority figure or even your friends to spend some time with yourSelf in silence?

When was the last time you believed in yourSelf, completely?

When was the last time you believed in your own decisions, independently?

When was the last time you did not second guess yourself?

When was the last time you did not blame yourself? I don't mean repeating what you have learned about your Self from others and saying: "I am so stupid. It is always my fault." I mean a healthy Self Search and examination and taking responsibility for your share of doing.

When was the last time you let your hair down and relaxed?

When was the last time you took a walk on the beach or at your favorite park?

When was the last time you said to yourSelf "I have done enough"?

When was the last time you felt free from obligations and instead of having to live life, chose what you wanted to do?

When was the last time you stood up for your convictions without ambivalence or guilt?

When was the last time you said "no" to something that looked very seductive and tempting just because you wanted to preserve your integrity?

When was the last time you felt whole without having to have a chaperon in life?

When was the last time you loved someone just because you liked them, not because you needed support, comfort or company?

When was the last time you wanted to do something and felt confident that you could?

When was the last time you did something that you knew would not look good to others, but felt good (without compromising your integrity)?

When was the last time you slept comfortably?

When was the last time you made love passionately?

When was the last time you controlled your impulsive anger?

When was the last time you laughed at your own foibles?

When was the last time you cried out your inner pain, loudly?

When was the last time you walked out of a destructive situation before it was too late?

When was the last time you tolerated delay of gratification?

When was the last time you listened, patiently?

When was the last time you gave for the sake of giving?

When was the last time you gave and received, gracefully?

When was the last time you forgave yourSelf and those who need forgiving?

When was the last time you responded flexibly to the imperfections of others?

When was the last time you initiated loving another, compassionately?

When was the last time you looked at the world through rose colored glasses, seeing everyone as deserving the best, equally?

When was the last time you felt your life had meaning?

When was the last time you were clear about your purpose, and had a purpose that included something larger than just daily living?
When was the last time you knew what made you hurt or angry?
When was the last time you could express your anger, calmly?
When was the last time you didn't feel you had to be the party clown?
When was the last time you didn't feel you had to cater to everybody to be worthy of loving?
When was the last time you felt life was a worthwhile adventure and you were the free bird taking off for exploration?
When was the last time you focused within and asked yourself what you felt was puzzling?

The list can go on forever. But these few are enough for now. If you are short of answering even one of these questions, you are not nurturing the Self within. That is how important it is to succeed in the business of Self before you can go on succeeding in the business of life. For the *Self is what life is*, and *living is what the Self does*, by merely *being*. You can choose to change any pattern from this moment on. You have taken the first step by acknowledging Self and beginning your process of Self Search. Your process can be a solo process as you become your own Self Programer, or it can involve another guide. If you choose to work with others, you may not agree with everything they say, just as I am sure you will not agree with everything in this book. I am a controversial person. But almost without exception I have found that those who have come to know their Self or have the courage or desire to, will find many messages I have formulated worth considering and focusing on. Only those intimidated by words of Self and Self Knowledge, who want control and power over others without much growth of their own try hard to find reasons for denial. If someone doesn't know how to see and demand their right then it is easy to take it away from them. There is no one worthwhile who can agree with everything about everyone. And there is no credible person who says everything that everyone will like. That is another key to success. You must *be* yourSelf, and words of wisdom or nurturance that stem from your inner beliefs and thoughts will touch others, or at least someone. Words that stem from clear Self are the golden path to universal truth. Words that stem from a confused person without a Self point us to universal evil. Thus, the path to *yourSelf* is the same path leading to *universal truth*. On this path, whatever you choose to do will be a success. Success means doing something well for others. And no one can do something well for others long enough if they don't know and have a solid foundation of Self.

Root to Success
Path to Spirituality

Self and Success. Self Search will give you Self, and I will be your guide on the path. Don't worry. I will also give you the ten commandments to success. I have been teaching these for years. But if you bear with my boundaryless vision that tries to simultaneously stay on earth and fly to the end of the universe, you will learn to do the same. It means absolute freedom of power and energy where you can be exactly where your vision wants you to be. I am a very practical, matter-of-fact and down-to-earth person who has a very deep philosophical and spiritual dimension. It helps to have a simple life that is meaningful and rich within. Yet comfort is bought with effort and societal success and it is a tool with which to enhance our connections. That is the easy part to attain in our journey and I promise that I will take you there. Fasten your seat belt, we are going to fly. But the take-off may be a bit rough. After all, we have been walking all our lives and are just learning how to flap our wings.

Self and Spiritual Excellence. Everything in life begins from within. The pain we go through in life in our process of searching for Self is the root to success and spirituality. There are no real or true answers that we can hang on to externally. The best guide can only teach you to find what you already possess within that may be temporarily lost or forgotten within a deep sleep. I too had to find my Universal Self. I too had it within, all along. But with all my sensitivity, I must say that there have been long periods when the Self within me was lost, forgotten, or in a deep sleep. I have shed tears as large as the ocean to cleanse my soul and to see clearly. Tears are the best healing tools anyone can offer; they are tools that come from within. They truly wash away the residue of pain and anguish. There have been times in my life when I felt like I was breaking. They still come and go once in a blue moon, yet I now know that I will survive even a hurricane. The more we can be flexible, let go and allow the waves to embrace us as tightly as they please, the more powerful, and the less hurt, bruised or dis-eased we become. The only thing that frightens me at this moment of history is the toxic power of ignorance and lack of Self Knowledge that threatens the survival of our great society and the future of our children and humanity. Although I have learned to remain objectively detached during my clinical training and at this time in my life I have no pain of my own, I still catch mySelf carrying the pain of the souls who are in silence, suffering. For as long as there is one person suffering in silence, there will be no victory for anyone, ultimately.

Thick Shells of Denial

In my work with individuals, when the thick shell of denial is destroying the person inside yet presenting a successful picture on the outside, I find mySelf gently but firmly guiding the person out of the Toxic Patterns of Need to Control that stem from fear of abandonment and rejection, while guiding the Self towards more power balanced, healthy and fulfilling patterns. However, at times of crisis when all family members are affected and their well-being and safety is at stake, a less process-focused approach, an immediate and painful break of denial by rocking the tower of unquestioned authority to save all concerned is taken.

Old patterns must be deleted from a life file in order for new, more progressive patterns to be copied and saved. Old patterns are there because new patterns have not been taught. People want change and are now willing to come out of their shells of denial, for they are in the tremendous pain of victimization stemming from the Power Imbalances of our society. The bully and the victim are both suffering, yet presenting their pain, differently. The resistance is nothing but fear and the lack of knowledge of what to do to create change. The more the fear, the thicker the wall of denial, the more the need for creating chaos before a true and lasting order can take its place. There is a shared denial that lies within the fact that chaos is presented in a false frame as "order."

I have never seen more chaos and absence of boundary in my life, under the name of democratic freedom and the rights of people, as leaders freely infringe upon other people's rights and privacy. Is this civilization, or are we falling downward into the chaotic times of the medieval ages? Who, in your analysis of our societal calamity, should take responsibility? The parents who are told what to do in their own bedrooms? The family that is dictated to about what will be? Or the child who seems enraged by it all and cannot live any longer in denial by acting happy and carefree? Or can we dare, once and for all, to search for the real roots to our problems of humanity? If we dare, perhaps we can help our children and family exist on some level of consistent societal harmony. And who knows, we might even be able to make a difference in our society and share the power on the path to advance humanity.

Both sides of Pendulum of Imbalance suffer. There is no true peace of mind for those who rape as well as for those who have been raped; for those who have abused as well as those who have been abused; and for those who have robbed as well those who have been robbed: of their privacy, of their sacred right to boundary, of their credibility, of their right to their body and mind, and of their right to Power Balance and equality. Again, the Patterns of Suffering are the same. The Patterns of presentation take different forms each time. Many times, in working with individuals and families, I must ignore the rejecting, careless, and arrogant omnipotence flashing on the surface of the person while the little neglected child is crying inside. I don't buy the old Patterns; I am not controlled or intimidated by them. Both sides of the pendulum suffer. We must find out how and why, so that we can put an end to this societally enabling toxicity that has spread its wings and cast a shadow over people's lives.

The Universal Law of Power Balance

Power Balance within means when all the patterns we have inside, no matter how different, live in harmony side by side, and we don't have to deny one for the sake of nurturing another. Just like our relationships outside of ourSelf when abundance and prosperity for one must not cause victimization of the other, it is the same law in the relationship between our own inner patterns. For example, a calm and spiritual person can have a successful life without compromising her or his principles. Power Balance in relationships and families means to be heard, respected and accepted, equally, regardless of role or position in the relationship or family. And of course we can have a Power Balanced society in which all people are treated equally and can live next to one another in harmony.

The key to success is to adhere to this Universal Law of Power Balance: to nurture all that surrounds you, non-selectively and without monopoly, and to embrace and accept all of your Self without fearing knowledge or experience. The same law holds true for successful relationships and societies. All crisis stems from the turmoil we feel inside. From family crisis to the universal crisis we witness on the streets, it is caused by the imbalance of the power within us and in our society, and the imbalance of power causes chaos in the universe. I began teaching and training *power balance therapy* and *pattern change programing* twelve years ago for the purpose of creating power balance within individuals and in their connection with others within the framework of their relationships. I have raised my children with the law of wisdom and nurturance that I have learned from the Universal Parental Law from which I feel a constant embrace. It has not been easily achieved, as with any pattern of substance.

Within my own family, we reap the fruit of our labor. There are no occasions of Power Struggle because there is no need to fight for equal respect and power; it is an accepted right for all. Everyone's welfare, feelings and rights count, regardless of age, gender or authority. It has created miraculous harmony between us. I have made it a general pattern to give my children as much respect as my most honored colleagues and friends. Consequently, they respect themselves and respect me. I have watched people suffer within, relationships fall apart and families act like enemies while they cared about each other deeply. I was sensitive to the experiences of Imbalance within each person and the roots of those experiences. I was also sensitive to the imbalances that occurred in the relationships, and the root they stemmed from, which was always the Imbalance of Power: within themselves, with others, and with society.

I share the pain. I come from the people's pain and have shared the depth of Imbalances and Block Patterns of Life: a pain I not only understand, but also cherish. It has only been through my own pain and suffering that I have come close to those I love and to those who come to me with trust. We can never see through the flesh unless we have lost our own thick layers of skin. My life has never been easy, but I don't believe that anything of value ever comes easily. Anything of value needs nurturance and polish: that includes ourSelf, our relationships, and our family.

And I share the joy and mastery. I have reached a path in my life that I myself never imagined. I don't mean recognition or wealth; although I have had my share of both among colleagues and in my community. I mean a power balance where I feel both connected with my loved ones and whole within. Balance in life has always meant everything to me. It has been a lifetime search and it has become a miraculous reality. By balance, I don't mean the societal box of "normal" that at times seems the least of what the "norm" represents to me. I am referring to what the mind, body and spirit feels; from a little Persian girl to a woman who created her own destiny in a country where even the natives have a tough time succeeding as she experienced in her filed; a woman whose children are whole, yet connected to their family, with a mission of embracing humanity. I feels she has everything I need within, and have healed mySelf of the addictions, indulgences and dependencies my world had imposed upon me. My life joy after searching in the world with all its magnificent seductions is to walk to the beach and feel the sun above me and the sand beneath me. My ambition, after preparing a powerful groundwork of prosperity, is to die feeling that I have made a difference and to live with joy and dignity. For me, it was fighting for my choices and finally having them all, that brought me peace within and made an honest woman out of me. Or so I clearly believe.

Self-Programing
Success and Spiritual Excellence

In my Seminars on Success and spiritual Excellence I teach the steps to Self-Program Power Balance and Excellence towards a Universal Self. As our own guides and Life Programers, we must learn to rise above Self Ignorance and experience the wisdom and nurturance we possess inherently within. We must work towards polishing our inherent forgotten patterns of strength before we take away the Adopted Patterns that over the centuries have been imposed on us. In my books entitled *Self-Programer* and *Programing Excellence*, I teach in detail how to become your own guiding light and that of your family and children. We must delete from the repertoire of our life file the adopted chains of victimization, dependency, addiction and need for authority so that we grow up, and not remain regressed children forever. As guides and spiritual leaders, if we truly believe in people, we must assist them, however we can, to find their true Universal Self through knowledge and not keep them as whims to soothe our own addictions and fulfill our secondary gains. We don't have to lie on the couch for thirteen years to find our Self, nor do we have to walk like zombies full of drugs and medicine. As much as we can learn from others' words of wisdom, we certainly won't learn about our Self and become independent in mind and action through focusing outside of ourselves and worshipping external golden and silver gods of our own illusion, or by becoming vulnerable to anyone who claims to have godlike patterns. We have already been given the gift of life by our universal powers and we need to begin to perform our tasks with the power of the mind and body connected with our spirit.

Pattern Interruption. Regard for the core of the person does not mean lying them on a couch for thirteen years and letting them wallow in their old Patterns while we dream about our own abundance pouring from the umbilical cord of their dependency. It simply means having enough regard for the core of the person to not play games or humiliate them out of their Patterns. It means, instead, simply to honor the core of who they are, and to interrupt their old, outdated and, in the case of today's societal crisis, the harmful and habitual familiarity directed to them by Societal Programing of imbalanced power and supremacy.

Finding the victim within the bully. For those who have spent a lifetime victimizing others, I would simply guide them to the victim within themselves. For it is that victim who is somewhere stuck, on the other side of the pendulum, acting like a bully, from fear of all over again becoming *the feared.*

Transformation of the forgotten Self. The bully we hold within us must see that the victimization is, indeed, the act of continuing to be a bully, not of becoming a whole person. Connecting with the vulnerable child as well as the strength within and accepting the forgotten and denied Self, the miraculous transformation and blossoming Universal Self emerges, enabling us to not only embrace ourSelf and those we love, but with a larger purpose outside of ourSelf we can embrace the injured patterns of humanity. Following is a simple generalization of the stages of Self-Programing:

A. *Individual Balance*. The purpose would initially be Individual Balance, which brings success in the material world and in relating with others, and teaches Preventive techniques to have crisis-free Life Patterns.

B. *Power Balance of the individual and the universe*. The next level is a higher level, and involves acquiring Power Balance, which is the balancing of all dimensions existing within, enabling one to see the inner and outer world clearly, and to transform the world one wants to live within, embraced by the inherent Power Balance of the mind, body and spirit, transcended, by the powerful method, tools and techniques of Pattern Change Programing.

C. *Spiritual Excellence and Universal Embrace*. Excellence is the collective of all Patterns in Power Balance, merged with Universal Wisdom and Nurturance. It is the Ultimate Formula for Existence in joy, mastery, happiness, peace and abundance of prosperity. It is reaching the point and process wherein the individual is no longer traveling towards a personal journey, but towards a larger mission, with the intent and purpose of changing the downward direction of humanity upward and towards progression of universal peace and prosperity. I believe that when we reach wholeness within, we are embraced by the paternal and maternal power of the universe and become a whole part to the ultimate wholeness that is embracing us, within. And that is another *Universal Law of Success and Spiritual Excellence.*

Two

The Forgotten Self

The Forgotten Self. The *Forgotten Self* is the "sinned" Self according to our religious background: the one that sees, feels, desires, hopes, wishes and wants. Having lived a life where we are constantly told that we don't count and that we must be selfless as individuals in order to be spiritual beings, the Self within, our true Self, suffers, becoming oppressed and forgotten. Our Adopted Self which is programed by our religious upbringing feels guilty for being selfish and for *sinning.* The multidimensions of our being begin to shrivel and hide in each and every corner. At times we even deny to our own Self that many patterns of our being exist. When life approaches us with many patterns of itself, and when love embraces us with many of its own shades, we are not equipped to fully function. For we have spent a lifetime denying and hiding our Universal Self. In fact, we have existing within us now an Adopted Self, a self consisting of all the rules and roles and expectations of societal programing and patterns, and a Forgotten Self who shies away from unusual experiences. The Forgotten Self exists on the back shelf of our mind and subconscious, imbalanced and disconnected from our Adopted

Self. In fact, they don't see eye to eye. The Forgotten Self is the neglected child within who never became the adult: the child we must now commit to, nurture and love. This child must feel whole and must grow up before and if we want to have a child of our own. The only way children will be safe is by having adults in their life who have also been nurtured and loved.

Universal Self

Through the love and nurturance of the child within us we can polish our Self and our soul and evolve to become the Universal Self; a transformed and transcended Self; a Self that has gone through the evolution of Self Search, analysis and recognition and has found the polished soul within; the forgotten child that once nurtured, little by little grows up and grows out of the whims of the adopted Self.

The *Universal Self* is the Self free from all obligations and expectations, thus blossoming to become real, true, independent, free and responsible. It is a Self that no longer has to rebel, or be oppressed: a Self not limited and bound to one place, although she can choose to make a home where she feels best. The universal Self has no biases, no prejudices and no discriminatory patterns towards others because she no longer lives limited to blind loyalty to her birth place; she flies where she chooses to nest and her home is the entire universe. Thus her sisters and brothers are all the godlike children of humanity: a family with which she feels the closest.

The Universal Self within each and every person is free from dependencies put upon the person and thus chooses a path of independence of thought and action regardless of the position they choose to be in. It saddens me more than it frightens me, however, when I watch governmental leaders merged with prejudices, and time-inappropriate limitations of dogma. Our democratic leaders are being evaluated, judged and even discredited based on interpretations with the absence of democratic rights of every person and against the laws of our Constitution. In this charade, the true losers are the people on all sides of the aisle of life who have been used, misused and abused, just to empower corruption. The bottom line of Universal Truth is that we are all equally blessed with the inherent power of wisdom and nurturance within. We are all equally embraced by the Universal Power that holds and nurtures and guides as we open our arms to its unlimited and everlasting presence.

I believe, from personal and professional experience, that those who want everlasting abundance and prosperity must go back to their roots and give back the power and dignity to the core of their Self. This applies to couples, families and even nations, who must give the power back to the people.

The root of any person or nation. Our root is not in our language or culture, nor is it found in our skin color or the piece of land we were born on by accident. Our root is in the common core of our inherent power and dignity within: the inheritance we all equally share. Only when we recognize that we carry our roots with us wherever we travel, in whatever language we speak, can we begin to appreciate and nurture everywhere as our home for inner peace and serenity. The walls are down geographically, but in order to tear down the walls of our hearts to others, we must begin to appreciate and respect the core of all people and embrace them as members of our extended family. This is the pattern of a Universal Self: a Self without limitations of prejudice but with boundaries of unlimited ethical compassion.

Regressive Imbalance Pattern: Idealization. I have repeated myself many times, since this concept is the most significant factor in my theory: the need for equalization and balance of power. The idealization of authority by people, and the abuse of power by the leaders, has created an imbalance in the system and swung it towards a corrupt and destructive path, and it must change; the survival and power balance of every society depends on both the acceptance of responsibility by the people, and the generosity and willingness to share power by the leaders.

The backwards Swing of Pendulum. We take things in life at face value. We are told not to question authority, so we have stopped questioning altogether. We hardly analyze the past or look at the present so that we can predict the future. We hardly recognize our ability to know the unseen.

Learning from Past Patterns and history. We know that our fathers thought the earth was flat; when some wise men said that it was round, others wanted to kill them. We know that when the airplane was invented, everyone thought that gods were coming down in the big, silver animal. We know that we are far from Darwin's time, and yet we still look for the missing link that he was searching for a long time ago; as for us, we are it. The missing link to humanity is the regressive slide to its ancestors' patterns of absence of using the mind. We have done it in the past, and we have the power and inherent capacity to do it now. Maybe, just in time, we can reverse the patterns of regression and revolutionize humanity.

Create, initiate and lead, instead of follow. I believe in the mental health profession as the leading torch for the survival of humanity, and as the entity that must go through its own reform and accept shared responsibility to empower the people, not to enable them and act as another yet societal agent of our corrupt leadership. I will begin my Root Analysis of Societal Imbalances with its leading authorities. Looking at our Past Patterns as they continue into the present, with our miraculous advancements in technology, what can we come up with as the final analysis by deductive reasoning? I cannot help but imagine that if Freud, our father, was alive today, he himself would no longer be using the method of treatment appropriate for a hundred years ago. I am sure that by now he would have come up with a treatment plan that he was hoping one of his followers, after one hundred years, would have creatively initiated. I am sure, if he saw us now, that he would be concerned about our Habitual Regressive Patterns of seeking familiarity at any cost and our absence of innovativeness, let alone flexibility, as we, a hundred years later, offer our clients the same outdated and incomplete method of therapy.

The root to Toxic Pattern of blind loyalty. What are the roots to the Imbalance Pattern of rigid, fear-stricken, unquestioned blind loyalty with its devastating absence of calculative risks and initiating futuristic thoughts and actions, that can graduate us from our parental figures and take us out of the eighteenth century? If patterns of obedience and unquestioned following of authority are seen amongst professionals in the field of mental health, where there is supposedly an abundance of Knowledge of Self, then the question is, what has caused blind obedience to become such an ingrained part of individual beings? These are Patterns that, for every mental health professional sitting on the other side, are clearly "characteristics of dysfunctional families" that the profession tries to heal. But if we, the health promoters and educators, are continuing our own blind loyalties and singing rigid and unquestioned "follow" songs, instead of leading, what do we expect from the rest of society?

Deeply-rooted, engraved Programing: religion. Our religious expectations, orders and suggestions have always been blind obedience to authority, and follow with guilt, fear of punishment, and the bribe of reward. The pain of "sinning" and abandonment, not only from immediate loved ones, but from eternity, can make anyone follow for life and give up one's own rights and power of the mind, no matter how knowledgeable. No wonder even our professionals and the healers of the soul have learned to obey and follow the great Fathers of the mind. The guilt of abandoning our fathers, of becoming more aware than they, of losing love if we are different from them and from all the Patterns that Block the ordinary person on the street from becoming successful at his or her own endeavor of having a creative and independent Self, is what makes the change most difficult.

The common boundary. The common boundary and Pattern for humanity requires acceptance, understanding, love, respect, and compassion for all, regardless of differentness in age, race, color, gender or selected systems for expression of belief.

People, not objects. One of the biggest crimes of the century lies in the fact that those who are clear enough to become leaders of some sort treat the people who follow them as objects. One of the most paralyzing wounds of humanity is the victimization of individuals by their own kind.

Philosophical Self

Power of the Self as cause and effect. We all have the power to change: change our Self, our relationships, our society, our world , and our destiny. We are capable of being the *cause* and the *effect,* of bringing everything to balance and harmony. We are *whole* within; we are a *part* of the universal entity. Until we feel whole within, we cannot connect with the power that surrounds and embraces us with universal generosity.

Everything we see, everything we take at face value and try to change by medicating temporarily or denying, is only a symptom, an effect. In order to find the cause, we must have Self-Knowledge that comes from the brief analysis of the past, of the Adopted Self, of the present of our Forgotten Self, and of the future of our Universal Self.

The Formula of Balance. Every living organ has its own Formula of Balance. Imbalance in nature and society is not a natural phenomenon. It occurs as a result of ignorance and lack of practicing the principles of Power Balance.

The collective formula. I would like to share with you the collective formulas that I have found, however unpolished they may be because of their newness. Let us together begin the process, and let others come and add excellence to what seems to me a necessary step towards giving the power back to the people and preserving dignity. It is a necessary step towards cutting the umbilical cord that keeps us attached to past Programers and their habitually repetitive, regressive Programs that intentionally keep us in childlike dependency and toxic fears, inappropriate for developmentally mature adults, serving as blocks to healthy progressive Programing, incompatible with mastering the mission of peace within ourselves, with others, and in society.

Individual Power Balance. Harmony, connection, peace and congruity within all dimensions of Self creates individual Power Balance. If the Self is disconnected with the dimensions within, toxic and imbalanced power will be created. Power Balance is created if the Self is congruent with all dimensions and perceives itself as the *cause* and *effect.*

Philosophy teaches us the larger meaning and purpose behind our actions. When we separate philosophy from the tools used to understand individual beings, we ignore the meaning of existence. Even if psychology had not failed to introduce health, prosperity and success instead of sickness to individuals, it would still only add up to a shallow "how-to" workbook if it did not give the reasons "why" to the journey of existence. The truth is that we are here, and it is up to us to give life the meaning we feel we deserve on our journey. We deserve to live a life of dignity, and to be treated as such.

A sense of purpose to life. Will we have a mission and purpose of Excellence in humanity, or an animal-like existence without leaving a footprint? The choice is ours; it is the difference between ourselves and animals. We eat like them, sleep like them, make love identically, and come and go just as they do. If we do not distinguish ourselves from our animal friends by having a sense of purpose to our coming and going, we will leave the earth just like them, without making a difference or leaving a footprint for others to continue where we left off. A sense of purpose outside of the fulfillment of our basic needs enables us to see life in a larger picture, far less complex and difficult than a life in which every action determines a rigid, black-or-white sense of self-worth.

Acceptance of Self as a whole. We cannot change what we have not already acknowledged, recognized and accepted. As part of the process of Pattern Change, I believe in Self Acceptance of our whole in totality before any decisions of change can take place. We must know where we are, accept our position as it is and embrace it if we want to change and move on to another choice destination.

Power Balance: a natural Universal Law, a Life Pattern. There are inherent Power Balance Patterns within individuals and in the universe. Power Balance is the natural flow of life. It is only when the flow of natural Patterns of Power Balance is blocked that we find ourselves with unnatural Imbalance Patterns that leave us disillusioned with life and with the living. In an environment where the balance of power is equally divided and shared, there is always harmony, both within the individual and in society.

Excellence: societal, familial, individual. Pattern Change Programing can teach children the self-discipline they need to increase the capacity and flexibility that comes from experiences of pain, without inflicting pain. If we learn Patterns of Excellence, we need no longer resort to abusive tools for teaching humanity. Children can learn in childhood to be responsible, ethical, moral, and compassionate without punishment that has caused negative backlashes of rebellion and denial.

Crisis: an unnatural Imbalance Pattern. I see crisis as an unnatural Imbalance Pattern existing within us, in our connection with others and in our world. Traditional mental health experts have described crisis in teenagers as a natural state. They believe that every child will run away from home only because rebellion is part of being a teenager. I believe that there is no such a thing as a natural state of crisis. Crisis is created only as a result of Imbalance within the environment.

Patterns of Pain. Pain and suffering stems from the lack of knowledge and tools handed down to us in our Past Programs. If we raise our children with the knowledge of appropriate parenting skills, they will not have to go through the pain we experienced as children. The pain of growth is a necessary process. But the pain we go through as children as a result of our parents' lack of knowledge during their development is a pain that blocks the development of Power Balance: Power Balance that later on we must go back to create by becoming our own Self-Programers.

A prediction of our choice of destiny. Looking at Past Patterns enables us to transcend them, experience more Power Balance in our present Patterns, and move on to Excellence Patterns that will predict for us our choice of destiny.

Societal Self

Freedom-Responsibility Program. The definition of freedom in my theory of Power Balance and Pattern Change Programing is not considered in the absence of the Pattern of Responsibility. In fact, freedom *is* responsibility. One without the other will not survive. Freedom of one cannot be considered with the absence of the freedom of all, and vice-versa. Any freedom that infringes upon that of others should automatically be void. The exercise of true freedom must automatically be accompanied by sensitive consideration for the freedom of others.

Individual as symptom, not as problem. Pattern Change Therapy believes that instead of the traditional approach where physicians waited in their offices for clients to show up, then drugged them and put them away not to inconvenience the people who paid the bill, the physicians should learn the Prevention of such imbalances by changing the harsh and victimizing societal patterns. Only then will their "patients" heal.

Society as the patient. We have always taken at face value that the symptoms are the problems, even though every physician should know, theoretically, that the symptoms that occur in one member of the family are the results of dysfunction within the family. In the case where there is universal crisis, the absence of protection and safety and the Imbalances existing in every society must be warning enough for every professional to consider their patient to be society.

Change Agent? Or a Societal adjuster. The mental health profession seems to be working as an agent for society, helping people adjust to their dysfunction instead of utilizing knowledge on a larger scale and demanding change from toxic programers and leaders who cause Imbalance in individuals and society.

Societal responsibility: focus on the larger scale. This has never been looked at, on a larger scale and bigger picture, insofar as the individual is carrying the symptoms of society's problems. Just as dysfunctional families focus on safe topics, frightened of rocking the boat and uncovering the true relational problems, blaming the most innocent among the crowd, the mental health profession seems to have closed its eyes to the real problems of humanity.

Society and the Individual

Family Power Balance. Family Power Balance creates health and individual freedom as well as individual responsibility. Parents who allow their children freedom will no longer be burdened by their children. Society, too, must Balance the Power of freedom and responsibility. I tell the parents who control, overprotect and, as a result, paralyze their children, that once they allow their children freedom, they will become self-sufficient. Parenthood will then become a joyful journey, and there will be plenty of time for connections that truly create Excellence of the family. It is the same with the leaders of society.

Unquestioned Patterns. It is not the Pattern's fault that long after serving its initial purpose, we still hang on to it and never question its validity. We are Programed by our cultures and sub-cultures not to question much outside of what does not take much intelligence and utilization of our minds.

Indulgent society. We are brought up so overindulged that we give up on anything that takes a bit of thinking to figure out. Our movies spell out everything, our books leave very little room for imagination, our schools have very little time to develop deductive reasoning. We grow up with everything we want in our friendly local supermarket at our disposal.

Appreciation or abuse? It is wonderful to live in such an advanced society where things are easy to come by. It gives us options and choices different from other oppressed societies where there are neither options nor the freedom to exercise them. When we live in an advanced free country, we are given the option and time for introspection, creativity and curiosity of our inner Self, unless we become preoccupied and lose ourSelf in the power struggle of life imbalances and survival patterns of our chaotic and evolving society.

Freedom and responsibility of choice. In our culture, we have the choice of responsibility to challenge our minds and create room for decision-making and deductive reasoning. So many options and an abundance of life treasures to enjoy easily leaves us with the choice of either appreciating or abusing what we are granted. Freedom gives us an honest choice of our own and a screening of patterns we have *adopted* and those we *own.*

Societal Freedom-Responsibility Program. Societal Freedom-Responsibility not only proposes that freedom *is* responsibility, but that the reward for responsibility must be freedom instead of the punishment or fear and guilt that creates rebellion, regression and destructiveness. Toxic Patterns created by outdated Societal Programing, followed obediently and blindly by parents, have been instilled in our children. To do right by oneself and others is an intrinsic, altruistic Pattern oppressed by the authoritarianism and natural rebellion of people from the forceful demands of blind obedience to authority.

Conscious decision of inner ethics and morality. That was what had to be told to the primitive beings who had no knowledge of humanity and societal responsibility, which translates into doing right by oneself and doing right by others. Meaning, do unto others what you want them to do unto you. It is far too primitive to obey for the sake of punishment or reward. This proves the primitive and childlike nature of fanatic religion that is based on guilt, fear, punishment and reward, where there is no internal locus of judgment, nor demand for personal commitment and the conscious decision of inner ethics.

Programers, are individuals, institutions, organizations, and any entity that has had significant influences on the individual's Life Patterns. They are either chosen by individuals in various ways (i.e. by choosing to idealize an idol), or given to the individual without choice (i.e. parents.)

Programs, are life paths set by Programers of our lives. Patterns are developed throughout our lives by influences of the different Programing by various Programers. There are several types of Programs. The main or Mother Program is the Power Balance Program.

Power Balance Program (Path). The Power Balance Program is a Program of individual, relationship, familial, societal, and universal harmony and balance. It involves not just the individual but also the environment in which the individual is nurtured. The Power Balanced individual is enabled to experience fully all aspects of Self, and connects harmoniously with the environment.

Patterns. Patterns are a series of processes existing within an individual that create the presentation of the behavior we observe. The cognitive and emotional processes affect the actual patterns of an individual. For example, the person we call passive may not be passive in nature at all. She or he may only be demonstrating a behavior that stems from patterns of guilt, shame or other thought processes programed within the individual that exhibit a passive presentation. Patterns are developed and written from the programs of programers of our lives.

Shades of Patterns, are the factors that establish character patterns of a person. These factors are:

Societal influence. The perception, interpretation and reaction of society to genetic tendencies existing within every individual, and how it is handled by the family and society. For example, hallucinations can be perceived as a creative tendency, a spiritual connection, or a schizophrenic thought disorder. The way we treat the individual accordingly will have three different life impacts on the individual. One becomes Beethoven or Shakespeare, the other becomes God Himself, and the third ends up in a mental institution numbed by anti-psychotic drugs, fighting for life.

The Patterns of Life Analysis. Patterns of Analysis of the individual's life experiences are significant in the establishment of character. In cognitive theory, Aaron Beck believes that not the event, but the interpretation of the event, causes depression. I agree with Beck's deductive reasoning for solutions.

Deductive reasoning. I also add that individual interpretation has a great deal to do with the power of deductive reasoning, which I call *Analysis Pattern*. For one, deductive reasoning, or Analysis Pattern, of her life leads her to believe that she has gone through a great deal of pain to prepare for a mission of peace, while another who has given up a long time ago thinks that life has been, and always will be, unfair.

Wisdom of Power Balance. It is not so much the power of positive interpretations of life, but having the wisdom that Power Balance provides, that enables one to see the bigger picture, including tolerance for delay of gratification and a lack of need for external rewards or punishments. Power Balance allows one to experience an independence of mind and action.

Seeing a bigger picture. There is a distinct difference between a positive interpretation of things and events by giving a flowery feel to tragic happenings, and seeing a bigger picture by knowing what makes life events and experiences connected, meaningful and objectively outside of ourSelf, separate from our existence.

Experiencing life without disintegration. That is how we are able to get through crushing events without getting crushed; we experience painful feelings without allowing the pain to devastate us. When we see ourselves as a Part connected to Whole, there is a pleasant process of sharing both the pain and the joy that makes the experiences of pain and joy less traumatic, and the intensity not disintegrating. It is enough to feel the high without becoming overwhelmed, intimidated, out of touch, impulsively arrogant, or out of control.

Adopted Patterns. Individuals adopt a series of Life Patterns that are a result of identification with, or rebellion against, all characteristics of the Programers. While individuals assume that they are being themselves and are unchangeable, they are actually living Life Patterns that do not belong to them and are borrowed from others.

Adopted Patterns do not belong to us. Adopted Patterns feel uncomfortable and cause stress and disconnectedness with Self. These Patterns *are* changeable and deletable because they are not a part of the true Self. In fact, to go on living these Patterns that do not belong to the person will only bring disillusionment and far more pain in the long run than the pain of facing the truth and leaving behind what does not belong. Even if individuals choose to keep the adopted Patterns after they recognize where they come from, the ability to choose will set the individual free, as opposed to being driven by, and at the mercy of, unwanted and unchosen Programers.

Significant Influence: a phenomenon measured by several factors called Significant Influence Character; it means when a person has had an impact of some kind on a child who grows up with Patterns that have been influenced as a result of the contact with that person. We can also be significantly influenced during adulthood. Programers are Significant Influences of our life.

The making of Programers: are the factors involved in the making of significant influences of our lives, our Programers. People become our significant influences through a) contact, b) role model, c) action impact, and d) security source. Knowing how people become influential in life makes evident the responsibility of the Programers of families and society, and the substantial impact of their choices that pave the path of humanity.

The power of Self. By utilizing our fullest capacities, we are capable of achieving our highest aspirations. Only by being the best of who we can be, which is our Excelled true Self, can we bring to reality our own dreams. There is no other power but the power of the individual who can bring the fantasies that have been dreamed into reality. To deny that power of Self and to be at the mercy of false promises is a choice against that which humanity can do for itself.

Universal Power Balance. Leaders must relinquish freedom and responsibility to those to whom power and responsibility belong. Another reason for the emphasis on the Programers, leaders and makers of the individuals, from parents of a family to the parents and leaders of society, is that unless we hand the ultimate responsibility of the making of humanity to those to whom it belongs, we will always only be mending and manicuring the fingers of a hand that is attached to a dying heart. Or we will be curing a heart attached to a hand holding a knife that is tearing the heart apart.

Pattern Changes: Scientific Dimension of the Individual. Pattern Change Therapy defines life with scientific understanding and empowers individual functioning. It is a scientific theory and tool for excellence and defines the individual as a scientific entity. By defining individual functioning with scientific predictability of computer-like existence where an individual can change patterns like a computer yet enjoy their depth of wisdom of a philosophical being, Pattern Change Therapy provides a tool for independence of thought and action for people to understand themselves, control the direction of their lives and create their own destiny.

Psychological Self

Change: an inevitable life pattern. According to the Power Balance Theory, when individuals are passive, it is not because they are born that way, or because that is their type. It is because they have not developed Power Balance, which enables both passive and active patterns of relating, or any other pattern they wish to develop and use appropriately.

Excelling in the science of relating. If a relationship is not working, it is not because the two people involved are not meant for each other. It is because they have not learned individual Power Balance (which enables them to go into a relationship with clarity, strength and tools to make it work.) They thus cannot achieve Relationship Power Balance, which enables them to overcome problems and excel in the art and science of relating.

No emphasis on predispositions. If an individual is having thought distortions, it does not mean that he or she is an incurable schizophrenic or a lifetime drug addict. It means that the physicians, who have not experienced their own Power Balance, have become frightened of working extensively with a person with difficult and unusual Patterns Programed due to oversensitivity to harshness of the people around, and by the ignorance of the profession that labels him or her as incurable. The responsibility lies on the professionals and their ability to help change what is changeable without preconceived notions.

No inferior or superior genes. The Theory of Power Balance believes that people are different not because some were born superior and some inferior. People are different because they have been given different Programs in life. For that matter, they can change their patterns and become whomever they choose. They are not doomed for life with patterns and characteristics they did not choose for themselves, just as they are not doomed with the clothing they put on that they don't like, or the relationship that was put upon them by circumstance, or the country they were born in, or the language they grew up speaking, or the religion given to them without choice, or the myths and beliefs Programed into them without their acceptance.

The choice of change. The choice of change must belong to the individual, not a system or organization trying to convert them into what they think is good for them while forcing them out of their individuality. Differentness must be accepted by others and challenged only by the choice of the individual.

Patterns of Arrogant Supremacy. Arrogant supremacy occurs as a result of inner feelings of inferiority which are compensated by the external presentation of arrogance and supremacy. The more ignorance and prejudice, the more need for supremacy. It is the most toxic, dangerous and antihumane pattern that has ever existed in humanity. Its origins stem from ignorance that creates rigidity and fear that breeds discrimination by race or belief apparent in several countries. Germany, with Hitler, as well as the Eugenic Colony here in our own country are examples.

An example of arrogant supremacy is an intelligent leader and staff member of previous administrations appearing on national television and talking of teaching his own stamped religious and partisan values and virtues to the multicultures of this country. We can accept that from a prejudiced preacher or an ignorant and limited person on the street who sees everything in one color. This action clearly indicates rigid and biased thought patterns of supremacy. If it weren't for the balance of Attorney General Janet Reno, a woman of fairness and integrity who was also enraged by such presentations, an aware audience would have lost hope in the future of this country. And these are the people who have ruled this country for years. I only hope that the people see through their facade of virtuous self-righteousness and see their contempt and fear for anything that reminds them of their own inadequacy. It isn't any wonder we are in such state of agony. He proceeded to say that if Hindus do not like honesty, they should be cheated and stolen from so they can come to understand what "family value and virtue" means. As if people of other cultures were born without values. Other congressmen have continued this bazaar pattern of undermining ethnicity, creating a regressive movement against diversity by the far right, inappropriate to say the least for an advanced, free country. Someone should educate and inform some of our politicians who are native to this country and have limited global knowledge that people of other cultures are the integral part of this country and some have lost their strong moral foundation and values by being exposed to boundaryless patterns of today's Western society. If the answer is, "Then tell them to go back where they came from," as has been the popular phrase of many politicians in our free country, we must also inform our dear but misguided friends that these people *are* home: a home that must begin to welcome them and stop denying them of their core and uniqueness; a home that must reform and change to suit all of its people, and equally honor and regard the core of all beliefs.

As long as there are victims, there will be bullies. We are certainly approaching an era where if we don't recognize our inner Self and regard it, fully, we will witness, as a nation, a great deal of bullying. We must know that as long as there is a victim, there is also a bully, and that patterns of victimization stem from not having a Self or having a poor sense of Self.

All values of substance are universal. Values, if they are any good, have a universal nature that don't humiliate or discriminate against anyone and are shared by all. No one has a monopoly on universal values; they existed before any entity or organization arrived. We just alienate them by our primitive laws that inhibit their natural flow. It is this kind of ignorance that causes arrogant supremacy detrimental to the survival of peace and humanity. I owe my life to the field of psychology and to my education. I truly believe that it is this field that ultimately saves people from the regression that stems from lack of understanding the inner Self, and the lack of knowledge to apply its potential to our everyday life experiences. I am only offering new dimensions to the one-dimensional field of psychology we have known in the past in order to emphasize its significance as a multidimensional science, for it is the path to peace among us, and to progression in humanity. Everything begins with Self, and everything ends that exists in the absence of Self. The multidimensions of psychology bring us the Knowledge of Self with a depth and speed deserving of the current time and history.

Depression program, a Pattern of change. As a natural process of unconscious change, or a need for change, one can experience depression. Patterns of depression in an atmosphere which enhances and seeks change is a positive experience. It is a way the individual communicates to Self and others that the status quo is no longer acceptable, and that the process of change is under way. It is a warning and alarm system of the mind, body and spirit that the individual needs to adhere to and respect. Of course, one does not have to become depressed every time there is a process of change. By the mere recognition and experience of feelings, and making change a conscious choice, the experience becomes a fulfilling one.

Depression as an effect of change. In my own initial process of change I noticed that the depression stemming from fear of change paralyzed me more than the actual change itself. Therefore, in my practice with my clients who came to me depressed and their life story showed changes and adjustments they needed to make and their reaction to them with anxiety and fear, I would immediately tell them that their body and mind is communicating a need for change, and the depression they are experiencing is the unknown they fear facing.

Brightness: Power Balance of darkness. When I explain this to people, they immediately get out of their depression and begin to change. After they go through the process of change once, they are able to see that at the end of every confusion there is peace, balance, stability, joy, and a true feeling of power. Just as clearly as the brightest days follow the darkest nights of the soul.

Shared pain, shared strength. If I could get to my Power Balance and the process of Excellence, anyone can. I always tell people working with me, at the first session in their own process of becoming, that if I could arrive at where I am, anyone can. I come from ultimate oppression, victimization, lack of personal freedom and absence of tools to deal with the anguish that stems from my pain of lack of control and helplessness in my life.

Pain as a Growth Pattern. The fact that I can now see, up here, what I would have never been able to see down there, I owe to the pain it took to be down there that made me want to climb. I also owe it to the tools I picked up on the way while climbing and sliding that have enabled me to look around fearlessly, choosing the next mountain to climb, consistently.

The magic of transcending from pain to joy. There is a magical, addictive quality in transcending from consistent pain to consistent joy without using any tools of denial, but only those of clarity. Anyone who experiences it will fall into the entrancing path of becoming.

Power Balance Theory (Program.) Power Balance presents the Theory of Power Balance versus Imbalance and Block, as a Program towards peace and harmony within individuals, among individuals relating with loved ones, and among all nations. The theory of Pattern Change Programing and Power Balance begins within each and every individual, and spreads to the connections without: with others and society.

Patterns of Trial, Patterns of Failure. Making many mistakes polishes us, while making the same mistakes over and over will ultimately dissolve us. It is when we repeatedly make the same mistakes, and not when we make many mistakes of different nature to form our Patterns of Character and find our true Self, that we will fail to truly choose our destiny.

Repetitive Patterns of mistake. Only by analyzing the past can we prevent our habitual, repetitive, self-dcfcating patterns. When I see people of compassion and intelligence repeatedly going in and out of relationships of the same Pattern, repeatedly placing themselves in the same situations where they have been hurt before, I see people who have been so busy blaming themselves and feeling guilt and shame, that they have not had time to analyze their own Past Patterns, let alone the Past Patterns of those with whom they are involved. Therefore, they are left vulnerable and not in a position of learning from their mistakes and controlling their life direction. Mistakes are investments towards success, until we keep investing in them as a habit. Then they become our liabilities and take away our life assets.

Psycho-Physiological Self

The psycho-physiology dimension. The root to most of the physical illnesses that people have brought with them to my office stems from patterns of suppressed anger, guilt, helplessness, shame, hopelessness and denial. My client diagnosed with Epstein Barr (now known as Chronic Fatigue Syndrome), healed from her muscle problems and migraine headaches, and I know of others in the healing profession like Bernie Siegel who have healed cancer wounds, and many other physical problems. By gaining Power Balance and, as a result, releasing the suppressed anger that was turned inward, poisoning their physical organs and blocking oxygen and power, people are able to restore and maintain their physical health.

Process work shortcuts healing. The first homework, which I call process work, that I give to my clients who come in depressed, is to set up a program where they walk daily. This immediately affects their psychological state of mind. It is not possible to ignore one and tend to the other, as the understanding and respect for the interrelations of every dimension of being is an integral part of the ability to help the person in his or her totality.

Working with all of the person, not just one part. To neglect the psychological, philosophical, spiritual, scientific or physical dimensions of the Self only because of pride or prejudice of specialty, is the root to long-term and costly modalities, as well as the disillusionment of people for the healing profession.

Three

My Computer, My Self

Past Programing and Habitual Life Patterns. Like a rabbit, I have been running for the past fifteen years through life: teaching, training, coaching, and guiding many people and professionals who have come to me as well as creating balance in my own life with my children and family. The process has by no means been easy. The struggle, the pain, the blocks and imbalances were there to overcome and to learn from for me to become a better person. My Life Patterns and Self Programing turned out to be the most pleasurable pain as a constant challenge of moving from one point to another. When one loves the climb as well as being on the mountain top, the mere pleasure of discovering life challenges and experiencing it at its fullest can become an addictive indulgence, detrimental to moving to the deeper and finer dimensions of being: a deeper commitment in the process of Self Transformation and making a difference in the rise of the Self of the masses through spreading Self Knowledge. It is easy for someone who has no recognition of the joy of life to reject such passion and seem self-sacrificing. Yet for me who loves life it has taken Self-Discipline, Self Control a process of an active development of other excelling patterns far beyond my own imagination. Besides, the joy of being involved in materialization of my vision daily; of people changing as they saw themselves through me, learning, crying, laughing, embracing life, embracing one another, and blossoming right before my eyes, made sitting in front of a computer and writing the books I had already published years ago in my mind, a far away mission. How could one so involved with life sit in front of a computer: a cold and emotionless machine that lacked emotional patterns of a warm connection and introspective feedback?

From living the change of pattern, to writing about them. There are many teachers who have offered great wisdom to the world, and I admire their Self-Discipline. It is difficult to give up living fully emeshed in patterns of joy and mastery just to tell others about it. It takes a different level of dedication and Patterns of Self-Discipline for an even larger purpose than merely having a successful life and profession. But above all is the dedication to face the truth: the truth of telling not just what goes on in our outside world, but what goes on within the walls of our harem, our personal confidante, our multidimensional Self. As we polish our Societal Self to others - the sophisticated, the flawless, the mighty, the kind and the virtuous Self-are we willing to equally search within the inner Self, the child, the parent, the adult; the needy, the feared, the not so perfect and polished, the Forgotten Self that uncontrollably appears in sound-bites or in moments of miscalculation? If so, then we have the potential to achieve Power Balance: a place of harmony where the *whole*, all of who we are inside, is accepting of each pattern; nurturing and guiding to make it a *part*. If we are willing to experience life stark naked and away from denial we are worthy of sharing our experiences with others. But the world is full of con artists instead of true teachers, unwilling to seek the truth within their Self, hoping to hide their own denial beneath the layers of their impressive titles. In today's world there are thieves and robbers in all walks of life, and Robin Hood look-alikes don't always hide behind the bushes to steal the jewels from the rich to give to the poor. We have advanced in all patterns of life, even its patterns of toxicity and corruption. But as our faith in humanity begins to fade in this critical time we live in and we seem to want to give in to the fast cures just to feel safe, our Self Knowledge and recognition of our inherent power to make a difference, will save the day. Or if we are seduced to join the corrupted coalition, our Inner Code of Ethics and Universal Law of Success and Spiritual Excellence enriches us beyond the need for or glitter at the cost of our honor and saves us from sliding into the seductive multi-million dollar Western industrial gutter of the marketplace of fame. And if we look even beyond what is right, we can see what we truly need to see. There is always a lesson to learn from the discomforts we feel about the life-injustice, and taking them lightly, externalizing and projecting them defensively, is rejecting the opportunity for excelling. In my times of anger of betrayal when I was robbed of what principally mattered to me, I have searched back to my root, of my mission of spreading the words of peace and progression. Within the core of my being there was no room for externalization of what was happening. I had to forgive the imperfections of my Self with which I was still struggling to gain compassion for those whom I had a hard time forgiving. During long hours of Self Search I have found myself hymning: "the closer to the Self we become, the closer to others we can be." We must be willing to live the Change of Patterns, the Laws of Success and Spiritual Excellence and the truth of our own being in order to be ready to write about them, genuinely.

Recognizing Regressive Patterns of the world. But we must also be willing to recognize the *pain* to feel the *joy*, we must acknowledge *imbalance* to recognize *excellence* and *spirituality*, we must *question* to become *clear*, we must *separate* from *familiar* to become *a part* of the *universe*, we must allow *chaos* to find the true *order*, and we must be a *part* to become *whole*. Yet as we must advance in the information age to fly on the wings of technology and learn the scientific dimensions of our mind and body, the denial of victimization going on around us, keeping our heads in snow and our vision limited only to what we see and hear, existing in our bodies disconnected from our spirits and keeping our minds away from our feelings can slowly turn us to cold computer-like beings living to be safe, only.

A calling from within. What changed my process of living Patterns of Life and instead pulled me towards writing about them were the Patterns of Imbalance in society and the world that I have been witnessing. The universal crisis unfolding before us for the past several years was a painful observation that created a shared existential anger among many. Witnessing constant war and power struggle among nations, and crime on our streets and in our sacred homes encouraged by those who call themselves leaders of peace and progression became an uncontrollable calling within. It felt like the people's voice of fear and anger needed a trustworthy facilitator to burst out in the open, and connect to and share thoughts with a larger audience. Whomever it is that is trying to speak through me awoke me from my comfortable and nicely programed life into an unknown interruption that could cost me my peace and security. I have been the voice of the people for a long time: sometimes even when they didn't want me to be. I am afraid this time, too, there will be many who will feel that way. Some of us cannot be appreciative if woken up from a deep sleep by someone asking us to leave the comfortable zone of our bed, and get out to the cold reality. I have felt like a mother who pulls her child back from crossing the street full of careless cars that pass by without the intent of stopping for the innocent pedestrian and only with the intent of getting where they want to get, while the child cries and feels it was the mother who was cruel for pulling her away from that which was to destroy her. The pain of ignorance is far more familiar and comforting to us than the pain of growth: the pain of standing tall and carrying the responsibility of our lives, on our own. It is difficult for us, in the midst of our need for affection and love, to recognize those who smile gently and lend a dependable hand that is attached to the chain of time. Yet this cruel chain of time, a timeless chain of time, a regressive chain of time, holds us back, as far back as we can regress, only to satisfy our endless needs for familiarity, security, and love. My mission to write for peace, promotion of the Institution of Self and empowerment of the people as I have explored and shared in my first book, *Pattern Change Programing: Creating Your Own Destiny*, on the first day of January 1994, does not come from feeling that I have all the answers. It comes from a sense of urgency within that the answers I do have must become available to as many people as possible who can and want to hear them and who hopefully put them in heart and action.

I am the voice of those who feel betrayed in today's society, those who have trusted it by holding their arms out and accepting those lending hands that are chained to the ancient time machine, pulling them back to the depth from which they came, from where they ran away, and in which they are still struggling. I could be misunderstood, again. For I have far too much compassion to rule out anyone on my list of those who deserve love, forgiveness and generosity. And that includes the victim as well as the bully, the guilty as well as innocent, the white as well as the black, the Christian as well as the Jew, Moslem, or Buddhist, the American as well as the Irish or Persian, the Republican as well as the Democrat, the therapist as well as the client, the preacher as well as the educator. For they all bear the common core of being human. I have an inherent weakness in seeing the cause before I see the symptom, the effect, or the fault. And there are causes for every fault, which makes the fault just another handed down handicap. So for me, personally, there is no anger, but only sorrow from the observation of pain: the pain of others who have no voice to release, nor the philosophical and psychological understanding and perspective. When there is no urgency, one can become the voice of those in pain in a softer process, as I have repeatedly encouraged. Yet now I see the world in an urgent crisis where not even the rage of an angered God would seem to be heard.

I feel there is only time for Power Balance so that the race of humanity can begin to exist side by side, in harmony. I could have chosen to ignore that voice, that Existential Anger so as to not risk my credibility, but I have not. For as much as I believe, in our age of computers, that we can learn to become as objective as machines, as predictable in the outcome of our destinies and Life Patterns and Programs, I still believe there is a humanness within all of us worth treasuring. When I said this in January as I began writing, many laughed at me and in silence with all due respect, and thought I was becoming paranoid in my old age. Three months later, after night and day writing as I had finished my book, two people told me that it was too intense. Since then, I have been watering down my intensity, as I have been confirmed in my each and every thought as I watch the course of history.

Person-to-person connection with a computer. Ever since I have had a person-to-person connection with my computer, I have learned a great deal about the common patterns between this multidimensional machine and an individual. I learned that not only is an individual capable of having the scientific patterns of a computer, but a computer also has the subjective patterns of a person. Maybe it is true that one takes on the patterns of his or her creator. If that is the case, we are in a far better place than our computer.

The process of Pattern Change. I would not have believed it if someone told me that computers truly do have feelings. Yet they are just as temperamental as people are, they get tired and careless, just like people do after long hours of being slave-driven, and they punish and reward their writing partner, holding the same Patterns that people have with their life partners.

Computers have feelings, too. Knowledge stems from the recognition of Past Patterns and the observation of present experiences. I have gained a great deal of wisdom from long hours of relating to my computer, and have learned to respect, understand and have a great deal of appreciation for it, as well as being careful not to abuse it. Computers do not punish, but withdraw their connection if one does not appreciate them and treat them respectfully.

The ultimate punishment. For someone who is tamed by another, withdrawal is an ultimate punishment. I know. I have experienced that pattern of pain before, among the other Patterns that pain has to offer. Loss of a loved one in one way or another is a form of withdrawal of love from the body of the one who loves. It is the same pain when we experience the loss of one we love through uncontrollable life accidents, or when we lose them because they have lost themselves, or perhaps because they never had themselves.

Pattern Change of our choices. In this Pattern, the pain is so overwhelming at times that it feels like one's stomach is in a knot, or that the entire body will disintegrate at any given moment. But we do go on loving and yes, we do go on using our computer. It is the only way to make sense out of our lives.

Analysis of Past Patterns. If we analyze our losses and understand the roots and causes of our pain, our knowledge about ourselves changes: not only about who we are so that we can gain strength in our Patterns of Relating, but also what we want, in order to make changes in our Patterns when bringing people into our lives. We will then be able to choose people who have a Self to connect with, and who do not have an unchangeable past to bring into the relationship, just as we will hopefully use a computer that is already upgraded and does not take a great deal of work in order to advance.

Patterns of Pain. To love, regardless of the pain that may be involved, is one of the risks necessary for a trance-like meaning in life. "To love and to have lost is better than not to have loved at all," is almost as popular a slogan as the billboards for Virginia Slims cigarettes that say, "You've come a long way, baby." As I stated earlier, there are many Patterns of Pain, just as there are many rides when one goes to a fair.

Chosen or adopted Patterns of Pain? Patterns are both inflicted upon us by others and inflicted upon us by ourselves. Adopted Patterns can hurt us and push us down a regressive path, sometimes with no choice to return, and some hurt us only to prepare us for wider paths waiting to take us on a higher plane. The pain of loving is the latter. And so is the pain of refusing deadly rides on a one-winged plane.

Believe me, the pain of connecting with our computer, too, is one of the same. The Patterns of Pain that we choose to inflict upon ourselves, if analyzed, teach us more tolerance, and as a result, we gain. The Patterns of Pain inflicted upon us by others are Adopted Patterns that victimize and paralyze us, and take away the power to learn.

Computers cannot be taken for granted. The law of the Universal Swing of the Pendulum truly applies to everything. I have come to respect this in my observations of a lifetime, as well. Every time I abuse my computer and don't treat it with grace, every time I think to mySelf that I shouldn't be concerned with this machine's feelings and temperament since I have two other computers I can use, it responds to me as if it heard me, and treats me just like a senseless, cold and machine-like person who can play dead in the middle of a magnificent love affair.

And each time I make sure I don't abuse it or load it up more than I think it can handle, it treats me like a person who knows how important my work is to me and is mature enough not to get jealous and throw childish tantrums. It actually becomes helpful, almost miraculously. I call that the Power of Compassion for all the living things. And maybe for the labeled "non-living things" as well, if we believe in the power of healing.

Power Balance and Imbalance in a computer. I am sure you know that computers, too, can start acting out and develop Imbalance Patterns just as people do. When an entire chapter got wiped out, my computer analyst explained to me, "It must have gotten a virus from one of your guest disks and must have not liked it. Until you get it cleaned up, it will give you problems." I said, "But I have not introduced anything foreign to it since last month."

Computer crisis. He said, "It doesn't matter. It decides when it wants to act out. It's smart. It decides when to behave the way it wants, and that can be any time, without advanced notice." I said to him, carelessly, "Well, it hasn't done anything to my other disks, so I will go on and use it for now until Monday." He said,

"Then expect it to cause you problems somewhere, just when you won't be ready to handle it."

Program overload. I said, "But only people do that. They collect all the Programing from others and go on without introspecting and thinking whether or not they like it, or if it is working for them. And one day, when they are overloaded with Imbalances and Blocks that have paralyzed them, one button gets pushed and sets them off. A crisis is created so that they must stop whatever they are doing and take care of the problem at hand." He shook his head and said, "That's it, that's your computer. You better take care of it now or you will be sorry if you wait till Monday."

Knowledge, discovery, pattern change. I was amazed. I was even more amazed when I had several files open at once and it made remarks that it was overloaded. I ignored it and went on. I thought to mySelf, what could really happen? What happened was that it dropped the entire application and shut down altogether. I said to mySelf, if computers can feel the way people feel, then not only must we change the patterns of relating towards people we treat as objects, but the other can hold true; we can function as objectively and scientifically as computers, and still feel as subjective as we want. The Balance between the Patterns of Cognition and Emotion creates the Power Balance we need within us to prevent crisis and move towards Excellence.

Learning from computers, leaping beyond. Since then I have learned a great deal more about my computers and have learned that even in relationship with a computer one must have Power Balance. If we don't know as much, and can't handle it with ease and the Self-Control of someone who knows the Patterns that are Programed, we are at its mercy. Otherwise it becomes a strong ally and enhances our life and Patterns of Liberty.

Now that I have hopefully begun Programing the Change of Patterns in your relationship with your computer, and perhaps your relationship to yourSelf and the people you connect with, as they are all interchangeable, let's begin to observe and recognize our similarities with computers, and our ability to function as a computer. Let's begin to learn from our computers and hopefully leap beyond their capacity to function as a person.

Self-Programers of our own Life Patterns. Owning all of our dimensions and Self-Programing Patterns of our own choice is not the impossible function of intelligent beings who have invented computers. As I mentioned before, they told us it was impossible when we said the earth was not flat. Let's not let them degrade us or keep us in the dark ages in spite of our abilities again.

Self-Programing our own destiny. Destiny is a by-product of the Programs and Patterns we choose during our lifetime. Self-Knowledge, and the utilization of our mind which bears the fruits of our thoughts, is everything. Any other commandment we hear in life is nothing but man-made Programing designed originally to assist us in our lives, and yet unfortunately, because of the lack of Knowledge of Self, has caused the very things that were supposed to help us, become detrimental to our Life Balance Patterns of happiness and success, let alone our ultimate pattern of existence: the Patterns of Excellence.

Excellence: independence of thought and action. We cannot excel until we begin to recognize independence of thought and action from any external existence, and teach our old Programers to Change their Patterns of dependence on our lack of Self Knowledge and ignorance to appropriate and helpful skills needed for our time. The destiny of any being is in the mind and the hands of the one living it. Any definition for destiny other than the one we make for ourselves is an imaginary story told by others and adopted by us as our reality. It is interesting that in a civilization that insists on living in reality and confines those who don't by calling them mentally ill, we have given ourselves an umbrella of unquestioned blind obedience to believe in myths and imaginary scripts.

Science has taught us that anything is possible. Science has taught us that with Patterns of openness and creativity, we can discover anything there is to know about the mysteries of existence in the universe around us. Science has taught us that there is an explanation for everything if we look for it objectively and methodically. Science has taught us that we can do anything if we put our minds to it.

We can even mold and forge our destinies by sending men into space, whereas Programers of Ignorance have taught us that human beings are worthless and can only look up to worship, while preparing to climb beneath the ground. Science has taught us that fanaticism and the regressive tendency to indulge in patterns of addiction, dependency and ignorance has taken our patterns of objectivity and scientific strength away from us and is blocking us from taking responsibility for our own mistakes as well as successes, and thus from creating our own destiny.

Individual as computer. Individual beings and the world around them function like a computer. All happenings are Programs set to function scientifically, based on controlled or uncontrolled inputs into the computer. Unwanted and Unchosen Programs can be deleted, just as Chosen Programs can be copied and saved. The scientific results are the Patterns of individual, herein called the Individual Computer.

Components of Individual Computer

The Brain is the central processing unit of the Individual Computer. The Individual Computer brain interprets and analyzes the information received.

The Eyes are the Individual Computer monitor. They display the results of our instructions. They also act as the mouse and keyboard. The information is received (input system) through the eyes. All other perception and sensory organs are part of input and output systems.

Memory is the temporary storage of the Individual Computer. There is long-term and short-term memory in the Individual Computer. Individual memory storage functions differently. Some remember things from long ago far more than the lunch they had an hour ago.

Conscious Memory, RAM, is random access memory, which is the memory when the Individual Computer is on. Almost everything Individual Computer sees, feels, touches, or smells, goes right through and becomes conscious memory for a while, until further notice.

Unconscious Memory is the application running the Program. This application, or unconscious memory, cannot be seen and yet has total control of the Individual Computer's path of Life Patterns, Programs and ultimately, destiny.

Functions
of Individual Computer

Individual Computer functions. Past Programs and Patterns can be Deleted, Copied, Pasted, Saved, Printed, Shifted, Controlled and Alternated in the process of Pattern Change Programing. New Programs can be Self-Programed or Programed with assistance of a Pattern Change Programer.

Delete. Unwanted Programs can be Deleted. Past Patterns are Recognized and, if not working in the present, can be Deleted and left where they belong: in the past.

Copy. Wanted Programs can be Copied. That is why we need effective role models in life, for we unconsciously Copy many Life Patterns whether they are constructive or not.

Paste. Copied Programs are Pasted anywhere. The collective of our Life Patterns gather up and act together in different Programs we choose. Programs function collectively with each other as well. The more an Individual Computer has flexibility, the easier that Paste and Copy will be obtained.

Save. Save is when the individual collects the knowledge, recognizes Past Patterns, and chooses to Save them as Present Patterns instead of Deleting them and leaving them behind. Many unconscious memories are Saved memories that are not in the Life Files of our Self-Control. Controlled and Saved Patterns remain in our consciousness.

Print. Print is when the Individual Computer utilizes the knowledge and materializes it in the real world. The printed Self Knowledge is the collection of our actions.

Shift. Shift can be used with any function in order to add to the functions. Multidimensionality of the Individual Computer is equivalent to the Function and Control Keys of a computer.

Control. Control can be used with any function in order to gain control of the function. Control of a computer is the Self-Control of the Individual Computer, managing the Life Patterns and Programs to be printed out appropriately.

Alternate. Alternate can be used with any function in order to have alternatives and different choices. Likewise, Individual Computers must be free to choose the alternative choices laid out before them on a life path.

Life File. Once we know what our Life Patterns are, we can keep them in our life file and utilize them as necessary. If we don't know what our Life Patterns are, we cannot have a Life File for them and can have no control over what we can do with them.

Computer language. The Individual Computer language is Self-Knowledge. Self-Knowledge is expressed as thought. Individual Computers are blind and ignorant and can only function based on its input. The language of the Individuals Computer (knowledge expressed as thoughts) need to be developed and clearly understood by the individual, and must be Self-Programed into the Individual Computer. Otherwise, others will put their language (thoughts) into the computer, and the individuals will be at the mercy of what other Programers choose to input.

The Individual Computer backup. The Individual Computer backup is a combination of all present and past Individual Computer's knowledge, conscious or unconscious (input.) It consists of the energy already existing in the world that the individual can always tap into if she or he knows how to operate the Individual Computer.

Function D: Destiny. This is the outcome of Programs. It is a scientifically designed path, Self-Programed by the individuals.

Embedded within it are many other functions to create the future, focusing on the Individual Pattern Change Programing. Different Programs have different functions.

Individual behavior. Individual behavior is similar to Individual Program. It consists of a Pattern or set of Patterns developed from Programs fed into the Individual Computer by its different Life Programers. As a result, since such Programs are not as ingrained in the individuals as they seem and their roots are Societal and from other Programers, they are changeable by Deleting them and Pasting Self-Programing.

To know thySelf, know thy Programers. It is partly for that matter that, in our attempt to bring back the power to the individual by Pattern Change Programing, we will study closely the Programers and makers of society and the world. To know thySelf, one must first know thy Life Programer and Pattern Creators.

Programers. Programers are the source of program input, and the carriers of the Individual Computer knowledge or thought. There is a variety of Life Programers in an individual's life span. Some of these Programers who have significant impact on individual Life Patterns are:

Programers: Power Balanced or Imbalanced:
    Parent Programers
    Societal Programers
    Teacher Programers
    Peer Programers
    Role-Model Programers
    Religious Programers
    Media Programers
    Leader Programers
    Government Programers
    Self Programer
Pattern Change Programers (Specialists): Power Balanced.

Patterns. Patterns are developed and written for Programs by Programers. They are the multidimensional manner in which the individual goes through life paths. They are the scientific results of the Individual Computer. Patterns can either be chosen or uncontrolled.

Chosen Patterns are in harmony with the individual's true nature. Chosen Patterns are those we choose consciously and keep in our consciousness. Many times our unconscious patterns brought into consciousness are chosen once become conscious. A Chosen Pattern is a Pattern of Self-Control, and takes conscious choice and effort to Program it within an Individual Computer.

Uncontrolled Patterns are not chosen by the individual. They are usually Adopted from other Programers during early childhood, and are not in harmony with the individual's true nature. An Uncontrolled Pattern would be the Toxic Pattern of Hate. Hate is not a Choice Pattern, but and Adopted Pattern by the Individual Computer from old Programers, like a virus that spreads without our choice by toxic programers of our society.

Programs. Programs are entered from (language) thought input into the computer by sources of those thoughts, the Programers. Programs are established by different Programers throughout the individual's life. There are several types of Programs. Programs are chosen or uncontrolled.

Chosen Programs, like Chosen Patterns, are consciously established, while Unchosen Programs are often Adopted without conscious choice. Among the Chosen Programs are Freedom-Responsibility Programs that must be consciously chosen and Balanced within Individual Computer. Another Choice Program is the Program for Healthy Living, the Power Balance Program and the Excellence Program. Programs that need the individual's conscious choice enhance individual functioning and capacity.

Unfounded or Unchosen Program. The path that does not belong to individuals and has been put upon them without their choice and consent will continue to function within the individual habitually and beyond control, forming toxic energy that creates anxiety and tension. Unfounded Programs will seem to flow through the individual on automatic pilot and without control, while not feeling to the individuals that they belong to them.

Example. The Imbalance Program of guilt, hopelessness and helplessness, will create tension and anxiety within individuals because they were put upon them by other Programers without being a choice Program.

Another Unchosen Program would be the Sensationalism Program, where one discriminates based on feelings towards a traditional and adopted sentiment handed down by Societal and Life Programers. Unfounded Programs are usually established for the purpose of forming groups, by peer groups or other systems with institutional encouragement and pressure. They do not necessarily benefit the enhancement of individual inherent capacity. They usually promote ideologies, political interests, or a common interest group.

Choice Paths. Paths, or Programs, are collections of different types of Programs established and chosen by people willingly and consciously, which bring them harmony and balance. A Choice Path would be the Path of creating your own destiny.

Unfounded Paths. Unfounded Paths will not flow, and will not feel like they belong to the individual. An Unchosen Path would be to follow your ancestors' Programing blindly and without question. The footprints of Unfounded Paths are found in history, whereas Choice Paths are progressive, futuristic, new, creative, innovative, and free from old, outdated Programing.

Power Balance Program. Pattern Change Programing is the scientific tool and application to the Program of Power Balance and Excellence. The Power Balance and Excellence Program is multidimensional. It is the natural and inherent functioning for individuals. It is a universal law.

Power Imbalance and Block Program. Power Balance changes and Deletes Power Imbalance and Power Block Programs that are Programed as a result of a lack of knowledge of individual Life Programers. The cause of all individual, familial, societal and universal crisis is Imbalance and Block of Power within and among individuals, in society and the world.

The Mother Program. Power Balance Program is the Mother Program for the application of Pattern Change Programing. The Mother Program is a formula for individual Balance, health, successes and excellence, and balance and connection with others and the environment. It is an individual's inherent formula for existence. It is the Universal Law that governs all the living things. Imbalance Programing inhibits Inherent Power Balance, puts it in unconscious, until Self-Programing brings it into consciousness and polishes it back into action.

The Scientific Program: Pattern Change Programing

The scientific explanation. The Power Balance Theory believes that there is a scientific explanation to everything. This also applies to psychology and to the understanding and healing of the wounds of individuals and societies. And that two plus two becomes four, if that is what one is looking for. And if not, one must be sure, and know what to do and what Patterns of Analysis to use, or otherwise someone else will. And that, too, becomes one's own decision by the utilization of the Withdrawal Pattern.

Simply put, we are given the scientific tools of the power of the mind. We must utilize our mind's inherent capacity towards the Knowledge of Self. By searching the Roots of our Patterns through Analytic Patterns of Deductive Reasoning, we will be equipped with the tools to Program and build Future Patterns, Programs, and ultimately our Path of Destiny.

Science has taught us to be objective. Science has given us the tools to be precise, exact, and to make our performances objectively unaffected by our circumstances. In science, the output is greatly influenced by the direct input given to receive desired outcomes. In scientific experiments, one can be confident of the outcome if one knows exactly what the input consists of.

Becoming objective beings, not being objects. Just as objects can gain individual functioning, capacities and characteristics, the individual can likewise gain objective functioning and capacities.

A computer is a scientific pattern, a phenomenon: a creation of the mind and of advanced thought processes of individuals who believed in their process of creativity. Computers have been so advanced as to be mistaken as real people, in their scientific yet flexible thought processes.

Science gives power to the individual. In the theory of Pattern Change Programing, scientific explanations and knowledge are used to give scientific credibility, reliability, and predictability to the deeply-rooted multidimensionality of beings. The scientific tool often used by the individual to give power to the objects, like a computer or a missile, or an atomic bomb, will be used to empower the individual Self.

Patterns of Analysis of history. Nations can only predict Future Patterns, or Program Excellence, from the analysis of history and its Repetitive Patterns of trial and error, or just plain mistakes. Individuals, too, hold the same simple, yet taken for granted, golden rule for establishing clear, calculated Programs for the destination of choice.

Patterns predicting our choice of destiny. Looking at Past Patterns enables us to transcend them and experience more Power Balance in Present Patterns, and to move on to higher, Excelled Patterns that will predict for us our choice of destiny.

Fear of chaos and disorder. Is it the scientists' fear of chaos and disorder that has kept them away from the individual: the unpredictable and, at times, chaotic machine? Thinking of the physics chaos theory, I have concluded a theory of my own that might assist our scientists in becoming interested in pursuing the psychology of the individual as a science.

Power chaos theory. Order stems from chaos. This theory proposes that any true order must welcome chaos as its catalyst. We must create chaos by rocking the boat in order to achieve Excellence that arises from a challenged order. The fear of rocking the boat for creating change contributes to a consistent Imbalance in life. Power Balance requires Power Chaos for the process to be ignited. In a Power Balanced family or society the boat will not rock destructively unless the forces and powers existing within it are victimizing and toxic. True leaders of families and societies welcome change even if it is different from that of their own blueprint.

Tolerance for chaos and confusion. For individuals to progress in interpersonal endeavors and aspirations as much as they have succeeded in science, they must take chances by asking scientific questions that enhance change, and to be tolerant of the confusion and chaos that always comes before balance and order. In the chaos theory in physics, it is proven that chaos brings about change. One must never sacrifice what one must experience just for the sake of keeping order.

As in the Universal Pendulum Theory, I believe that the Pattern on the opposite side, or even side by side, of every Pattern that we see as positive, is important to the Power Balance of that Pattern. If we strive for order at any cost, there will never be true order and balance in our lives. Chaos by itself is not a valuable Pattern to own. However, chaos for the purpose of acquiring order must be seriously considered. Unless we experience the night, will we never truly understand the day, nor will we be prepared to fully enjoy it.

Order after chaos represents Power Balance. Order without the challenge of chaos becomes a Pattern of Rigidity, not Balance. Wonderful and intelligent people avoid change because they fear the risk, the confusion and the lack of stability and order that exist in any worthwhile and profound change. As I stated earlier, in my own initial process of change, I recognized that the depression I felt prior to bringing about any change scared and paralyzed me more than the actual change itself. It was the *fear of change itself* that created the depression, not the fear of what I needed to change. When we don't know why we become depressed, the depression itself becomes the root to the fear we experience. Anything, if explained to us negatively and toxicity, will not only lose its merit, but also creates fear and lack of harmony.

In my experience with my clients, I recognized that my mere permission to embrace the fear of change and even the depression that arose from it not only alleviated their feelings of depression but lifted the fear itself. When they understood about why they became depressed and what it meant to them, the Pattern of Crisis was over and they could utilize the same pattern as a Preventive and even Excelling Pattern to proceed and succeed in their lives.

Depression: a natural pattern of change. Depression, the sad and empty feeling of exhaustion one experiences and fears because of the strong label it has been given by our fast-paced societal race of active participation even at the cost of Self, is a natural pattern of change and is actually a natural process, and can therefore become a positive emotion.

Scientific Programing for success. There is a theory and assumption in Pattern Change Therapy that people functions as computer; we are our own creation, in predictable patterns of cause-effect. Empowerment and the programing of individuals with scientific knowledge enables the outcome of their actions to be unaffected by circumstances outside of the individual power or choice. Self-Knowledge is everything. It enables people to become clear about their path, and to gain the power in the universe.

Power Balance: Universal and Individual Law. A scientific eye cannot deny the wonders of universal and individual order. The consistency and accuracy of the chain of events within the mother universe and its embedded children of identical patterns and components cannot be avoided by one who understands the deductive reasoning of science. Denial of the Pattern Changes of day to night, cold to hot, snow to rain to rainbow, and the entirely accountable and predictable evolutionary process of the universal components and parts including the individual and the predictable, time-ticking inner system and automatic changes of Patterns, is only caused by the fear of learning, succeeding and excelling as species of freedom and responsibility.

Science used as a hypnotic suggestion. Pattern Change Programing defines the individual as a computer that has the power to change the Programs and Patterns inputted by others in the past. Since today the average person, including young people in educational institutions, are dealing with computers daily, its comparison will be to them a consistent reminder of their own inner personal computer. Therefore, it can be used as a tool of Self-Control. Unlike Programing used to remind people of their doomed, hopeless destiny and worthless existence it guides people to become empowered, competent, self-sufficient and healthy creators of their own destiny.

Scientifically predicting individual functioning. Pattern Change Programing helps individuals to imprint their own destiny. It enables them to cease seeing themselves as victims of circumstance, of incurable diseases, and of other labels that traditional Programers make people believe is their fate. Fate, in that context, is viewed as a predisposed, printed Program that the individual has nothing to do with. It follows a set of future programs that suggests destiny is unchangeable, robbing people of motivation and responsibility to gain control of their actions and their lives, and change the outcome of their past Programing.

Individual with scientific capacity. Pattern Change Therapy assumes that individuals possess the scientific capacity of their own creations. It defines individuals as computers capable of printing out chosen Life Patterns that lead to the choices of life paths and destinies.

Development of scientific functioning within Self. Since the individual created science, the individual can develop scientific functioning within Self. I believe that individual functioning is very much a scientific process. The focus of scientists has not been one of gaining scientific objectivity and advancement in regards to the individual. The mere reason is that our scientists, too, like any ordinary individual on earth, have preferred to seek answers outside of their Self.

Science used as denial and escape. Even though it is the individuals who have been the scientists and creators of much that is on earth and beyond, because of their lack of interest in using scientific knowledge to empower the Self, they have remained "powerless" themselves, at the mercy of their own creations. The fear of the unknown has kept scientists away from Self-discovery. They have abandoned ship and left it up to the people who have the intuition but not the scientific tools to bring the multi-dimensional creation called individual home.

Far past the moon, far away from compassion. For that very reason, we have passed the moon and yet remain regressed as infants, as far as knowledge and its application to interpersonal matters. It is no wonder that most people, as hard as they try, never quite succeed at becoming their highest Self. It is no wonder that our parents, as hard as they try, have yet to learn Prevention and Excellence in parenthood. It is no wonder that our leaders, as hard as they try have a universal crisis hanging over their shoulders without any true, applicable answer and find themselves going back to the ancient answers that for centuries, have been proven mistakes by history.

Four

Our Culture, Our Self
All Patterns are Cross-Cultural

Whole cannot exist without its parts. We can no longer afford the separation of powers, since we depend on each and every power existing in order to maintain Universal Power Balance. Therefore, an environment must be created where every individual being lives in harmony and balance amongst others, of all races, sexes and differences of belief, where everyone can experience all Self Dimensions. An individual who cannot accept the different shades of patterns around the Self has not yet accepted his or her own Self. It is what we hide within from even our own Self that we want to keep outside of our domain. Each and every pattern outside of our Self represents one on the inside and the only way to grow is to explore both the world within and the world without.

All relationships are cross-cultural: even within one family. Even among members of one family, I have observed patterns of cross-culture of various shades and depth: patterns that can only be endured by the power of love and acceptance of the core of each member. As a part of Preventive Family Therapy, we need to look at all relationships as cross-cultural. And we must observe that within our own Self and in our families, under one roof, we have cross-cultural differences. No two patterns within us and no two people are alike; aggression and silence, adolescents and parents, husbands and wives, and even twin sisters, have cross-cultural differentness. Everyone is unique. Understanding of that uniqueness requires flexibility and capacity and openness to Self. Accepting differentness in others is a path of philosophical and spiritual existence that guides us to extend understanding of our own relationships and our larger family: the society. Allowing and nurturing the *Power Balance of cultures* enables us connect with the multidimensions of our Self. To the degree that we can look at each other and instead of strange, black, Jewish, Italian, fat, or thin, we only see *different,* and to the degree that we can accept this differentness, we have learned to accept ourSelf, our families and our society; this is a process of prevention of dysfunction and imbalance of patterns on a larger scale.

Many virtues to any culture. There are also many Patterns that are detrimental to societal survival as well as its Excellence. If we set aside our biases and prejudices and create a power balance of cultures and differentness where we can choose the best of what universal wisdom has to offer, we will have swung the universal pendulum, and will have chosen Universal Nurturance. It is very easy to reject differentness. We can all pass justified laws or make familial rules to keep others out who are different so that no one can challenge our limitations. Yet what seems to be a tough challenge and difficult for many who are too rigid to be flexible is the answer to societal excellence: the cultural power balance of differentness.

Beyond
The Inherited Culture

When I see people who immigrate to the States while creating isolated islands among themselves, refusing to learn the language and what the culture has to offer them, I ask myself, why did they come here? It would have been far less complicated to remain where they were. I believe that people migrate, like myself, to stretch beyond what they have already outgrown and mastered. If not, they can find far more comfort and security in their own land, and will have an easier life with a familiar language. If we travel across the globe just to be competitive with others and are not willing to participate, we will pay the price of creating power struggle within our family members who do go out and grow further away by just being exposed to more than one culture.

Culture exposure creates wisdom of flexibility. Exposure to two cultures is a treasure and luxury not many people can afford, physically, emotionally or financially. But to be exposed and not to gain from it, to me, is a personal crime and irresponsibility for not following through with the choices one has already made. Some say they did not choose to become gypsies; it was their fate that drove them out of their homeland. True. Some people's choices are made by the corruption of systems that have failed. And yet once one is in the garden, with or without choice, it is a loss not to choose to smell the flowers.

Guest cultures as the treasure. On the other hand, I see that the native people of a land are often too hesitant to learn from or honor their guests, and often by the toxic influences of ignorant and inhumane politics see them as intruders who should never have left their own land. It is not only sad for the guests, but a tragic limitation for the hosts who close themselves to the sea of knowledge and culture handed to them graciously if they would only welcome the treasures that have come to them as holy gifts of Universal Maternal Nurturance. It is openness to differentness that creates the flexibility, understanding, respect and acceptance that we need in order to create a healthy balance of peace and prosperity for all beings in this magnificent melting pot of existence.

Eastern Culture
Timeless Path

Eastern culture and the lack of material indulgence. I, a philosophically-oriented being, understood the East far more than I ever studied it. Maybe it was in the clear and unhurried air I had to breathe daily for twenty years of my life in an Eastern society. In Eastern cultures, the lack of indulgence, from an absence of too many toys to play with, forces people to look within themselves and search for a meaning to life.

Eastern timeless life in a slow lane. They also have the time for it. They are not Programed to think that if they don't own a house, two children, dogs, a station wagon, and a membership pin to a political party and religious empire, their lives will have no meaning. They don't have multiple freeways running them on the maze of life, wasting half of their lives getting on and off the road, not being able to enjoy their true paths with those whom they love. Nor do they have to breathe the toxic polluted air that promises prosperity to a group of lobbyists while victimization to the rest.

Eastern culture's lack advanced tools. Eastern civilization lacks advanced tools to apply their depth to everyday life and living. Instead of using their philosophical depth towards more meaning and purpose, life becomes a meaningless philosophical fantasy, symbiotically enmeshed in their families and friends; they never quite claim a Self in totality.

A second chance and a rebirth. A democratic society is the best environment for development of Self, separated from the umbilical cord that connects us to the addictive indulgences and Imbalances mistaken for culture. People who migrate to other countries, especially to the United States, must appreciate and take advantage of the second chance they created for themselves in learning democratic patterns in a free country; of independence of thought and action. Once we become clear about who we are, and are no longer affected by the chaotic distractions of societal denial, we must look around and see the sea of opportunities that exist for growth, abundance and prosperity. For immigrants there is even more chance at developing their true Self because they are not held back by the chains of the handed down of this society.

Westernization
An Advanced Maze

Westernization: fast-paced maze, illusive reality. In Western culture, everything is provided in quantity but not with quality, with rush and not with thought, careless, not with grace, arrogant and mindless, not introspective with thoughtfulness. Life that is assessed and valued by performance and not substance becomes living fully on the surface, never even looking for the meaning to its fast-paced maze and overwhelming illusion of reality; living life with slogans and before long we begin to think of ourSelf only as numbers to promote a cause we never deeply thought about, questioned or believe in.

What is missing in Western culture. The time to introspect upon philosophical dimensions and to look for the true meaning to life is missing in Western culture. It is possible to be successful and yet not to be sold to material success. It is possible to own things and yet not to be driven by them to the point of losing Self. It is possible to become independent in thought and action and yet remain connected to those we love. It is all a part of the inherent capacity existing within all of us.

Eastern philosophy before religious influence. I grew up with the philosophical belief of "do unto others what you want done onto you." In the Persian Empire where my ancestors grew up before the influence of the Arab religion, we believed in goodness for goodness' sake. Do good, think pure thoughts, and have clear actions, was the commandment of the Zartosht belief that existed long before any religion came to play.

Philosophy of goodness for goodness' sake. The Persian Empire's exemplary wisdom and strength came from people who did good for goodness' sake, not for the fear of punishment, guilt, or shame. They lived by the law of inner ethics and the wisdom of the universe. They only lost when they began to mimic and copy what was popular and looked outside of their Self for the answers.

Philosophy of power and responsibility. Equality between the sexes, liberation of the mind, and the wisdom of happiness built on personal responsibility and power, were founded in old Persia: before corruption and ignorance of religion, and the indulgences and arrogance of the West forced her powerful wings down and seduced her into the dark caves of oppression. It is a tragedy that the world is paying for today; a tragedy that we, as a nation must learn from; not to follow a path, blindfolded.

The root of every person: Universal Self. I find the true Root to the problem of the lack of Power Balance of people who seem to have lost the strength, the principles and the grace they once had, is that they are being influenced by escapism and the denial patterns of the West, living the empty life of indulgence. The powerful, rich, and graceful heritage of Eastern territories came not from their folk dances, their language, their Persian rugs, their oil wells, or the queen's jewels that impress the Western world immensely; it came from knowing their Universal Self, accepting responsibility for the fruit of freedom and liberation embedded within their heritage. This same power, the inherent power of people, has been the force behind building a democratic empire in the United States. The miracle of embracing humanity with all its dimensions and colors and regard for the core of the person is the essence of survival of any civilization. We cannot build on the body and the souls of victimized people just as clearly as we have not been able to build humanity for centuries by franchising on the nails on the cross that hold the body of a great prophet.

Gaining back individual dignity. It is up to the people of each and every society to gain inner Power Balance so that they can gain dignity. The people of the Persian Empire, and all the lost cultures of the world, including the people of the lost cultures of our free society, must take personal responsibility by going back to the roots of their existence and nurturing once more. Persia needs the principles of Self-Knowledge and the qualities of joyful living with goodness, without the indulgences and addictions of a Western society. Otherwise, no matter what kind of leadership they choose or adopt without choice, Persia will repeat the mistakes of its own history.

Matriarchal Eastern societies. Eastern society, long before the humiliation of religious fanaticism cast a shadow on the equality of the races, was matriarchal. Women not only bore and nurtured their young ones, they also left them with their partners and worked in the plantations to plant the seeds and reap the crops to feed their families.

Lack of men-women Power Struggle. There were no Power Struggles, wars for dictatorship or one-dimensional and lopsided relationships. There was only love, protection, responsibility and partnership of equal and whole entities. Even now, when women in the Western world are fighting for liberation, Eastern women, although I don't quite know the root to such liberation, have kept their own last name and identity when they join a man with whom they share their destiny.

Power Balance of the sexes within and without. The Power Balance of the sexes existed not only between men and women, but also within the inner souls of men and women. Men were strong enough not to be afraid and intimidated by women, to share power and vulnerability. Women were not oppressed or sold into the victimized system of holding their true Self back, exercising vanity just to be an accepted member of society.

The Power Balance of cultures. People have been manipulated into becoming nationalistic isolationists and partial to their own cultures, closing themselves to others. By doing that, they are not only creating Power Imbalance and war among themselves, but also cheating themselves out of the Inner Power Balance they could gain by accepting all of humanity, and finding the Patterns of Humanity that exist within Self.

The War of Cultures

We live in a time of history when there is war of cultures not only on the streets of our free country but among the leadership in our constitutional democracy. We the people must become aware of such a significant swing of the power from nurturance of diversity to the present power-play of isolationism and claims of one race supremacy. This war does not belong to people. It never has. And even though in the end it is the people who pay the price, its root is the need for power and greed, which stems from ignorance, not of the people, but of the blind leadership. The civil war of the South and the North, for and against freeing the blacks in this country, was not about the people, either. It was about the absence of flexibility to change and experience the glory of shared power, progression and prosperity, in peace. The killing and bloodshed on the streets was not because people hated people of a different color. It was because they were not taught by their leaders, who did not know, how to accept those who had grown and who wanted a piece of the pie for the efforts they were making. It was about the inability and lack of skills of those who wanted to have equal power to assert themselves and demand power balance instead of aggressive tactics of force. It is all about the choice of either moving towards progressive negotiations to share power globally, with all the children of humanity, or to seek leadership through bullying and building more defense and offense and to continue the destructive war games with no one truly winning. There is no such war as a holy war; where there is bloodshed, there is killing, murder and pure inhumanity far from the claims of spirituality.

So for the war of cultures to end, people on both sides of the aisle of life must begin to appreciate one another and focus on what they are gaining from the presence of each other. Those who come to this country must appreciate the opportunities which expose them to the practical dimensions of Western society, and its hospitality as a host who has opened her arms to all people of the world. They must welcome the opportunity, and know that they are here to mingle and adapt to the universal languages and customs that can only bring them a deeper connection with their own inner complexity.

And natives must appreciate the sea of culture and depth of richness and opportunity handed to them as a result of being a host in the free melting pot of America.

One-dimensionality of one culture. It is not possible to recognize all our dimensions if we are closed to differentness and become one-dimensional creatures, fearful of the colorful world of difference around us. Only by exposing ourselves to the world of Power Balance and polarities do we find dimensions of existence within ourselves that extend to our external world and connect us to the universal ocean of abundance of differentness as well as similarity.

One-dimensional perception of reality. That is why people who have only experienced one culture can become limited and one-dimensional in their perception of reality. Easterners only see it in their dreams. Westerners miss it by passing it by at rush hour, trying to make a pretty picture to frame a lifeless trophy, without truly living in joy and harmony.

Depth to life. That is why both Easterners and Westerners, if not exposed to the balancing cultures that would help them see the larger picture, will go on living without knowing the meaning of life. For a Westerner, life becomes meaningless and is so easily taken for granted. Nothing without depth will ever have meaning. And for an Easterner, the depth is wasted in dreams. Chinese monks sleep whenever they wish to resolve deep-rooted problems. They trust their vision in their sleep far more than their vision when they are awake. They think that their earthy eyes may be influenced more by that which is meant to be seen than by that which is truly the reality.

Power Balance of cultures. Understanding the true meaning of life comes from balancing the depth offered by the Eastern philosophies with its adaptation into life with the scientific tools of the West. There is no reason not to live successful, prosperous and joyful lives with the depth and meaning that only comes from introspection and fasting from indulgences that corrupt our minds.

Embracing Differentness

The Power Balance theory and its application of Pattern Change Therapy does not look at people with predispositions and preconceived ideas. Each and every individual is unique, and as it is crucial to experience differentness, it is equally significant to make efforts to preserve one's original Patterns of Strength and Uniqueness.

Sameness is not a virtue: anyone can copy. Although it is wise to copy Patterns of Excellence and Power Balance in any culture, it is only from Patterns of Differentness that creativity can be developed. Sameness is virtuous when challenged, tested by differentness, just as order is a virtue when challenged and resulted from chaos. When we have been exposed to different patterns of life, and then consciously choose the Patterns of Strength shared by others who have gone through the evolution of change as well, in a path similar to ours, the sameness we have chosen is that of grace, and is a foundation for excellence.

Differentness. Differentness must be appreciated, encouraged and rewarded for the quality of sameness to flourish. People who feel acceptance for their differentness become open and willing to take on the sameness that can bring them even further strength, dimension and resilience.

Rejecting people creates rebellion. The Pattern of Rebellion has created a traumatic crisis in society today. It has always been the cause of war and inhumane action by ignorant and insecure others who condemn differentness because they fear a loss of power over what they don't understand, and consequently cannot control. When we condemn people for who they are, either the walls go up and they can no longer hear us, or the walls fall apart and the conformity we gain is the pseudo-success of an oppressor who will be rebelled against at some point in time.

For any change, the core must be nurtured. The core of the people must be nurtured and accepted before any significant change can occur. The core of the people must be accepted and nurtured for any positive change to take place. Unfortunately, some societal leaders who consistently reject others and want to create a uniform world of Patterns that weaken the backbone of humanity cannot be reached with firmness and nurturance, for they have long forgotten their humane qualities of openness, flexibility and deep regard for differentness.

Inhumane shield of dominance must be broken. These inhumane leaders do not seem open to suggestions, for they are so busy rejecting others that there is no room left for negotiations and civilized compromises for the welfare of humanity. They are in so much fear of differentness and lack of control that they have created shields of dominance, power and supremacy around themselves with Patterns of Intimidation and Control that must first be torn down before they can be rebuilt.

Universal Freedom and liberty

True freedom and liberty needs all people on its side. On the same token, Western culture must become aware of the gifts of wisdom and the enlightened nature of its guests who have left their own comfortable homes to become part of the making of the dream of freedom and liberty. It was all of us who built America, and it belongs to us all, without discrimination: the ignorance that brings greed and the need for exclusive power, war and hostility.

Culture wars: Power Imbalance within Selves. Only a one-dimensional person fearful of differentness would be rigid enough to reject the richness and beauty that the diversity of cultures offers humanity. In a free country as ours, culture wars have been declared by some of our political leaders who define democracy as an impractical ideology of the people on the other side of the aisle.

Tear down walls of ignorance and prejudice. Sadly, the melting pot of the world, where once the trust of finding freedom on the streets brought the cream of the crop of other nationalities and races from all over the world, is beginning to build the walls she helped other countries tear down.

There is Imbalance in any culture or belief. We must find Balance within ourselves. True freedom comes when we have experienced the ability to be free from the need for appearances of freedom that compromises its development in a true sense. A fourteen-year old cannot find inner freedom in the heart of the night on cold and ruthless streets.

In Eastern culture, where I was brought up, overattachment costs one one's soul and a separated identity, whereas in Western culture overdetachment does not provide an adequate environment to develop the Self fully. The need for the appearance of freedom simply takes away freedom's true essence.

Adjustment disorder from flight to a new culture. For a foreigner, coming to America is a shock to the system for a while: a condition that unaware therapist, unfamiliar with the situational crisis of this sort, can call schizophrenia and refer to a psychiatrist, who might immediately take out his prescription pad and prescribe the legitimate drug that makes a zombie out of an intelligent person who from then on, if not sophisticated enough, will be at the mercy of the diagnosis and labels written in a file. I did not go through this tragic process, but as a therapist, I have worked with many who spent half of their lives wandering in it.

Family of origin and Power Balance Initiation. Power Balance Initiation is a process of separation from old roots and embracing roots of our own, without rejecting our original roots. It is more difficult for people who grow up in Eastern cultures to separate themselves from their families and begin families of their own. Some of them forever remain the children of their families, always flying home in the slightest of conflicts and crisis. Most of them never leave home, but bring their mate to live with them, creating unhealthy power struggle between crushed identities.

Margaret Mahler's notion of graduation-individuation is the separation of the child from the mother that takes place in early years of life between two to five. Its unsuccessful resolutions leave either the helplessness of autism (attachment-depravation) or the anguish of schizophrenia: an unsuccessful symbiosis and over-attachment. Reading her material when I was in the process of painfully separating mySelf from my family of origin at an age far beyond the natural life process, as the experts determine it, dissipated my fears and created joyful empowerment. At twenty-one, away from the familiar and habitually loved attachments of my life, as painful as it was, I began to grow as an individual.

Too close to the forest to see the trees. I was a very late bloomer indeed, in every meaning of the word. A late bloomer in love and a late bloomer in life. For I had not been allowed to experience much. Separating helped me heal from Patterns of Imbalance of my own family of origin for the first time. When one is too close to the forest, seeing the trees is impossible. No matter how vivid to a distanced eye, the eye that is too close only sees the chips on the surface, the blend of everything together: so together that one usually sees only the faults in whatever is too painful to separate from.

Suffering strengthens and polishes the soul. The pain I experienced was my pain, and the joy I felt was purely the outcome of my own actions. This was especially true when I had none of my family members to share the most significant moments of my life, like when I delivered my children. I cried a lot for a couple of days, especially since the woman in the hospital room with me was visited by her family members. It hurt that my husband worked at a jet propulsion lab in Pasadena and could not get to Newport Beach until late at night to visit me, and had to bribe the nurses to see me. But somehow, when I got through crying over feeling that I was alone in this world, magically, for the first time in my life, I realized that I was home, and that I would never feel alone again. I had finally come to mySelf.

Pseudo-Savior Syndrome

Pattern Change Programing and the Theory of Power Balance puts the responsibility back onto people and takes away the pseudo-savior syndrome that disables people and prevents them from becoming their own saviors, taking responsibility for their mistakes and accepting the consequences for their actions. Pattern Change Programing does not teach people to live in a borrowed reality where any minute someone may appear and save them from their problems and take them to a better world. It does teach individuals to recognize the danger of encouraging denial existing within society: denial of problems they cannot run away from and leave behind, but which they must deal with and help resolve with dignity. The existence of a pseudo-savior image in people's lives in itself has created patterns that endanger the survival of our society; people relieve Self of responsibilities to make changes, losing rights to freedom that cannot exist without responsibility.

Selective Compassion that is spreading discrimination. The development of discrimination among people who hold onto an image that is supposed to save them has caused the spread of hatred and prejudice, provoking wars throughout history. What had been developed by people, to serve people, and to bring connection and harmony among them, according to Pattern Change Programing principles, no longer functions that way. In fact, its childlike and primitive nature has become one of the most regressive and destructive elements in the survival of humanity.

Role models for humanity. To me, a role model for humanity must have a choice of protecting and defending himself or herself from immoral, conscienceless and anti-humane individuals and groups. Otherwise, he or she cannot be an appropriate role model for humanity. A good role model for humanity will not hurt others, will not treat people like objects, and will not harm people for his or her own benefit at the cost of integrity, freedom, prosperity, or rights.

Inhumanity and cruelty should not win. Yet if a role model for humanity is in the midst of inhumane environments, he or she will not bend down and make people feel that cruelty wins, or that darkness is stronger than light, or that the truth will lose over each agenda of greed, need for power, or revengeful act of hate and prejudice stemming from blind obedience and ignorance of the ones exercising it. Cruelty and inhumanity should not win before the eyes of our children.

Children are the leaders and decision-makers of tomorrow. They watch us with utmost sensitivity and make decisions in their hearts and minds that will affect the course of destiny. As parents, we must not advocate them to role model after inhumane behavior, no matter how popular the perpetuators of cruelty may be. It must not be difficult to recognize such inhumane patterns today, in our society. Aggressively insulting innocent people who are serving our country has become a manipulative tactic of winning votes and popularity.

We must not be blinded by selective kindness of those who are only kind to us. We must demand from them a universal compassion and decency and guide them away from wrongdoing if they are so confused that they cannot see. We cannot afford to be shy or afraid of not joining in for laughing at the cruel remarks of another, thinking that it will make us an outcast, a disloyal church or community member.

The scars of an unjust, beaten and violated integrity are far more painful than the scars of a beaten and violated body. While in our society we have become conscious of violence and abuse and our government is actively after those who violate the rights of others, from the top of the hierarchy we still exercise and allow emotional slavery and brutality as a sign of strength, honesty and sincerity. We say "he is telling it like it is" to a guy who has a monopoly on manipulation and dishonesty.

Honorable convictions must be supported. The theory of Power Balance and Pattern Change Programing does not believe in the genuineness and authenticity of the Pattern of Kindness if one has not and cannot also exercise the Pattern of Strength and Bravery needed for people to protect the Self and their honorable convictions, as long as one's intent does not infringe upon the rights of others or intrude upon ethical boundary.

Societal Tough Love

Would we have been so merciful to a father who molests his children for whom he has responsibility, or trusting of a thief who robs us of our money, home, peace of mind, and security? This is the same thing, and to close our eyes and go along with it is a silent crime of today's society. If we raise our children with love and compassion and treat others with the same respect and acceptance we feel deserving of, there won't be a need for tough love: a method that our societal leadership today seems to be needing.

This is the result of our past programing of blind obedience to authority, and it is the cause of imbalance in our society. Authority in American culture today has become anyone who can come before the camera and say something. And we the people have learned to automatically honor or dishonor others according to the seat they take, without intrinsically questioning their intent and their integrity. Morality and ethics are not measured by what church someone goes to, if he or she goes to any church at all. It is measured by how they treat others and how they advocate others to treat the members of their community.

The Arrogant Culture
Hitler's Men

Millions of innocent people of their own country. It all began with a brilliant idea of arrogant supremacy: a tormented individual feeling inferior, alienated and lonely most of his adolescence and childhood, whose power gave him the unwise opportunity to play with millions of people's lives as he became a powerful and ruthless visionary. He planted a seed with his power of persuasion and waited to see the reaction of the majority. If he had not succeeded by the power of the mind and spirit of the people, he would have apologized and gone away feeling sorry for his lack of expressive ability. But he succeeded, and began his terrorism of morale and assassination of decency before ordering his clan to dig holes and throw in the bodies. A similar tragedy was once allowed in this very democratic and free country in the Eugenic Colony: a place where people were killed because of not looking like, and acting like, the masters and the majority of the society. The Hitlers of our time must be stopped so that history does not repeat its mistakes.

We must look within our own inner ethics. People have power and must be responsible for how they utilize it. It seems like we must carry the burden neglected by some of the leaders of our society. We must ask and become clear of the intent of each and every gathering where we are asked to be the cheerleaders. We must ask ourselves the purpose of our existence in that gathering. If some are terrorizing and assassinating the character of others, we must put ourselves in the place of whomever is being victimized. We must ask ourselves that if it were ourselves and our family and spouse they were terrorizing, what would we have expected from the rest of our community. Laughing at someone who is putting others down assists the accepted crime by any rules of ethics and morality. No showman or a congressman should be making millions of dollars at the cost of others, let alone be honored and awarded for intrusive bravery, by any club whose members are not the same as those of Sodom and Gomorra, without a conscience, but instead are decent people who truly mean it when they advocate and stand by their spirituality.

Five

11
Universal Laws
of Success-Spiritual Excellence

Laws of Multidimensionality

Knowledge of Self develops Individual Inner Power Balance which is governed based upon the Universal Laws. We are multidimensional beings, as is the universe, although unaware of many of our dimensions. All Universal Laws are driven from the universal multidimensional nature and patterns that in practice I call *Power Balance Therapy*. Our societal training has taught us to only adhere to one dimension of our Self while denying the others. Rigid old order that limits the vast power of being human has caused us much pain and confusion. I unfolded, in chapter two, the Forgotten Self: dimensions existing within the individual that we must nurture and embrace or they will stay forgotten and remain on the back shelves of our unconscious. When we become vulnerable, these inhibited and punished facets gain power over us, and we lose control of our actions.

Universal laws are driven from my source of inspiration and wisdom: the universe, an ultimate teacher. In my observations, its vast powers embrace the swings of Individual and universal patterns of existence. There are many Universal Laws governing this natural playpen. I will point out eleven which powerfully affect individual and societal patterns of excellence.

1st Universal Law
Law of Pattern Change

The core of Sky and earth, equally significant. Pattern Changes as a universal law; it clears the air of Toxic Power Blocks of all kind that impact the environment, by not only respecting the earth, but also fighting the Imbalanced and lopsided Patterns of relating altogether. The equality and significance of the sky and the earth symbolizes equality among all individuals, at all levels and classes that our cultures offer. It is true that one who works hard should reap the fruit of his or her labor, yet that does not put one on any higher level than one who does not choose success as the meaning for progression in life. A sincere and true choice cannot arise when we have but one choice and option.

What are Patterns? Patterns are processes of multidimensions existing within an individual that create the presentation of the behavior we observe. Patterns are whole within the individual and yet a part of the universal patterns of existence. The cognitive and emotional processes affect actual behavior and characteristic of an individual. For example, a person whom we call passive may not be passive in nature at all. She or he may be demonstrating behavior that stems from Patterns of guilt, shame or other thought processes Programed within the individual.

Patterns of Harmony. Are Patterns which exist next to each other or alone within an individual creating joy and peace. For example, when a person is watching a sunset or sunrise, the pleasure and joy of the moment is an indication that the person is in harmony at that time. If someone feels as though life is just like watching sunrises and sunsets every moment in life, even amidst crisis and the rush of everyday life, that person lives completely within the Patterns of Harmony. Harmony is a state in which many Power Balance Patterns exist side by side with the intent and purpose of peace and progression of Self and, ultimately, the environment.

A collection of Patterns existing in harmony. Patterns of Harmony at times can be entirely different from each other, or similar in nature, yet representing multidimensionality of the individual who exists in harmony. Power Balance Patterns that are of multidimensional nature existing within individuals in harmony, are indications of flexibility, versatility and clarity that only exists from the wisdom the stems from Self Knowledge.

Disconnected harmony. In absence of harmony in Patterns, or in the presence of Patterns of Imbalance and Block, the continuity and consistency of existing harmony is interrupted, and harmony becomes disconnected.

Existential Patterns. I would like to add to our awareness of what I call existential Patterns, the Patterns of Existential Health, Existential Power, Existential Clarity, and Existential Reality; the Universal Patterns and Laws of being. In all of these patterns there exists an inherent power, health, and clarity as the core, commonly embedded within all individuals. It is only because of a lack of focus and knowledge towards such inherent power, and misguided societal Programing that takes the individual outside of Self for sources of power, support and nourishment, that individuals have drifted from their inherent Patterns of Being.

Existential clarity: Universal Paternal Power Change Therapy and Programing is based on: a) the assumption that the healing process of individuals, families, and societies is directly related to their willingness and motivation to change their status quo, and b) the competence and the Power Balance of their guide. If the knowledge they receive is substantial, liberating, unbiased, and clear of specialist's own blocks and Imbalances, and if the guide has transcended the *part* given to him or her to *whole* "Self,"; an Existential, Universal Self. Healing is gained, in part, by an almost automatic transference of what I call Existential and Universal Clarity, or Universal Paternal Power existing between the student, and the guide; an Evolved Change in definition of existentialism; a Universal Law of Power Balance.

Existential Anxiety, Existential Power. Existentialism has focused mostly on vulnerabilities of the individual instead of the strengths, at least as I have understood it. I would like to change that Pattern and introduce new Patterns of Existentialism. Just as we have innate Existential Anxiety, we have Existential Power and capacity. The absence of focus on something simply takes the power away, temporarily. And the focus on the other, makes us all feel that anxiety is a natural state of being. Whereas the knowledge and recognition of our existing and inherent Existential Power acts as the support system we all need and seek outside of ourselves. It reduces Existential Anxiety, and produces Power.

Patterns, too, have minds of their own. Our Patterns, too, have minds of their own, and it is only when we accept, nurture, and understand them, that we can have control over them and change them if we so choose. To deny our Patterns means to be at their mercy for as long as we live, driven by the motivation that brought them into our lives, for the rest of our lives, even if the Programer of that motivation is long gone.

All Patterns have had true intent at one time. We cannot look at our Patterns as our enemies, even if they are destructive to us. Every Pattern is initially Programed into our general life patterns for a positive intent and purpose. It might have also been Programed just because it was there, and was not necessarily for destructive purposes.

All Patterns change. All Patterns change; the choice to change is the awareness of the direction and the guidance we take towards change. We are changing all the time. To know what one picked up on the path of life, what one rebelled against, and what one obeyed, is to know what we are made of and what we will become with a choice of the direction our changes take place. Where we are today can change position from regression towards progression, from lack of control to healthy control, from limitation to openness, expansion, and a dropping of the walls, from hate to love, from separation to compassion, from alienation to connection, and from the abuse of power of the institutions to the power of the people: the creators of those institutions, for their peace of mind and not their own destruction; if we choose to trust our Self.

Blueprint for Change

Patterns: Adopted or Chosen? We all know that great wisdom comes in simple definitions and solutions, not in confusing, vague and complicated labels and stereotypes. Pattern Change Therapy explains people's differences in the Programs and Life Patterns they have Chosen or Adopted. As a result, it simplifies the ability to change. It also provides tools for individuals to find the roots to Adopted Patterns handed down to them by other Programers, challenging the notion of widely accepted theories of genetic predisposition as the basis for mental illness or inferiority. Even further, by scientifically walking the individual through creating and forming patterns that have been stamped exclusive to a certain generation, race, belief, or even gender, it challenges the stability, credibility, and validity of many established beliefs that have been formed by others just like the individual, within and without his or her life domain.

This simplification of individual patterns releases the burden from the shoulders of the people. Individuals will find freedom from the labels of other programers who find power, pleasure and challenge in developing invalid grounds for creating competitive prejudicial separation between people by dividing them into boxes with names on them, glorifying some and humiliating others. It isn't any wonder that we are always fighting with each other to salvage our dignity.

No genetic superiority or inferiority. Life is but a collection of Patterns. The problems human beings experience are only the result of Patterns adopted; they are not caused by something they inherited or because they were doomed by the devil or blessed by the angels. There is no superiority or inferiority: only a collection of Patterns one acquires that if one sees fit, can be chosen or deleted. Just as easily, if we are not comfortable with the weight we put on, once we recognize the subconscious reason for keeping it on, we can easily lose weight: not for feeling less than a person, but because we seek our own best of health.

Genetics are real. But we can change our Programs so that they enable us to benefit from our gene selections, and thus control the nature of their functions. Genes, too sensitive to be read by neurotransmitters, exist. They will not go anywhere, so worrying about them will only deny what can be done to tame them. Everything, no matter how wild, can be tamed and changed by patterns of flexibility and tolerance of delay of gratification. Not what we have acquired in the womb, but what we do with it, even long before it is out in the world we invite it to, will enable us to take full responsibility. The power of the mind and the inherent capacity and desire to change our lives from powerlessness to Self-Control, are truly worth focusing on.

What is Change? Change is an inevitable Universal Law; its direction is a choice one can make. Change itself is not a choice; it occurs consistently and unconsciously. Every living thing is in constant change before our eyes, every moment of our lives. The ability to change is inherent and, in fact, more often without our conscious awareness. The direction of change is controllable only if we bring its process into our consciousness.

Example. When we walk into a room, if we don't decide where we want to sit, who we want to talk to, what our purpose is in the room with these people, and what we want to accomplish, then we will walk out of the room having sat where someone else suggested, talked about what others brought up, ate what was offered and left with what others dictated to us as an assignment or order.

Change with intent and purpose. The core of the individual or any living entity will never change. What the individual is carrying that does not belong and blocks joy, progress and prosperity, is changeable. People are terrified of change. They think that if they change, they will have nothing left, or that they might turn into some kind of monster they will have to live with all of their lives. But the fact is that people are right. They can't change. The core will never change. The core of every person is a shared, inherent goodness. What changes are the Patterns of Imbalance and Block that have been put upon them.

The blink of an eye is a change so automatic that we don't even think about. But if we learn to focus on the changes going on within us, we can learn a great deal from the meaning of the blink of an eye. The power is not in the changing; it is in understanding the meaning and direction of that change.

What does change do? Just as we watch someone who is dying of deprivation come to life as we give him or her oxygen, water and food, I watch people change from the death of a meaningless existence to the life of a purposeful journey, every day. And they make that happen only by change.

What does change look like? How does it feel? And how does it sound? I suppose we must first see and understand stagnation, to see change. During the process of Pattern Change, I see people for different purposes and in different times of their lives. In people who come to me during crisis experiencing hopelessness and powerlessness, I observe the pattern of literal death and dying in their faces and bodies. I see colorless faces without a glimmer of hope, love, joy or compassion, bent backs from heavy and uncontrolled life burdens, Imbalanced postures from a lack of awareness and Knowledge of Self, and suspicion and fear of others from the absence of trust in Self. Change, changes all that.

I see feelings, hidden, tucked away to where they are long forgotten; voices shaky and without firm convictions from being lost in a path they did not map out; without a guide; without their Self; and without a companion or friend; just looking for another excuse or legitimate permission to give it all up and go back to their custom-carved graves of stagnation they call *life;* doing nothing, being afraid of death. I tell them they seem to be already dead and it is up to them to be in heaven or hell. And then as I merely put my hand behind their back, lean towards them and say a kind word that stems from genuine care; when I guide them to see that change is near, I see their faces glow and their voices strengthen. They sit up straight, and I see *change.*

Patterns of Change needs no lapse of time. Change needs a focus of the mind to feel and to think as if there had been a lapse in time. Any time new answers, new methods, new approaches and new visions are presented, they must also go through their own process of Power Balance and Excellence like the individual experiencing it. But the process does not mean a lapse of time; it means focusing the mind, and using its flexible capacity to go from one point to another, in moments, as if there had been lapses in time. Pattern Change Therapy shortcuts the lengthy times spent with the lack of understanding the purpose, as well as the lack of knowledge of the tools and the process. The scientific step by step well defined process, enables not only the client to know where they are going and why, but it also creates demystification in the therapist or the guide who now can be clear simply because she or he has the answers and the tools to lead on the why, what, and how, of today's path of guidance.

Witnessing Pattern Change in moments. In moments, I witness them becoming open to hear and understand, their eyes clear up of fear and suspicion; their movements become lighter, they begin to breathe; they even begin to care. They loosen up and laugh a little. They begin to talk about their plans instead of their hopelessness. They gain a sense of purpose. Their voice becomes stronger and the ambivalence hiding underneath disappears. When I meet people, I can immediately tell whether they have a sense of appreciation and respect for change as an inevitable constant process of life, or if they fear, deny and constantly fight it. One way or another, its appreciation or denial leaves its footprints all over a person.

Change is only created by change. As I begin to change position in my comfortable seat, leaning forward towards my client, changing within mySelf from feelings of empathy for the person to wanting to do something about their pain, feeling no sympathy for keeping them in their thick shell of denial and prolonging their dependency, my intent becomes focused on the purpose of replacing their Pattern of Stagnation with that of Movement. And at that moment, change is created.

Change as a transferable phenomenon. I changed. I no longer accepted the status quo of another person in pain, knowing that pain was neither necessary nor natural. By my change, by leaning forward to lend my trust of the inherent capacity within my client, an immediate change in my client was created. After that, the knowledge of Patterns of Life and the Programs, techniques and skills to gain control and take charge of my life and destiny, brought about a constant chain of changes that are now part of the joy and mastery of my life.

Myth: Block between dreams and reality. Everything is simple when we begin the process. Only the illusion that change is difficult paralyses us from acting. We must realize that we are capable and powerful: not powerless, as some Programers have taught us to believe. There is no dream that cannot be materialized.

Questioning old and outdated Programing. The only thing standing between the dream and the reality is our doubt about the inherent power of our minds, our unquestioned beliefs, and our choice to remain ignorant of the Knowledge of Self. Knowledge of Self is the key to obtaining everything there has ever been, and anything there is yet to be.

Becoming the makers of ourSelf. We must choose what goes inside our bodies and our minds. We live in a free country where everything is easy to reach.. Abundance of information and opportunity is severely taken for granted in this country by its natives, and is far more appreciated by others who know that acquiring such vast knowledge is a difficult task elsewhere in the world. Accumulating knowledge is inhibited and discouraged by those who fear self sufficiency and independence in thought and action by people. No leader whose life savings depends on leading the blind will ever buy or encourage the purchase of a cane for that person. It is up to that person to recognize the hindrance of such dependency and to ask another to assist him or her into buying a cane, or to hold on to the walls, feel the light and walk out of adopted darkness of blind insight.

Becoming our own Life Programers. As a part of freedom without boundary, we are also exposed to unwanted or harmful information. But it is up to us to care enough about ourselves to feed our bodies and souls the nurturing nutrition they deserve. To the stockholder, we are only a body to fill with a toxic and wasteful product. To ourselves, we must mean a great deal more, or else we learn to become that which we are given.

We are what we consume. We become a collection of what we see, what we hear and what we eat, and the less we care, the more we are at the mercy of others who care not about us, but about how to use us for their own personal profit and agenda. The study which found that plants that heard classical music survived and actually blossomed better than the ones reared with pop music gives us part of the answer to the great mystery of the lack of control we feel in the way we become. Only because we don't choose the direction of becoming, and not because the process of growth is uncontrollable, do we lose Self-Control. Knowing that knowledge is power, and that the mind is the keeper of that power, we must begin to feed our minds the Programs we choose, consciously directed towards the intent, purpose and mission of our lives: becoming Power Balanced and Excelled Individuals.

Self-Program of Power Balance and Excellence. We must become the creators and Programers of our own lives, in full knowledge and capacity of functioning with choices deserving of our integrity. Life is but a chain of Pattern Changes that creates our destiny. Self Knowledge = Freedom = Responsibility = Power Balance = Program of Individual Power and Dignity. Power Balance and Excellence, a philosophical, psycho-physical-socio-universally Spiritual Self-Program, guides us towards the vision to obtain and maintain our inherent individual power and dignity. Pattern Change Programing is an application that scientifically teaches us why we should, shows us how we can, and trains us to maintain it.

Beyond the Patterns. By moving beyond the labels of the mental health profession and see the shades and the patterns of the individual as a part of the universe, we can utilize Change in a liberating, unlimited change process governed by Universal laws, scientifically, spiritually, philosophically and societally, allowing individuals the vision, and the mind/body independence of thought and action to take charge of their own destiny and not get lost in today's societal calamity. And by moving beyond the patterns we can connect with the core of the person connected with that of the universe: in mind, body and spirit.

2nd Universal Law
Law of Power Balance

Hymns of Harmony. Hymns of harmony are multidimensions of Patterns of Harmony: Patterns which exist next to each other or alone within an individual, creating joy and peace and mastery. For example, when a person is watching a sunset or sunrise, the pleasure and joy of the moment is an indication that the person is in harmony at that time. If someone feels as though life is just like watching sunrises and sunsets every moment in life, even amidst crisis and the rush of everyday life, that person lives completely within Patterns of Harmony. Harmony is a state in which many Power Balance Patterns exist side by side with the intent and purpose of peace and progression of Self and, ultimately, the environment.

Universal Pendulum Swing. In my Theory of the Universal Swing of the Pendulum, I suggest that the entire universe is in a constant, natural process of swinging: from life to death and back to life; from dark to light and back to dark; from cold to hot and back to cold. The Universal Swing of the Pendulum uncovers universal laws governing all living things, from the smallest cell to the largest entity, and provides us with the universal knowledge to heal the swing of the pendulum within and without.

Extremes in swing are Imbalances of Patterns. The Universal Swing of the Pendulum means that just as an individual swings from cold to hot, from kind to harsh, from compassionate to insensitive, the universe has also embedded the same law of pendulum within it. In fact, it is a part of Universal Swing of the Pendulum that individuals feel within. Imbalance of one creates Imbalance in the other. It is in the Power Imbalance of Patterns that the extremes in the swing occur.

Constant flow of Universal Power Balance. This theory explains swings of moods as a natural process of being. Extreme swings stem from oppression and denial of Power Balance between Patterns. It is much like the Universal Swing in that the extremes of the powers cause friction and imbalance in universal harmony and peace, and vice-versa; imbalance and harmony cause extremes in the swing. I believe that we naturally copy the Universal Laws within us just because we are a part of the whole Universal Program. There is a constant flow of Power Balance between the individual and the universe, its keeper.

The Swing as a natural Pattern. The Swing becomes a Natural Pattern of Existence and not a disorder that one must have medication to numb. Fighting natural Patterns causes their rebellion and exaggeration. Accepting, analyzing, and recognizing the roots from where they stem will lead them towards Power Balance, wherein one Pattern becomes an integral part of the other, both being necessary for inner peace and balance. Together, they lead to Success and Excellence. When it rains and flood rivers take over the paper homes of our sunny cities, when the earth angrily shakes and tells us we cannot have control of everything and must become a bit less arrogant, when the mountains erupt and the fire of their souls rise, just when we think they are dead, if we panic or rebel we will be damaged just as if we deny and neglect. The mere acceptance of our own fall before our rise, our own angry stormy nights before the inspiring sunny days, and the sheer understanding of their purpose and meaning in our lives, will empower us and bring out the best of the swing of our natural patterns, without the need to compromise.

Universal Power Balance and Harmony. All other Universal Laws mentioned here and many more that fall under their categories are embedded in this Universal Law of Power Balance. My theory and therapy of Power Balance is based on the assumption that everything in this world must have balance and harmony. For every cell, every organ, every leaf, every plant, every tree, every animal, every piece of dirt and every human being alive, there is a formula of balance. The ultimate balance is harmony between all living beings. A harmony and balance of each *part* creates harmony and balance of the *whole*, which is the accumulation of the parts.

Evolution of Power Balance and Excellence. Power Balance is the process in which all of our dimensions, within and without, live in harmony. It is a revolutionary evolution of mental, emotional, physical, spiritual, societal and environmental Balance, and a peace to life that such wisdom and nurturance brings, and its by-products are health, success, happiness and spiritual excellence. It offers a long-lasting life in prosperity and health in a balanced environment that embraces us within, as we embrace it without, as we humbly accept the universal law of the swing of the pendulum. Revolution is needed now because of the neglect of this law. The avoidance of a mental revolution of equality and justice of choice that brings global peace and progression will resort in destructive regression.

Harmony is Power balance. Only in the existence of Power Balance can we achieve true Harmony. When two whole beings stand together, next to each other, unafraid of the wholeness within one another, unafraid of dissolving in each other, in appreciation and respect and compassion, Harmony is created. Harmony within Self and others is true power. So often, the pretense of Harmony for the sake of survival, need, or fear Blocks a true harmony that could have been created if the fear or block of power was stripped and deleted from the true Self.

Harmony within Self. Harmony within Self is the state of individual Power Balance; it is liberation within the individual where each and every step is a Pattern of Choice, conscious and free of blocks of fear, procrastination and any other pattern blocking the Self from being clear. From the universal law of harmony the following Power Balance patterns are created.

Individual Power Balance. Harmony is a state of peace and oneness with all that exists, within and around us. It is a blending without dissolving. When I refer to Power Balance, I am referring to harmony. When our Life Patterns not only live together harmoniously and at peace, in spite of their differences, but also guide and assist one another in the process of inner balance, we have reached Power Balance and harmony. The rules for Power Balance within Self are just like the rules for Power Balance with others and in society. The objective is to create an environment where all the Patterns, similar and different, exist congruent to one another in peace, acceptance, appreciation, respect and validation.

Harmony with Others. Harmony with others is connecting with joy and progression of minds together, with the flow of Patterns between each other creating new Patterns, where the feeling of oneness without losing the Self becomes possible.

Joint Power Balance Patterns. Or Power Balance Patterns of Relating, are Patterns of Harmony and Balance with others, creating the Power Balance Program for relating, where one can exist with another, and while maintaining individual Power Balance and inner harmony, the individual can create the same in relationship with others.

Communication Power Balance. These Patterns are included within the various Patterns of Relating, where the Power Balance between couples is achieved through the tools of communication. Patterns of Relating are explored in my upcoming book, *Love Patterns*.

Power Balance of Reciprocal Sensitivity. This occurs when we feel the pain of having been victimized, yet feel clear enough to do something about it. It is when, just as powerfully as we feel victimization, we also feel the pain we have inflicted upon others. Nothing is more hypocritical than a person who is offended by everyone's rejection, and rejects others without even noticing. It is different from inflicting pain upon an entity or institution that holds unquestioned and imbalanced power, and thus the only way of reaching its denial is attempting to rock its authoritative tower. It is when one chooses other innocent victims to inflict pain upon: pain felt in a past that has remained unrecognized, and thus unhealed.

Familial Power Balance Patterns. These are the Patterns of Power Balance among family members, creating a Family Power Balance and Excellence Program. In such a case, all family members coexist while creating both inner harmony and family harmony in which nurturance, acceptance, validation and respect are the given Patterns within the members of the family. Family Power Balance Patterns are explored in detail in my upcoming book, *Family Patterns of Excellence*.

Societal Harmony. The Power Balance of success and spiritual excellence has been the theme of all of my theories and work. The lack of choices in life and having to be one thing but not the other had always troubled me. The limitation we put on ourselves along with *rigid societal programing* that wants everything in tight, neat packages has caused imbalance and limitations, as is evident throughout history and in the patterns of being. Just because we are women we can't be strong and just because they are men they can't be vulnerable. Just because we are kind and compassionate we can't have a Self and feel power; just because they are powerful they can't be sensitive and flexible. To be a good person, we cannot have our own dreams. In order to gain material success, we cannot be kind, compassionate or spiritual. Or we cannot want a comfortable life if spiritual. To be a good partner and love someone, we cannot have ourSelf; Self-sacrifice is the true sign of love. It is the same with success. If we have success we have to be cutthroat and lonely souls, forever intimidating and frightening others. And if we are spiritual we have to become monks and live on a mountain to prove our true identity. People are just not that single-dimensional or that black and white. Besides, having choice makes our tendencies true and honest.

Societal Power Balance Patterns. Societal Power Balance Patterns are the Power Balance of Societal Leadership Patterns and Societal Individual Patterns, within and between themselves.

Societal Leadership Patterns. The Patterns of Societal Leadership can be divided into those patterns relating to the societal leaders and the people, and those relating to the societal leaders among themselves.

Patterns of a healthy society. Patterns of healthy Societal Leadership refer to the safety and protection it offers, its compassion and guidance, its Power Balance, and its connection with its people. A healthy harmony between the individual and societal leadership occurs when equal balance exists between them; they are able to equally gain from each other, and one does not exist at the cost of the health or integrity of the other.

Patterns among leadership. Patterns among leadership must be those of objective cooperation with each other for the sake of people's environmental health, safety, and excellence. Political hazing and competitive enterprise at the cost of the people must be fully rejected by the people; otherwise, societal survival, especially with the fast-growing, downward regression of this country, is at stake. Our leadership must acquire the humanitarian Patterns and Patterns of Excellence necessary for role models of health and Excellence. These patterns include:

> ***Media-people Power Balance Patterns***
> ***Health profession-people Power Balance Patterns***
> ***Politics-people Power Balance Patterns***
> ***Religion-people Power Balance Patterns***
> ***Enterprise leadership-people Power Balance Patterns***

Societal individual Patterns. The healthy connection of an individual with society involves the ability to understand societal rules and games, and to enjoy societal appearances, as well as the ability to be successful in career and function comfortably in different environments, interact with others, yet not be dependent upon society for evaluation of self-fulfillment and self-worth. It also involves equally choosing solitude and focus on the inner Self to create inner Power Balance, in addition to developing knowledge and participating in societal decision-making to create Power Balance with societal leadership. Types of Societal Individual Patterns are:

> ***Power Balance of Freedom-Responsibility***
> ***Power Balance of Goal-Process Orientation***
> ***Power Balance of Strength-Vulnerability***
> ***Power Balance of Silence-Activity***
> ***Power Balance of Introversion-Extroversion***
> ***Power Balance of Openness-Boundary***
> ***Power Balance of Cognition-Emotion***

Environmental Harmony. Environmental Harmony is the awareness and harmony both between and of the blend of Patterns of Excellence and their interrelation with each other, and their totality within themselves. Only by becoming aware of the trees, the flowers, the birds, the air, the water, the sun, and the earth above us, behind us, side-by-side us, and around us, can we begin to understand the meaning of the Power of Self and inner balance. And only by focusing within, by hearing our own heart in silence, can we become aware of the Power Balance existing in the environment, embracing us as we breathe.

Connection with the Universal Powers. By feeling the universal powers within and around us, we feel that we are all one, without losing ourselves and remaining whole within. It is the graceful interference of universal powers at times when we feel we know everything and can control whatever goes on in our lives. It is in a passing moment of astonishment, when we feel a brush of air going through us, and we somehow know that which before was completely unknown.

Environmental Patterns. Environmental Power Balance refers to the healthy, ongoing connection between Self and the environment. Until we, as the children of mother nature, learn to respect and appreciate the kind and giving mother earth, and until we stop abusing her kindness (for she is too loving and passive to respond with violence), we will not be safe from her outbursts of anger; patterns of anyone who possesses one-dimensional, passive Patterns of Love and Tolerance.

Changing Patterns of Relating to environment. We must begin to change our Patterns of Relating to our environment. We are taking it for granted with neglect and abuse, without recognizing the consequences of our actions. If we begin to nurture the earth, who has served and embraced us since the beginning of life, we can become familiar with the miraculous rewards she has to offer us, her children. But we are only obedient to that which intimidates and scares us, while neglecting and abusing she who passively and forgivingly loves and nurtures us; that is the result of our Societal Programing.

Ocean demands Power Balance, earth gets even. We must learn to give before we are commanded to do so. We must learn to love those who love us without conditions. We must learn to be fair to those who do not demand it. On the other side of the Pendulum, we must learn from the ocean, who demands Power Balance while at the same time embracing whomever it connects with, instead of passively awaiting, accepting abuse, and silently getting even, like the earth.

We will get what we give to our environment. We must see the environment as a system, both independent within itself and connected with the whole. As a part of the whole, environmental Power Balance, or Imbalance, will affect us all, both the earth and the universe as a whole. Any system becomes Imbalanced as a result of the neglect, abuse or misuse of that system. The Imbalance of any system within itself and among other systems affects other systems related to it.

Environmental-Individual Balance. An individual, as part of the whole, will affect the entirety of that system. Understanding the impact of the environment as a system, as an interrelated part to the universal whole that we are a part of, will help us recognize its impact on the universe and on ourselves.

The Power Balance within nature. Nature creates natural Patterns of Swing of the Pendulum within herself to maintain the Power Balance necessary to survive and assist in the survival of natural order. Imbalance is created when society interrupts nature's constant, natural Swing of the Pendulum; by interrupting her progression, society jeopardizes the resilience of both nature and itself.

Environmental Imbalance. Cutting too many trees, polluting our water and air, and killing precious animals for the sole purpose of making room for more civilization will ultimately backfire. A balanced state of nature is a necessary Pattern for the survival of civilization. However, those who have exercised abuse, indulgence and exploitation, adopting Habitual, Repetitive Patterns of fast relief and answers, such as fast food, fast drugs, and fast cures, have no respect for the necessary balance of input and output between civilization and nature.

Environmental Swing of the Pendulum. Any system that is taken from without receiving back the same amount and quality of what is taken, will ultimately backfire and swing with the intent of making both the taker and the user the ultimate victims. That is how I explain our recent natural disasters, patterned unusual to what has been expected from nature. Even the most loving mother can withdraw from a child who exhibits destructive, sociopathic patterns by treating others as objects of personal without considering the consequences of those actions.

Reason. There are simple questions, however, that one must ask in the process of analysis of Power Imbalance and the occurrence of crisis of any kind. The question is: "Which came first?" The development of destructive patterns of the dependent, or the withdrawal of love and nurturance of the caretakers? Has the caretaker attempted in liberating the dependent freely, or has the dependent been forced to retaliate in order to obtain freedom?

Passive Boundary. In psychotherapy, the therapist builds a passive boundary with those who are damaged heavily and have no boundary of their own and treat others as objects without thinking about the consequence of their actions. Passive Boundary is a pattern of establishing and teaching others, creating a sense of clear boundary, enabling them to feel, understand and separate their own identity from the rest of what they see. This technique is essential in dealing with clients with severe boundary collapse, such as those who are labeled schizophrenic. They see everyone, especially those who get close to them, as a part of themselves, the hostile part they feel within. The key is in the paradox of the ability to enter the world of the person for establishing trust and intimacy, without intruding upon their boundary.

3rd Universal Law
Wisdom - Nurturance

Universal Parental Wisdom-Nurturance is the root to all universal patterns that need balance within their powers (Power Balance of Strength-Vulnerability), and between us and others (Power Balance of Whole-Part), and with our environment and the universe (mind-body connection with trees, spirits and even animals.) Together, these bring us harmony. The lack of harmony and Power Balance creates imbalance and crisis, as we experience today. Our universal theory of Universal Paternal Power provides us with Universal Wisdom and Nurturance at our disposal to help us recognize the universal connection we have with one another, with the environment, and with the universe, so that we can put an end to the existential loneliness that leads us to bond only partially with humanity. The Universal Paternal Wisdom and the Universal Maternal Nurturance qualities belongs to all genders, races and religious beliefs.

Universal Parental Power. I have proposed this theory because it makes scientific and intuitive sense to me. Universal Parental Power is the Power Balance in all levels of the universe. For every individual being and animal, there is a balance of male-female. Within all children of earth, one can find the Universal Parental Patterns of Wisdom and Nurturance, of the male and female. This does not mean that only females will have nurturance and only males will have wisdom. Within each individual, male or female, all Patterns exist if equally nurtured in society.

Universal Parity. There are pairs of being consisting of patterns of male-female, in the universe for the purpose of production and self-maintenance. Parity is a universal functional and survival pattern separate from the patterns of relating created by the people among themselves. *Reproduction* is an instinctual pattern, whereas intimacy and *relation* are *excellence patterns* of civilization. We must have a male-female anatomy to reproduce. But we can relate and love through the unlimited patterns of humanity. Parental love, and intimacy between two, require expanded souls beyond the limitations of the body. Thus as we find ourselves predestined by the universal laws physically to search for the body type or pattern to reproduce, we will find ourselves embraced with the choices of patterns of cognition-emotion and power balance when it comes to matters of love.

Universal Paternal Power. Universal Paternal Power is the universal mind and the wisdom of the soul (existential clarity.) It is the ability to have deductive and analytical reasoning and to see through the Programs and Programers so that one can act upon self-intent and purpose, and ultimately use other Programs towards independence, being unaffected by manipulations and intimidation that have taken power away from the individual thus far. When we gain knowledge of our surroundings, our inner capacity and outer connections, we are no longer at the mercy of others who try to Program our lives while focusing on their own personal gains.

Paternal Wisdom. We are surrounded by Universal Wisdom, and need to be open to its generous, unconditional gifts. Our Universal Paternal Wisdom is the connection of all existing wisdom in the world, past and present, that will never die.

Celebrating life instead of its destruction. It is the wisdom of celebrating life instead of celebrating the universe's destruction. The choice is ours. We can wait until someone appears and takes only a chosen few away from here, and instead of celebrating life and what it has to offer us, we can celebrate destruction. We can choose whatever we please, but we must bear the responsibility that where we are is all a matter of choice. We might even fulfill our own self-prophecy, if we think hard and long about it, and abuse this holy planet by taking it for granted, treating it like a sidewalk bar-joint to heaven, so that it eventually rebels and throws us up like a bad apple.

Spirit never dies. When our material body deteriorates and changes to another form because we have not yet mastered the preservation of the body and the prevention of aging to the degree that we can prevent death, our minds and the wisdom we have accumulated embedded within it flow forever in the universe. Although after death, we cannot use our wisdom to take action in the material world, we are able to lend it to those who are open to receive our spirit. That is why wisdom escalates and accumulates all the time: it adds to that which existed before, and opens more avenues to life at its best as it opens more eyes.

Mind-body openness to universal abundance. I have worked very hard to get where I am in life, professionally and personally, and in becoming who I am as a person. I don't want to undermine my efforts, since nothing has ever come easily to me and I have always been willing to pay my dues for where I have wanted to be in life. However, some people who have watched my Patterns say that often I learn through osmosis.

Learning through osmosis. I don't know about that mySelf. But I have noticed that many affirmations I need to learn, if I am on the right track, come to me in mysterious ways, almost as if they fell from the sky. Every time I go on my long walks on the beach and open my spirit up with my Universal Mind-Body Prayer, I am led to a sea of knowledge and creative expression, or to wherever I want to be which seems to be in harmony with my purpose and where I am destined to be. I think it is entirely scientific that if we leave ourselves open to the abundance already existing in the universe, we pick up not only affirmations of our own work from those who are on the same path with us, but, with a little assistance from the Power Balance of others who have been in our world before, we may even pick up from where someone left off without knowing that is what we are doing.

Thoughts are ever-flowing in the universe. I believe that the mind will never die. Thoughts are ever-flowing in the universe as they leave our tired bodies to rest. And if we sharpen our tools of Self-Knowledge and become the Universal Selves we are capable of becoming, there is no limit to our discoveries. I believe that the abundance existing in the air is rich, not only in wisdom, but in the nurturance of all who become clear enough to recognize it.

Universal Maternal Power. Universal Maternal Power is the Mother of all living things, the source of nurturance. As a mother who has spent all of her life being a true source of nurturance for her children, I feel that I can identify with the Universal Maternal Power. She is the creator of all individuals and beyond; all that She creates, She holds in her arms and rocks day and night. It is only a nurturing mother who could be so patient and have so much tolerance to love consistently and unconditionally.

Universe as the mother's womb. My theory is based on my discovery of the commonalty between the mother's womb and the many mysteries of the universe. Both together are a calculated, scientific, natural, systematic machine with little machines inside that govern by the same rules. The rules of one apply to the other.

Mother-like nurturance of the universe, and the cyclical and systematic nature of the universe, is all too significant to be accidental. I hope that scientists focus on this theory, for I think it brings us significant answers to humanity. Just as we don't have to run off to other cities or relationships to find our answers, we don't have to run off to the moon to find the universal truth we are looking for.

Universal Power Balance: life and rebirth. The process of death and rebirth is a constant process, not a one-time finality. The pregnant Mother of the universe is constantly giving birth to godlike, universal children of all kinds and types. Individual beings are as one. The temporary death of any kind must exist only as to the laws of Universal Power Balance: to generate energy for the life to come. This is much like sleeping at night, which is a mini-death of its own kind. If we did not sleep at night, then how would we look forward to the morning after?

Maternal nurturance. Mothers of the world can all identify with the Universal Maternal Power. They, too, have experienced maternal power when holding their child in their arms, having the tolerance to delay gratification for the sake of their loved ones. Only a mother automatically, naturally, and unconditionally puts her own needs second to those of another being. Only a mother can awaken in her sleep just by the sound of the breath of her child, and run to nurture her loved one in the latest of the night or the earliest of dawn. It is only a mother who hurts by just the thought of her child's pain, and feels endless joy from the sight of a smile.

In absence of nurturance of our own mothers. It feels as though there is nothing that can take the place of a mother's love. I know the feeling; when my mother died, I felt as though a part of me would die with her. But it didn't. For many years, I craved my mother's love and felt cheated by the absence of it, especially during the most vulnerable times of my life. When I was raising my own children, I missed her presence the most. I wanted so much to share with her the love and the experience that only she would understand. But she was gone, and there was nothing I could do (or I would have) to bring her back.

Creating Patterns of Nurturance. I learned to reach out to the Universal Maternal Power that somehow I felt even in the air. Many times, I felt my mother's ever-constant presence beside me, assuring me that she would be watching after me. Many times, I felt it was more than just the maternal nurturance of my mother that was holding me in her arms. For in the most critical times of my life, I was never truly alone. There was a power beyond my mother that was embracing me in her arms.

Embracing the Universal Maternal Power. I believe that unconditional Maternal Power exists all around us if we open our hearts and allow ourselves to feel it. This I call the Universal Maternal Power that embraces her children endlessly, night and day, and is always watching after them. It only takes an enlightened heart to feel the warm nurturance of her presence, and to learn from her and embrace her as a part of her own maternal soul.

Maternal Soul: the ever-existence of nurturance and love for ourselves in our hearts. If nurtured, the soul will flourish and spread its wings onto others as a natural Pattern of Living. I began to do the things for mySelf that my mother had once done for me. Doing so helped me feel her presence at all times. When I was ill she would get rice and chicken and make me chicken soup. She would also give me hot milk and tea at bedtime. This became my remedy for my children and mySelf whenever we came down with a cold. My mother has never left me, since I allow her to stay without material expectations and conditions attached to her presence. Persians have a saying that heaven is underneath the feet of mothers. I believe that is true right here on earth. For it is from the feet of the mothers that are created children: the heavenly souls. Power Balance is the natural, inherent state of being. The individual with Power Balance is in harmony within all inner Patterns of Self and the environment. Power Balanced persons possess multidimensional Patterns that work in harmony: one who is both goal-oriented and process-oriented; one who has feminine-masculine Patterns side-by-side that develop a whole Self; one who is kind and assertive, passive and active; one who has boundary and is boundaryless, depending on appropriate moments in life; one who is in harmony within Self, feeling inner peace and at the same time finding harmony with the environment with and others; one who creates peace and joy while never compromising the harmony within. A Power Balanced Self is a Universal Self: a successful spiritual being. To be Power Balanced, one must connect to not only both sides of the Pendulum within Self, but also to the Universal Self which enables the individual to connect with the Universal Pendulum: the Universal Wisdom and Nurturance available to all beings, based on the laws of the universe.

The key to Universal Abundance. The key to Universal Abundance is the development and nurturance of the Universal Self: the Self that exists in the core of each and every individual, stark naked, washed away from all denial and labels, with the holy water of knowledge: the truth.

In absence of the paternal wisdom of our fathers. In the absence of the paternal wisdom of our fathers, we can open our souls and our hearts to the wisdom of all fathers of the world combined: the Universal Paternal Wisdom. The Universal Father, just like ours, would spend hours patiently explaining the hardest matters to understand. He would take our hands and tell us about his worldly experiences, yet let us live our own experiences and make our own mistakes, and come to our own life analysis that is unique to us. He would neither punish nor bring us shame. He would suffer if we felt guilt for what is not of our doing. He would not blame or humiliate us for what we were born with. Nor would he favor any of us against the other.

My father never punished me. My father never made me feel guilt or shame. No father with a right mind would. I know this because that is how my father was, and that is how I know any wholly Universal Father would be to his children. My father, when he died well over the age of ninety-six, did not take with him the compassion and the wisdom that he had given to all of his children as a gift.

The greatest lessons to learn. He never expected anything from any of us but that we be happy in our own lives. He did not even expect us to become the best of ourselves. That was something he left to us, because he trusted that we would. I have copied in my mind and in my life my father's peaceful and humble appearance, and his tremendous wisdom about the meaning of life. He had a mission of honesty and integrity, and a promise of joy, throughout his life. I will never forget his philosophies, even though we did not talk much; greatest lessons are learned through watching someone else's Patterns of Life. Even his childlike naiveté, his trust in all who worked for him and who stabbed him in the back seems to be his best asset now. He did not have time to keep score, nor did he feel threatened to watch out for the bad guys. He knew what he wanted to do, what he wanted out of life, what he had, and who he was. I think my father kept the world as he wanted to see it, inside the little pages of the books he read, and in the holy marbles in his right hand that he constantly rolled with his fingers as he took his long and quiet afternoon walks. After all, what more can a person want?

Universal Power Balance. My Power Balance Theory holds also that the combined Power Balance in each individual being will develop Universal Power Balance. Without Individual Power Balance, meaning the people power of togetherness, Universal Power Balance will be non-existent. They both *give* and *receive* power from one another.

4th Universal Law
Law of Doing and Being

The *Universal Law of Doing and Being* is a path of experiencing, learning, engaging, participating, meditating, loving, and living life in a balance that allows us to embrace all dimensions of our Self and our existence. Patterns of Being are evolved in a process of ***becoming a whole person,*** thus being able to connect fully with others and with the Universal Power that is holding us within, creating Power Balance. It is an inner and outer harmony: a process where all patterns within are in balance and harmony. Thus, the individual can create harmony with all the patterns outside of Self. So when a person allows the Patterns of Being to flourish, and nurtures the Patterns of Doing as well, the patterns that evolve are ***Power Balance Patterns of Doing and Being***: a Universal Law that exists all around us if we become aware. This law exists within us, inherently.

Power Balance as theory, therapy and philosophy behind the tool of Patterns Change Programing, has evolved with the changes of the patterns in mySelf; it is a constant process of experiencing life and evolving the multidimensional Universal Self both within and with its connection with the universal powers without. Independent of the external objects of change, and at the same time connected with all that exists on the outside, the universal gifts and powers are at our disposal.

Power Balance of Success-Spirituality. Power Balance of Success-Spirituality is a Universal Law governed by the wisdom of the paternal and the nurturance of the maternal laws of the universe and Patterns existing equally within each and every person. The Power Balance of material success and excellence in humanity embraces spirituality in a linear process. In our fast-paced Western society, we need to feel success before coming to spirituality. In my personal and professional experiences in life, the Power Balance of material success and excellence in humanity which embraces spirituality is a linear process. I believe that until one has choices to satisfy one's basic needs and dreams of success and progression, the ultimate process of Excellence will not be an honest and meaningful one; having a choice alone makes all the difference in a true arrival to any direction. Likewise, without satisfying the basic needs of safety and hunger, one cannot move towards finer aspects of Self. It is very easy for people to say that they don't want fame and fortune if they don't know how to obtain it. When they gain the options to fulfill any dream they want, and then decide otherwise, they have made a true choice. But not having had the options and rejecting materialism self-righteously while feeling envy inside is a Pattern of Denial that hurts the person as well as others who happen to be around the toxicity it creates. It is much like wealthy leaders of institutions, supported by the people, who preach that materialism is a "sin." It is not the absence of presentation of a pattern while hiding it somewhere in the corners of our subconscious mind, or coming out with it in the dark of the night, but it is the clear lack of the need for it within that is significant to our clarity and wholeness.

Patterns of Being. Patterns are a collection of cause and effect processes within and around us that change constantly. But they are governed by master Universal Laws, and as parts to the whole Universal Laws they possess the same nature and principles. Patterns are ever-changing and ever-present. By recognizing and acknowledging them we can control their direction. We all live by Patterns. They exist in everything and everyone; from deep within our inner Self, to the vast and endless ocean of the universe. Patterns embrace us as they embrace our environment and all parts to the universal whole. They are a series of processes existing within that creates the presentation of the behavior we observe. The cognitive and emotional processes affect the actual behavior and characteristics of an individual. For example, a woman whom we call passive may not be passive in nature at all. She may be demonstrating patterns that stems from guilt, shame or other thought processes Programed within her. On the same token, the patterns of a mountain are not necessarily those of being still and calm. Inside of a calm and motionless mountain may lie a roaring lion awaiting to destroy and kill. Only in the presence of acknowledgment and balance of all patterns can we truly be safe, for ourselves as well as others.

Patterns of health, abundance and spiritual excellence. Patterns in harmony within Self, with others and with the environment, are congruent. To be one in thought, emotion, spirit and action is one of the known signs of mental health and excellence beyond the societal expectation. Patterns of Crisis occur when the individual feels no hope or no way out of a critical situation, feels no energy or motivation, or feels too much uncontrolled energy in the wrong direction, and can think of no solution to relieve the paralyzing stress, anxiety and feelings of helplessness. Our mental health theory and practice up until the present has focused on disease rather than health, on putting a bandage on crisis rather than exploring and learning about long lasting prevention and instilling individual and familial patterns of excellence.

Based on my brief therapy called Pattern Change Programing and my in-depth theory of Power Balance , I have developed key patterns and tools to achieve patterns that guarantee success and abundance, spiritual excellence within individuals, families and societies, and embrace humanity. In my books entitled *Pattern Change Programing: Creating Your Own Destiny* and *Power Balance Therapy,* I explore these theories and techniques with you. In *Self-Programing* I teach how to become your own Life Programer, outlining all preventive and excellence life Programs. This revolutionary path has not come to me overnight. Although it has only taken me one year to write nine books with the mission of becoming a strong voice for the masses. In this history-making time of societal calamity, I have been personally searching and exploring as well as professionally teaching it for the past twelve years. I am thankful to my clients who have trusted me, and to other professionals whose curiosity for clarity has empowered me. This is just the beginning of an evo-revolutionary era in which the power of the individual and the inherent dignity forgotten and oppressed within each and every godlike child of humanity will be the focal power of rewriting society's current downward direction of humanity. If we all rise from the death of ignorance of the Forgotten Self and the God within us, we will not only prosper in abundance, but we will also be able to reach out to the universal wisdom and nurturance and embrace the orphan child of humanity who is held hostage by oppressive old order within its attacks on liberty.

Societal one-dimensional Programing. We live in a rigid, perfectionist and one-dimensional society in which we are taught to choose one way or another. In a way most societies and cultures are one-dimensional. They either advocate patterns of being and leave the doing to other cultures, or go out of their way in patterns of doing and forget about being, as in America. As a result, we are left with only a single, flat dimension of our Self. That is why it is truly a blessing to be exposed to several cultures in our process of becoming whole within.

Patterns of Success-Altruism. The options must be created for an honest choice. The process of Excellence begins when an individual has satisfied both basic physical needs and basic psychological needs. Among those basic needs lies the need to succeed in a material world. The cost becomes evident only when one has a choice between material success or an altruistic purpose. To obtain both, if possible, is a fine art and scientific endeavor that becomes the purpose in the process of Change of Patterns.

Pattern of Self Expression-Preservation is the key behind success. To succeed in a long-term period and to maintain it we must learn about our Self, gain Self-Knowledge and then learn about how to express and apply all that inner wealth to the reality of our lives and the needs of our society. We must learn about who we are, what we are made of, our emotions and our thoughts, and our patterns of connecting with our Self and others in our family and in society. To learn about Self is the key to learning about the business of success tailored to fit us, in the making. In order to devote Self to others through creativity and self-expression, we must first learn the art and science of health and self-preservation. If we don't have a Self, we cannot devote anything to others. The selfless people who go on being a victim of others' ambitions and needs will only burn out like a candle. Power Balanced individuals who are on a mission of serving humanity, or have any purpose outside of Self, cannot be preoccupied by the judgment of others. If we need the judgment of others to feel good about Self, we still don't have a Self to offer. Creativity does not flourish in an environment where judgment lives. In order to keep humanity alive, we must allow self-expression.

Power Balance of Freedom-Responsibility. This sacred Pattern is only developed when we are given the power to act, the freedom to choose, and the responsibility to sit back and analyze the consequences of our actions in relation to ourselves and to others. Freedom is only a true life pattern and more than an illusive denial after we first master the Pattern of Responsibility.

When powers come together in harmony, we can do anything. We can have our cake and eat it too. We can be joyful and happy, loving life with all the passion there is, while having short-term and long-term goals towards creating our own destinies. Many times, people get stuck in Patterns that are one-dimensional and create lopsided-ness everywhere in their lives. Although they are intelligent and work hard, they end up feeling cheated in one way or another by not paying attention, by not nurturing all of Self and feeling whole.

There is nothing wrong with having it all. What would be wrong with having it all if you could enjoy, create, gain mastery, give, receive, produce, and make a difference in one life span? When we learn about all of the dimensions within ourselves and in the scientific world around us, we learn to embrace life with all that it has to give us, without holding back a part of ourselves from fear of being different; from this we will find both success and spiritual excellence.

Patterns of Giving-Receiving. The Universe embraces us all unconditionally. She gives power, but while *giving* power she, too, is *receiving*. Success at any cost is a cold place to be. I know. I have been there and have helped many who find themselves at the top of the ladder of success without happiness, joy, balance, or even the treasured feeling of mastery. Ultimately *the Universal Law is that we cannot exist for external rewards* for too long and not end up paying the price of losing the essence of Self: our integrity. We *can succeed materially and societally when we have a purpose with an intent that is first aimed at the pattern of giving.* There must be always something more meaningful to us than collecting the green bills. If that was happiness, we would all be aiming at becoming wealthy. Perhaps most people are, but not all. It isn't because they fear success or because they don't want to pay the price. It is because it is difficult in this era to maintain our spirit while we succeed. But in this book I would like to show you how. It all begins with *giving without the calculation of equally receiving*. The art of giving is a path to success and spiritual excellence.

Patterns of Openness-Boundary. We are open to the universe and the more open we become, the more we can define our own boundary, and vice versa. The interrelation between discovering wholeness within and recognizing wholeness without is a magical pattern. Only by the process of expanding Self are we able to see the whole, the vastness of our surrounding. She who sees Self as a small person will never see the aggrandizement of the world in her vision. Thus, openness to Self brings openness to the universe and simultaneously defines the boundary of Self.

Patterns of Activity-Silence. Like the universe, we are giving while *active,* and charging and receiving while *silent.* Silence is voice of the soul and the hymns of the spirit trying to heal us, while activity is the presentation of our existence in its intensity.

Patterns of Feeling. Hidden and unexpressed emotions cause Imbalances detrimental to the healthy Self. When we learn how to feel our emotions and express them appropriately and openly, we will be able to not only prevent many Imbalances, but also to feel more whole. I have watched people grow, literally; their bodies get larger once they learn to express themselves. I have seen people shrink, developing cancer and ulcers as they keep inside a chest full of emotions unexpressed. Emotional harmony does not mean hiding our emotions and appearing as though we are at peace with one another. It simply means accepting and connecting with all Patterns inside of ourselves. It means understanding and respecting ourselves in our totality for, and in spite of, making changes to get closer to our universally true Self.

Patterns of thinking. With Cognitive Harmony, we become capable of utilizing all cognitive powers (the power of the mind), and thus function fully in that regard. Then we not only prevent many Imbalances, but also contribute to our lives and the world around us with Power Balance and Excellence. The Power Balance Program enables individuals to function in full capacity, with all aspects of Self. First, the individual recognizes all dimensions of Self, and secondly, there are no Blocks, Imbalances or Toxic Patterns driving us to inhibit ourselves from functioning with our full potential.

Power Balance of Thinking-Feeling. Power Balance of thinking and feeling is when Balance Patterns of cognition and emotion connect in harmony and create not only the ability to create one's own destiny merely with the power of the mind, but also to enjoy life by feeling each and every moment while mastering life.

Swing of the Pendulum of thoughts and feelings. When the individual recognizes all dimensions of Self and lets the pendulum of thoughts, feelings and actions swing freely to find the Power Balance within Self, he or she experiences Power Balance. Imbalance in any dimension robs people of experiencing all of Self, which we all deserve and are capable of experiencing. In Power Balance, the opposition of Patterns is not significant. Power Balance Patterns can be Patterns of similar or entirely different nature.

Process of Self-Control versus controlling others. To the degree that we can expand ourselves to recognize and express all that there is within us, subconscious and conscious, we have moved towards Power Balance and can express Patterns as we choose, and not as they choose to come out without our control. Obtaining Self-Control to replace the need to control others is the process of gaining Power Balance.

Patterns of Goal Orientation. This means the person is focused, self-disciplined, self-confident, clear about long-term dreams of life, able to selectively choose activities and is willing to pay the price.

Patterns of Process Orientation. An individual with Process Oriented abilities has no boundaries of time, place, or goal; she or he simply processes life events and feelings. Like a channel for life, the person has no specific agenda but to enjoy the path that embraces life.

Power Balance of Goal-Process. When a person has Goal-Oriented Patterns, she or he has embedded within the actual presentation of being goal-oriented, other thought processes that result in an end-product of goal orientation. The same with the process-oriented person who processes life without having a goal in mind, and thus all the patterns he or she embraces swing towards the joy of process and away from end results. When one is in power balance, one experiences both the joy of process and the fulfillment of embracing the materialization of vision: seeing the effect of the cause.

5th Universal Law
Assertion - Compassion

The mother nurturer of the universe has embraced us within her arms for decades. She also asserts herself at times. The power balance of such assertion and compassion has been behind all elements and patterns of the universe; like the ocean that intrudes upon the sands of the shore proudly and at times with arrogance; like a mother who provides us with the most basic necessities of life in order to survive on earth. It is the pattern of assertion by the universe that makes her nurturing yet not enabling as she expects her children to grow and be responsible just as she teaches the same to all the mothers. This is how we learn to assert ourselves by standing up for what is rightfully ours, and are at the same time sensitive to the rights of others. We must be sensitive to our own feelings and equally sensitive to the feelings of others. We must have passion for our own convictions and yet think twice before we slash someone away as a human being unworthy of life and living just because that person does not fit into our adopted self-righteousness. It is easy to have selective compassion and love those who love and obey us. *But it is true spirituality to have sensitivity for those who reject us.* Assertion becomes an inhumane pattern when it crosses the boundary of thoughtful assertion, which is when one will not compromise one's right and dignity but respects, just as equally, that of another. The repeated crimes of centuries have been justified as the "assertion of right" when actually it was a distorted intrusion upon the rights of others. It is crucial not only to our inner balance, but to the balance in our world, to relate to our inner Self while connecting with others. Meaning, do unto others what you want done unto you. When the Power Imbalance is in the other direction, we are treating others better than we treat our loved ones or ourselves. We truly must assume at all times that when we are relating to our Self or those we love, we are indeed relating to our best friends.

The Universal Law of Assertion-Compassion is love without need, without addiction, with respect of Self and others, with softness and certainly without prejudice and discrimination. We are the most advanced species, which means we can analyze and think better than the rest. Otherwise, we all act alike and at times we are more primitive than the worst animals whom we claim are dangerous. But it is indeed quite a miraculous scene to watch the mother of any pattern or nature. My son and I were watching the Discovery channel recently. They had a program on penguins in Siberia. It was amazing how the penguins fed, nurtured and protected their children until they no longer needed to be protected. Yet there was another pattern of female penguins who did not have any children that tried to steal the little ones to the point of endangering their lives. Many little penguins were killed because some female penguins were in need of maternal possessions. Need in any form becomes a destructive pattern and its toxicity takes away from wisdom and nurturance. I have seen so many parents whose lives depend upon their children to the point that they constantly defend themselves against their children's independence. The same pattern is seen in institutional enablers whose need and addiction to people forces them to keep students dependent.

Asserting oneself is an act of love and nurturance, not an act of intrusion and violence. In assertion, we respect ourselves, and those who respect their Self cannot disrespect the Self in others. Aggression, conversely, spells out the anger within of a Forgotten Self who must be self-indulgent, intrusive and violent only to feel. In the absence of compassion we become distorted and our intelligence is utilized towards corruption and destructive self-indulgence. Compassion softens our unpolished edge of primitive, childlike impulses that have been instilled within us as reactionary rebellion from the neglect of our Self by society and our parents. In fact, what we end up doing is continuing the same neglect by maintaining the act of rebellion, which most often is targeted against our own better sense. With assertion, unlike aggression, there is a flow of Self-Knowledge absent in dark dungeons of victimization of anger, and ever-present in the transcendent light of Self.

That is why the angry God, sculpted, painted and worshipped by those who promote and breed victimization is only a manmade God and does not fit into the universal laws of transcendence. No Father of wisdom would wish harm to any of His children and no mother of nurturance would intentionally scold them even if they talk out of order. Anger and the self-righteousness of ignorance are the evil corrupters of our minds, and we must fight them. We learn best by the power of love; we remember only the power of love, we are driven truly by the power of love, we live for the power of love, and we transcend by the power which we receive from love, giving and receiving that which already exists plenteous enough for all. There is truly no need to fight. When I look at people, often I see a collection of experiences of pain and, if they are lucky, I see some shades of joy and even behind the presentation of the indulged and the corrupt there is an innocent soul that must be nurtured. I have hated in my life before. But I can no longer imagine or feel such a toxic and poisonous pattern that has nearly destroyed our world. Even at this moment I am a more compassionate person than the moment before; that I have found as the power of turning inward which is strengthened by the powerful tool of writing. At this moment in my life, I already feel pain for those whom I have hurt intentionally and those whom I have hurt unknowingly. I hope I live long enough to make it all up. Indeed, compassion softens our heart and makes us vulnerable to love: a feeling that may be too frightening for some. Anger at times serves to cover up the tenderness so that we can feel safe temporarily and not feel too overwhelmed with inner anxiety. It is temporary because if we don't heal from our pain and let go of our fear, ultimately no shield will protect us from our own inner toxicity. I know. I have been there. Fear can bring out the evil in everyone and we must fight it together. If we all at once put down our weapons and hold out our white flags, the world will be one. I hope to live long enough to see that. For I truly suffer inside from such deeply rooted separation of mankind. I suffer when I hear people rejected for their difference in color or religion or belief. If they are wrong, we must try not to get hurt by their ignorance by learning even more of how to be right. But we have no right to end their precious lives or to be the judge that they are not worthy enough. Who are we to make such judgments? Are we all pure and flawless? Have we never been human? Then let's be fair and assertive, but for God's sake, let's not lose human compassion and fairness. All flowers of the garden, thorn stricken or thorn free, must be watered and nurtured. The gardener of the garden must water every flower; the speaker of the house must speak for everyone to be empowered; the teacher must teach all students; and the masters must be humble to the slaves, for the pendulum may swing and the master may become the slave and the slave may become the king.

6th Universal Law
Part- Wholeness

Universal Self: whole within, part of the universe. I see the universe as a whole entity that like a parental figure embraces us with its Maternal Power of Nurturance and Paternal Power of Wisdom. I see the individual as Part of the Universal Whole, carrying all the Patterns of the universe, within. Thus the individual becomes a part of the universe and holds the same principles and patterns of the universe. By carrying its parental patterns of Wisdom and Nurturance as an inner capacity and inherent pattern, the individual too, becomes whole within. Since the universal pattern is to be whole within and yet connected with the individual, then the individual is also whole within and yet connected with all other beings, in mind, spirit, body and emotion connected with the universe.

I thus help individuals who have lost their sense of connection with the universe as well as their sense of wholeness within Self to become their Universal Self, whole within and a part of the universal whole: complete alone, and connected with others and the universe. They find their Self beyond the local and external signs and languages that confused them, disconnecting them from others as well as themselves, and left them running in a maze without ever getting anywhere. I help them see the universal map and the universal law of the road that lights the path for everyone to see, and is wide enough for everyone to travel. I help them make their own signs with their own language, and to create their own paths so that they know where they are going: traveling towards a joyful destination, mastering the purpose of connection within and without, and at all times, *whole* within themselves, while they are a *part*. We share patterns of the universal *whole* as we are a *part* of its miracle; a state of Power Balance. Power Balance is the harmony within all existing universal patterns, within and without. Harmony exists between the day and night with their interrelated connection as well as their separate wholeness. And the same holds true within us as a part to the universal power. Today we live in universal crisis because of the lack of societal and universal power balance that is creating individual imbalance, and vice-versa. Thus we create patterns between ourSelf and the universe that carry themselves to other relationships in our lives.

Awareness: path to sacred connection. It is humbling to know there are other powers and patterns of relating and being, known or unknown, that at times work with us, and at times work against us. Yet it is comforting to know that through our own Power Balance we can connect with the Universal Power Balance and Excellence Program, and that the Universal Patterns of Being can enhance us and take us to even higher levels of being: levels unknown to the ordinary. By ordinary, I mean those who do not know their universal Self: the Self that is at all times connected to the universe, with or without our awareness. Yet only through awareness of Self, and of the Universal Power, can we feel the presence of, become a part of, and utilize this sacred connection.

Power Balance of Togetherness-Separateness. Within our wholeness we are a part of the universe and others around us and yet with our part, we are apart and separate from others, whole within. The requirement to feel a part is, first and foremost, to feel apart. In other words, in order to feel connected with others and the universe around us we must first experience Self and become who we are. If we abide by the Universal Laws of Power Balance, we learn to become whole within and move not only towards everlasting Patterns of Success, but we also embrace an eternal Spiritual Excellence. I will unfold for you, one by one through my books, the wonders of such Power Balance existing within and around us and the miracles that we ourselves can make happen by not selling our souls to the manmade golden gods and the misrepresentation of the great prophets, but to adhere to the true nature of the universal spiritual connection and power that nurturingly, maternally and wisely surrounds us, as we open our minds and hearts to the miracle of non-selective and unconditional love.

Self: part of Universal-Whole Program. Individual beings can no longer afford to deny the interrelationship they have with the universe and the power they reciprocate with one another. Nor can they afford to deny the fact that as part of the whole universal power, they, too, are complete within themselves, and need to enhance and maintain inherent Power Balance within themselves.

Clear, Programed Paths. In order to accept ourselves as a whole, we must first recognize and analyze our Present Patterns, identify the Programers who helped Program those patterns, and then make a conscious choice to save or delete those patterns. Nations can only predict Future Patterns, or program Excellence, by first analyzing their history and their repetitive patterns of trial and error. Individuals, too, hold the same simple yet golden rule for establishing clear, Programed paths that lead to the destination of their choice.

Change as a Universal Pattern of Existence. Change is all around us. It is a Universal Pattern of Existence and an inevitable state of being. The darkness of night changes to the lightness of day. The waves can't sit steady for a moment. They constantly arrive, coming to shore strongly, impatiently, passionately, and intrusively, while, like an unfaithful lover, they simultaneously plan their departure, leaving us with the certainty of coming back. The flowers open and close, die and blossom again as we begin to think it may be their last time.

Everything is constantly changing around us. And so are we. Everything around us is changing with the ever-constant ticking of time. We, too, are not exempt from this perfect order of the universe. We are in a living universe. The moment something stops changing, moving, and growing, it falls into the regressive path of disintegration and, ultimately, death.

Only in stagnation and death is there no change. To simplify this, I can give an example of my feelings when I am watching environmental awareness programs offered on the Discovery channel. The saddest happenings occur in places where there has been no change. The hippos are dying because there has been no rain to fill up the dried sea. The fish are dead because the water has been stagnant and polluted.

The wisdom of Wholeness, the nurturance of Part. The interrelation of all laws of the universe is the strong affirmation of its wholeness; all parts work together as they work apart and independently. Wisdom and Nurturance as the ultimate patterns of the universal entity connect each and every part to one another with the compassion and firmness of a true parent. In fact, if each and every parent learns from the Laws of Wisdom-Nurturance, there will never again be a victimized Self or a child who feels deprived of love of the parent. As we explore the next law, we will find even more evidence of the Part-Wholeness of the universe and our interrelations to it as a *part* that is *whole*, within.

7th Universal Law
Chaos - Order

Universal Law of Chaos-Order. Whenever things are not going exactly the way I planned, when I feel out of control and don't know exactly what will happen, I know that something good is about to happen. The key is in not panicking and thinking that it is the end of the world if the order we are familiar with is swung to chaos. ***Chaos and confusion are requirements for true order and harmony.*** For individuals to progress in interpersonal aspirations as much as they have succeeded in science, they must take just as many chances by asking the scientific questions that enhance change, and must be tolerant of the confusion and chaos that always comes before balance and order. Just as in the chaos theory in physics, where it is proven that chaos brings about change, one must never sacrifice what one must experience just for the sake of keeping order.

Order at any cost creates Imbalance. The problem with our society and our families is that there is a great deal of rigidity governing our rules and laws of existence. In psychotherapy, dysfunctional families lack flexibility for change towards balance. Whether in our personal life or professionally, or within members of our own family, the ability to move forward and the willingness to change are among the most significant success keys. I teach many Patterns of Success and Excellence Seminars, and in all of them I find people who are the most successful are those who are still *searching to change* in order to compete, not with others but with themselves, in order to own their inherent excellence within. As I indicated in my Universal Pendulum Theory, the Patterns on the opposite side of every Pattern that we see as positive are important to the Power Balance of that Pattern. If we strive for order at any cost, there will never be true order and balance in our lives. Chaos for the sake of chaos is not a valuable Pattern to own. However, chaos for the purpose of acquiring order must seriously be considered. Not unless we experience the night will we truly understand the day, nor will we have had the preparation to fully enjoy it. It is adhering to the patterns that I call *Universal Laws of Power Balance* that bring us closer to ourselves. I have learned that miraculously, all universal laws apply to individual existence: the *part* contains all the properties the *whole* has within.

Many wonderful people have lived a life of one-dimensional and flat indifference only because they dared not experience the moments in-between the life of order. It is in those in-between moments that we find our Self and a true connection with others. There is nothing more mistrusting and horrifying than the presence of those who will not move from fear of making waves. Even the dead body changes and decays. But the dead mind is one that will not wonder and will not question. I can tell the psyche of an individual by the way they move their body. Likewise, I can tell how someone feels physically by the way they think. There is such an strong connection between the health and movement of all our dimensions of mind, body and spirit that if one stops moving in one dimension it will hinder the movement of the others. The Universal Law of Change and Movement is the most significant key to success and spiritual excellence. I will explain to you my own mind, body and spirit experiences which have helped me gain my Self. If there is not enough on this subject in this book, please read *Pattern Change Programing: Creating Your Own Destiny*. You will know what I mean by mind, body and spirit movement once you read chapters one and seven. But here as well, I will explore with you not only the Laws of the Universe, but also the Patterns that carry such laws in one form or another to action. Do not fear the depth to which I dig, for there is no end to the depth of a person. But I hope you find deeper meanings to my lighter sentences. The deeper you recognize who you are within, the deeper you can recognize and seek the same in others. People are afraid of the words "depth" and "meaning." They think they are heavy. I beg to differ, for I believe that only in the *lack* of depth is there heaviness. Spirit is light when we see deep within and through things and people, not remaining on the surface. We float in the air in spirit without having to rely on any superficial substance. The problem with humanity is that we take things as we feel inside, and inside we see darkness, only because we are terrified to turn the lights on. I have never met anyone who found less than goodness once he or she began to search through patterns that were adopted unknowingly, and found his or her true Self beneath all the layers.

Chaos-order Power Balance Program. Chaos and confusion are requirements for true order and harmony. For individuals to progress in interpersonal aspirations as much as they have succeeded in science, they must take just as many chances by asking the scientific questions that enhance change, and must be tolerant of the confusion and chaos that always comes before balance and order. Just as in the chaos theory in physics where it is proven that chaos brings about change, one must never sacrifice what one must experience just for the sake of keeping order.

Excellence is not perfection. Rigidity of our society has created a rebellion that we paid for during the sixties and are currently paying for again. Societal rigidity, rules and expectations are combined with boundaryless intrusions that have confused not only our own people but also the people around the world. Everyone is angry for being put in a golden cage of society, being labeled with only a part of them acknowledged. I know the feeling; I lived a one-dimensional life and have worked with many who have experienced the same tragedy. The world is rebelling against it even when it hurts to rebel. Throughout the centuries, people have spoken that without clear choices there is no peace and wholeness in humanity, only the presentation of pseudo-order before the chaos necessary to bring a healthy and true order back again. The sad part is that if we live by the Laws of Nurturance and Wisdom, our people will never have to pay such high prices and our nations will never have to watch the painful scene of bloodshed of their children. Chaos is the nature of the universe and man which reflects an intuitive attempt at harmony and Power Balance. We can have constant peace and harmony if we learn the art and science of prevention, where there is no longer a need for drastic measures. Only then can we constantly move towards the future without being held back by the past. Only then can we finally get as close to ourSelf as we are to the moon and proudly call ourselves a species of advancement and progression.

Power Imbalance, Block, Balance, and Excellence. These are the Programs that can be chosen by individuals or adopted without conscious choice. Although the Balance, Power Balance, and Excellence Programs require conscious choice, the Imbalance and Block Programs are most often adopted without conscious knowledge. I am sure that no one chooses to feel like a failure in life, to lose all that he or she has worked so hard for, to feel disconnected and alienated even in a crowd of friends and loved ones, to be hateful towards others, to be prejudiced, or to judge and control the world and ignore looking within. All of these Imbalance Patterns are adopted by people as a result of their Past Programing, lack of Self-Knowledge, and influence of Programers of their lives.

Imbalance of Power among the people. We must not forget the Societal Imbalance of Power among the people themselves. Some are called followers and some are called leaders. Imbalance is created by toxicity of the power that is not appropriately divided, and Imbalances are created by societal leadership's abuse of the power given to them by the people. Whenever there is Imbalance, there is patterns of victimization, oppression, relinquishment of responsibility, idealization, corruption, crime and war.

Societal Power Balance. Societal Power Balance is when there is equal regard for the core of each and every person, and what separates them is only the given task, not inappropriate power over their life paths and destiny. People are given equal knowledge and equal opportunity to have equal options in life. The fear of authority is not a motivating factor to do the right thing, but individual responsibility and integrity is. People are color blind, differentness of beliefs and political preference optional, and compassion laden. That is the definition of Societal Power Balance.

8th Universal Law
Feminine - Masculine

Men who come to me for consultation often ask me similar questions. They come from all walks of life, and all ages. Some are just getting out of high school and others are in the midst of their success and happy marriage and family, and some are in the depth of loss of everything. They all ask me:

Rose, please tell me, who am I? Who do I want to be?
What do I want from life? How do I feel? What am I
doing here? What is my purpose for all that I have done?
And why is it that with everyone around me I still feel
lonely and unloved, and with all that I have accomplished
I feel overwhelmed with anxiety and fright?

When I begin to guide them through their own process of Self Search and when they begin to feel safe enough to cry, they feel shame, awaiting my judgment of them as weak and foolish; judgments we all are so quick to make and so quick to tell; judgments they have been used to hearing from their fathers, mothers, teachers, preachers and even their wives and children; words everyone feels liberated to pour out and smear. The biggest crimes take place by the people who love us the most, have the best intentions for us and have no knowledge of how they are hurting us. When we fear love, we breed pain.

Men and women in every culture. We have all been handed the short end of the stick. No one wins when who they are is dictated to them. They become their own walking *make believe*. It almost always develops a sense of rebellion that shows up at some point in one's life. The reason for that is because everyone who is raised by expectations and rules and rigidity challenges them, passionately, even if they represent who the person truly is.

The true Self rises from the challenges that the individual puts himself or herself through: the challenges of stretching beyond the agreed-upon societal roles and finding one's genuine life patterns and identity. People who fail to challenge themselves will never know who they truly are. They will forever be at the mercy of cultural expectations, ramifications and labels given to them for the gender they were born with, the country they were born in, the religion they were born into, the career they were told they should pursue, the talents they were told they should have, and the mates to which they were lured, because they simply don't have a Self to make their life choices with and to decide.

The Male-Female Power Balance in all of us. Masculine Patterns require the cognitive operation of the mind, and feminine Patterns are all those that require emotional operation. This does not mean that only men operate cognitively or only women operate emotionally. It is only a definition for a set of Patterns. For instance, goal orientation is a masculine Pattern, whereas process orientation is a feminine Pattern.

Men don't come from Mars, nor women from Venus. Aside from a bit of physical difference that now, by the women's fitness movement, has made obsolete, I don't believe in a substantial difference between men and women. Furthermore, I don't think men come from Mars and women come from Venus. I think we, as a society, put them there. With expectations and definitions, we put people in boxes that most often don't fit, but which people must pretend fit or else they are alienated by their own kind.

Traditional masculine Patterns. A man is born with a set of rigid expectations. His family, his culture, his religion, his friends and his women want him with such specific Patterns that, by the time he grows up, he almost always ends up being somebody he is not, or somebody he does not want to be.

Incongruent with his true Self, he becomes detached from the feminine, soft and tender dimension within him, ashamed of his oppressed emotions and sensitivity that make him doubt that he is indeed a man. Feeling guilty about who he is casts a shadow upon his life. He indeed becomes more of a man than society allows him to be, and more of a man than women know he can be.

Disillusioned men. Many men do not wake up even amidst their success and picture-perfect happiness, never noticing that they are disillusioned, confused, and lost. The only reason that the years from forty to fifty constitute mid-life crisis is because men, after a lifetime of slavery by their families and society, finally get a chance to think about who they really are and what they really want. Unfortunately, this happens after they have already received the whole package, wrapped up with their names on it for the rest of their lives.

Running in a lopsided maze in life. Before that, they are in the maze of life, running without knowing what they are truly after, achieving only what the maps made by different Programers tell them to achieve, feeling only what they are told to feel, without having any time to question this lopsided and bad deal in life they have received.

When we have learned to "follow." Beginning from when we are tiny children, we have only two options even in a free society: to follow and miss out on being our true Self, or not to follow and be our true Self with a great deal of Imbalanced Patterns because of the guilt, fear, alienation, rejection, and lack of love and validation that we carry with us by disappointing others who love us and who expect us to be who they wanted us to be.

What does it mean to be a man? Don't cry, don't be a sissy. You have to be tough and strong, and you can't show emotions. You have to be brave and protect and defend everybody, including your country. You have to go to war and get killed to be a hero. You have to provide, you have to be rough, and you have to be tough. You have to be polite and considerate and honest, but you have to be shrewd and cut-throat in business. You have to care about your parents and be just like your father, even if your father was a cruel man. You have to be close to your mother, but you cannot be as tender, caring, or feminine as she. You have to care about your wife and be close her, but you cannot tell her everything. You should have a mistress on the side if you can, and treat your wife as an equal, but you have to provide for her and don't forget to open the door for her and be a gentleman. You have to be sensitive but you can't have feelings because you have to be strong, and you have to be responsible for everyone, but you are so lucky because you are a free man. No wonder men come to me confused and disillusioned and ask: "Tell me, am I a real man?"

Men live in prisons built by past Programers. From the songs that tell them what they are made of, to the commercials that tell them what they should be, what they should do, and what they should feel, men encounter the do's and don'ts from every direction, losing touch with their sanity and a peace of mind.

What would you have done differently? If you knew what you know now in the beginning of your life, what would you have done differently? This is a question I often ask men who come to me in pain after losing everything, or at least everything that meant something to them, and want to go through the process of Pattern Recognition and Pattern Change Programing towards Power Balance and Excellence, which will allow them a more fulfilling and harmonious lifestyle.

Analysis of life Patterns and a rude awakening. After analyzing their life Patterns and discovering how they have only followed in the footsteps of others to get approval without truly being connected to their true Self, every one of them get tears in their eyes and says: "I would have done it all differently. I would have studied a different subject, I would have married a different wife, I would have treated my kids differently, and I would have had a completely different lifestyle. I would have felt a lot happier and fulfilled than I do now." This, for a seventy-year old man, is a lot more painful to recognize than for a man of twenty or thirty years.

No winners in a life without a true Self. Yet that recognition sets them free to change the Imbalances of their Patterns and their lifestyle, and to move in the right direction for themselves and everyone involved. A man who does not know who he is or what he feels, and is burdened with guilt and obligations instead of joy, compassion, vigor and passion, is not the only one suffering in a relationship or a family unit. Everyone else suffers with him and pays a price one way or another. One can never reach or connect truly with a person who is not connected with himself or herself. The Blocks can only create hurt and pain for all involved.

Men must become free from the moment of birth by the influence of loving and nurturing parents who lift all expectations and misconceptions of manhood and put them only in their photo albums as memories of the past that belong just there: in the past. Men and women must be raised as individuals that are unique and different from each other and from the parents: not different by their sex, but different by their life choices, Patterns and preferences as people.

Parents who raise liberated men. Daily interactions should never include how boys should behave, or how they should feel, but only with the loving and nurturing questions of: "Honey, how do you feel? What do you feel like doing? How do you feel about what I said to you? What do you think about this subject or this event? Who do you want to be when you grow up? Who do you like among your friends? What made you like them? What do you like to do? Where do you like to go? How do you like be? What do you like about me? What do I do that offends you and hurts your feelings? Please, sweetheart, be sure to tell me whatever bothers you about anything and everything, including me. And don't forget: I love you for exactly who you are, right now, and I will always love you no matter how and who you decide to be."

A free man or a free woman. A man or a woman who has not heard these questions while growing up has not truly been nurtured, loved or validated for who they are, and has not been guided to learn about who they want to be. Fortunately, it is never too late. At any time and moment of life, individuals can begin the process of healing and becoming their true Selves.

Process of becoming liberated people. Asking oneself these questions begins the process of healing and excellence. Becoming the unconditionally loving, nurturing parents, and the wise, objective significant Programers you never had, is to work towards the process of Power Balance, freedom and independence of mind, thought and action. These are qualities that every human being must embody in order to become true beings and free men or women.

Universal Male-Female Power Balance in all of us. The true (and frightening to some) experience of being human is that for every Pattern we possess, its opposite also exists in us. To deny our own opposite Patterns is to deny our Power Balance and to cause our own Imbalance. Thus, for every man who possesses male patterns, there exists in him equal female patterns necessary for his well-being and are significant for his Power Balance and Excellence: Patterns that are crucial for accomplishing his mission of success, happiness and prosperity as a person alone, and as one relating to others.

Fear of who we truly are. When a man denies his female side - the femininity, softness, and tenderness - he denies half of himself, and thus only functions with one half of his being. Doing so causes ignorance, rigidity, Power Imbalance and block in his process of becoming. He lives in fear of finding out who he truly can and wants to be, and that if he did so, he would not be acceptable to others or to himself. It is that fear that will ultimately cause his downfall, for one cannot forever continue to be someone else successfully on the stage of life.

Living a lie, lonely behind the mask. No person who is not completely himself or herself will ever truly be acceptable to Self or others. No person, no matter how hard he or she tries, will ever be accepted by everyone. The secret is that if we become our true Self and are happy with who we are, we will have a clear and positive power without toxic Blocks; this power will attract people to us no matter who and what we are. The key is to know, understand and accept ourSelf with all strengths and weaknesses and uniqueness that belong to us. Otherwise, we will be living a lie that, no matter how successful, will leave us lonely behind the mask, disillusioned in our success.

Men and women want the same things. Men should ask themselves if they like women who have no feelings. Do they like women who are so rigid, invulnerable and out of touch with themselves that they never cry? Do they like women who are so fragile and dainty that cannot become true partners in the thick and thin of their lives? Do they like women who don't have minds of their own? (Some of these Patterns might be fun and intriguing for a while, but almost all men ultimately like women who are not stuck with what society has told them they should be, and are instead Programers of their own lives.)

Challenging cultural colognes within ourselves. In that case, what makes men believe that true women like their men to be the ones who adorn cultural colognes and lack Patterns that make them complete human beings? Both men and women want mates who are capable of sensitivity and tenderness as well as strength and masculinity. I am not saying that every man or woman must be all these things. I am, however, saying that all individuals must challenge their own cultural myths. It is only from that challenge that they can recognize their true Self. The sacrifice for being who they truly are is not half as painful as living a lie and being their own second best for all their lives.

Masculine Patterns in women. Masculine Patterns are Patterns of logic, goal orientation, assertion and action. A woman who denies her masculine patterns denies a dimension of herself. The absence of such a dimension will handicap and paralyze any woman throughout her life.

Downplay of Masculine Patterns in women. The masculine patterns of goal orientation, assertion and action have been criticized in women of multidimensionality, and society has left them feeling disillusioned and guilty only because they did not have the cultural limitations set upon them within their families. Their upbringing instead has enabled them to flourish and become whole human beings, not just products of social expectations.

Outdated societal Programing. This society takes its orders from the limitations of outdated and old books written by men who had not developed their own strength enough to appreciate and encourage strength in women. Hence, they limited women out of the fear of being dominated and controlled by them, while ultimately feeling lonely and overwhelmed in their roles as the sole providers. They resented women because they themselves did not have the ability or the time to nurture themselves, and felt left out because of the role given to them without considering their true abilities and desires for being true partners with their women who should have had an equal chance for fully participating in life.

Feminine Pattern. Femininity has been described by many authors. It is a fascinating subject for men and women alike. The conclusions about what constitute a "woman" truly depends on the writer, the writer's past, and the writer's perceptions based on his or her experiences of femininity.

Patterns of Femininity (female power.) In my vision and experience, femininity is a pattern that has embedded within it many intriguing patterns. Without these various patterns that create the dimensions existing in women and men who possess feminine patterns, one cannot see femininity operating at its best and fullest. These Patterns are as follows:

Pattern of Softness. Softness comes from wisdom and the peaceful silence existing within a person. Aside from the fact that softness comes from process orientation, which is the ability to feel the here and now and the joy that life has to offer, anyone (man or woman) who does not possess the pattern of softness will suffer from a lack of grace, tenderness, patience and tolerance, creating an unconscious distance in relationships not only with others, but with oneself. Furthermore, the absence of patterns of softness develops rigidity and blocks that make a person prone to physical and mental illness. These illnesses can paralyze a person, for without softness, the person also lacks the flexibility and resilience that creates true strength. It is only in a soft and slow process that one can be flexible, and flexibility creates resilience.

Harshness, the opposing pattern of softness, is a significant pattern embedded within the patterns of detachment existing in the absence of intimacy. When one touches softly, man or woman, one leaves traces of emotion, energy, and power. Yet these traces get erased when one touches harshly and hurriedly, without focus on tenderness and attentiveness. Softness, then, has embedded within it the pattern of process orientation, strength, flexibility, resilience, patience, tolerance, and attentiveness that together add to the dimensions of feminine patterns. Attentiveness is the unhurried manner in which we exist within ourselves and with others.

Feminine Patterns in men. Men will lack resilience and strength without feminine patterns. Without patterns of softness, process orientation, flexibility, resilience, strength, attentiveness, patience and tolerance, there is no substance in a man or a woman. This is the core of the significance of Patterns of femininity. Men and women are both robbed when society dictates to men not to be feminine. In doing so, society tells men not to be soft or attentive or tender, and not to have substance in the patterns of touching others.

Patterns of Submission and Passivity. Submission and passivity are also among patterns embedded within the pattern of femininity. Many men lose their relationships only because they don't know when and how to remain passive about issues that are simply irrelevant to the making of a relationship, or even the true substance to life. The burden of remaining alert and active at all times, as society has demanded from men in matters of control, both robs them from the joy of equally sharing responsibility with their mates, and robs their mates of having reasons to give equally and feel equal in societal responsibility. Unfortunately, some women have far too much of these patterns, and others have rejected it altogether because of rebelling against the demands of societal Programing.

Patterns of Nurturance. No man without patterns of nurturance can survive any relationship, or their own un-nurtured Self. For in the absence of patterns of nurturance for their mates they will not have connection and intimacy, and in the absence of nurturance for themselves they will become too vulnerable, dependent, and needy.

Toxic Patterns should be omitted. True nurturing does not involve nurturing the Toxic Patterns of another or of Self. Loving Toxic Patterns is neither love nor nurturance, but rather an enabling, sado-masochist Pattern that will end up in resentment, hatred, and lack of genuine intimacy. Keeping score, paralyzing a relationship that would have otherwise had the chance to change with the power of love, nurturance, and firm stance on refusing to accept the Toxic Patterns, will result in destructive Patterns of relating, and disillusionments of intimacy.

Patterns of Sensuality. Sensuality, like nurturance, is love and tenderness towards oneself as well as one's mate. It is caring for one's body and soul with the joy and acceptance of one's totality. To be sensual means to be vulnerable to, and to nurture all parts and aspects of Self; this is necessary if one wants to nurture another. It is impossible to truly love and nurture another if one has no idea what it means to love and nurture oneself.

The Sensuous. A sensuous person shows the ability to love and nurture through the softness in his or her touch. One cannot possibly be out of touch with loving Self, and be nurturing and sensuous to another.

Sensuality. Traditional men have been deprived of sensuality. In the midst of their love for another, their goal-oriented, impulsive, indulgent Patterns of compulsiveness manifest, depriving them and their partners of feeling the love and tenderness which is the ultimate joy in connection with another. This same Pattern is the reason for indulgently wanting more food after just finishing a full meal. The inability to focus and capture all that there is in the moment, which requires self-discipline of the mind and body, causes them to seek the next meal while eating the one in front of them, missing out on the entire deal.

Breaking stereotype and Pattern Selectivity. Not all men are non-sensual, for I would like to break the Patterns of stereotypes and pattern selectivity. I myself learned the art of sensuousness through men, for I was a goal-oriented woman initially, occupied with accomplishment instead of feeling, existing, and being. Goal orientation can become a Block Pattern to intimacy, stemming from the fear of connecting.

Pattern of Sexuality. Passion and excitement are patterns embedded in patterns of sexuality. Sexuality is a pattern of body awareness, for without awareness of our own body, we cannot possibly actively participate in a fulfilling connection of sexual and sensual patterns with another individual. The closer we get to our true Self, and the more we appreciate and nurture our own mind-body connection, the more fulfilling, passionate, healing and spiritual our patterns of sexuality. It is limiting the vast power of being human that has caused much pain and confusion.

9th Universal Law
Responsibility - Freedom

There is no freedom without responsibility. We must find Balance within ourSelf. True freedom comes when we have experienced the ability to be free from the need of appearances of freedom that compromise its development in a true sense. A fourteen year old cannot find inner freedom in the heart of the night on cold, ruthless street, nor can a man or a woman in the arms of a stranger. Freedom is only found within; even in the confinement of a prison.

Freedom is a misunderstood and misrepresented words in the vocabulary of the Western world. Unfortunately we live at a time where we can distinctly see such misrepresentations at the cost of the future of our children. People, including mySelf have passion for what they believe and seem to infringe upon the freedom of others with a lack of boundary of their own perceived freedom. Freedom is no longer freedom if it threatens that of the same of others. For by its own pattern and nature only exists in absolute wholeness as a part to that of another. I am not free if my freedom has put a chain on your hands; you are not free if your freedom is surviving by breathing my air. Freedom is kind, compassionate, and fair even in its rage of anger; freedom is responsible and it must be earned and presented by the totality of its nature.

Taming Basic Instincts

We are born with basic instincts. Like animals who eat, sleep, have sex and release themselves of all their toxins and protect and defend themselves in cases of danger as they instinctively feel necessary, we, too, universally share their basic instincts with the same level of intensity. Our basic instincts are so powerful that if not trained and polished we can find ourselves more and more similar to the animals we hold and admire as pets. What makes us different from animals is the power of our minds that can be put to action calculatively, and the power of our spirit that can polish our immediate needs and basic instincts. As I said earlier, our basic instincts are to feel fed, safe, rested, relieved and released of all tension and toxins accumulated, in sexual forms or otherwise, in our body. I will discuss sexuality as an example, since sexuality is one of our basic instincts that has been inhibited. Our culture allows sexual exploitation and legal forms of prostitution of the soul. However, it condemns healthy, guilt-free sexuality. Thus in our culture we turn to food and exaggerated patterns of satisfying our other basic instincts that are not inhibited. That is why Americans suffer from obesity. It is not a natural pattern of being to abuse food and neglect our health. The notion that people gain exaggerated weight by merely enjoying eating or that it is a natural pattern does not seem reasonable to me and only the justification of the self indulgent without self discipline; unless they indulge themselves for feeling deprivation of other needs for which they lack the training to feel self-contained. There are many countries that inhibit sexuality, but we live in the only country with a distinct schizophrenic double bind in patterns of sexuality, which is sexual *exposure* and *inhibition,* simultaneously.

Sexuality as an instinctive Pattern. We accept sexuality as an instinctive Pattern within animals of all kinds. Sexuality must also be seen as an instinctual Pattern of humanity, for its oppression and lack of fulfillment has created malfunction and emotional depravation, leading people to severe effects, causing Imbalance within society.

Sexual balance and clarity. People who have clear minds without guilt about their sexuality can go about their lives without entangled energy that could have been used elsewhere. They feel clear and free and can accomplish whatever they want in life without toxic Patterns of frustration and Power Imbalances that inhibit healthy development and mind-body progression.

Sexuality must be a choice. Sexuality must be a choice combined with Patterns of self-discipline, self-respect, and guilt-free ethics and morality. When we raise our children with healthy

Patterns of sexuality by teaching them about their sexuality while at the same time teaching them about their integrity and self-respect, and when we teach them Preventive and Excelling Patterns of being, we have raised children who will grow up not only as whole people, able to enjoy who they are and what they are capable of, but also as safe people for our society.

Societal neglect and abuse of sexuality. Sexuality has been neglected, abused and misused in both Eastern and Western societies. The swing of the pendulum has been so severe that both cultures suffer deeply from a lack of understanding of sexuality, which is a significant part of the dimensions of both the male and female totality. A dimension that has not been nurtured for the intent of nourishment for its own sake, and has been used, exploited, and abused and at the same time inhibited and guilt-provoking in Western culture, while neglected and ignored in Eastern culture, creates crisis and Imbalance within individuals and society. Its lack of a healthy and Balanced existence has a great impact on the absence of safety presently encountered in families, communities and society.

Sexual depravation. Sexual depravation is like oxygen, food, and water depravation. When we put a person in a room and deprive that person of food, when that person is free to get out, he or she will seek to satisfy his or her food depravation at any cost. When we deprive people of the oxygen they need in order to stay alive, they die. Lack of an appropriate amount of water in body causes severe malfunction of the body, and ultimately death. Depravation of any kind creates people willing to kill and exploit in order to satisfy their basic needs, depending in their level of tolerance for frustration and for delay of gratification. We must learn and teach not to physically, emotionally or psychologically indulge in food or, for that matter, sexual gratification. This is a pattern of excellence not achieved by inhibition but by training the mind, body and spirit to have voluntary Self-Control of the patterns of mind and action. This training is not only missing in our families and society, but also lacks substantive presence in the depth our most sophisticated spiritual teachings. We cannot beat and punish the universal nature out of human beings. Because we have not known up to date anything about training them to go beyond such basic life patterns and move towards patterns of excellence, we must neither deny them of being human nor hold them responsible for not knowing. But as teachers, parents and preachers we must begin to admit to our ignorance and lack of appropriate training, and *begin to learn and teach.*

Background and ideology. Any act of sexual violence that has been reported and witnessed in the history of humanity and has captured the headlines of news and media, where people have been raped, molested and murdered by another, is conducted by people with a classic background of sexual depravation, sexual inhibition and guilt, or sexual exploitation that also created guilt within the person.

The roots of sexual crisis. Sexual guilt, shame, and inhibition creates societal and individual sexual crises. Let us look at the type of people who become societal liabilities as a result of sexual Imbalances. A sexually deprived and inhibited father rapes his own daughter. A sexually deprived, inhibited and guilt-provoked preacher rapes innocent children who turn to him or her for guidance. A sexually deprived and guilt-provoked man without adequate societal skills and sexual maturity becomes a hillside strangler.

Prevention of damage of societal safety. For instance, a boy witnesses his mother's sexual exploitation and lack of boundary at an early age, and has had no proper guidance and education to put his mother's Imbalanced Programing into perspective and arrive at an interpretive analysis that would separate him from the premature and frustrated needs and desires of his childhood. If his questions regarding this issue were answered appropriately, the classic domino effect that almost always results in damaging societal safety might be prevented.

Sexual deprivation creates Imbalance. People with healthy sexual life Patterns who can satisfy themselves sexually without guilt will not go looking for someone to rape or murder on the streets, or exploit their own flesh and blood living under their own roof.

Victims of sexual assault. Many become perpetrators of assault only because they have copied the Pattern from another. The act that has been done to them has been so traumatic that it has become a part of them in order to survive the pain of having been intruded upon in such a tragic way.

Perpetrators: frightened victims of lack of Self. Some victims choose to victimize others only as a way of preventing the repetition of the tragedy in their own lives. For it is a universal law to swing the pendulum to the other extreme that we have experienced in life, as an Imbalanced Pattern of dealing with our pain. Once one has experienced pain, if it is not dealt with fully, with the Self rising with clarity, one can becomes a danger to others, for she or he may repeat the experience on the other side of the pendulum.

Guilt and shame: cause of all Imbalances. How many healthy people who can buy their food, go to stores and steal it? Those who do so have emotional Imbalances of guilt about something that makes them feel unworthy inside. Stealing becomes proof of the truth of the messages of unworthiness they have received from others. It is a way of punishing themselves for the "sin" they feel they have done and no one else has discovered. It is a way of proving to themselves that they are able to even hide their feelings of inferiority from themselves.

Sexual identity confusion. At times, compulsive stealing is a reenactment of the past, where the individual did suffer from an absence of basic need and food depravation. It can also be a cry for help, for they are showing that they have no control of their impulse that has been Programed into them by societal Imbalance. It is the same with sexual perpetrators who rob people of their rights and exploit without Self-Control. All of these perpetrators, in my experience with people who possess these Patterns, are coming from feelings of guilt, most often because of confusion about their sexual identities and Imbalances.

Oppressed sexuality becomes toxic power. It is created as a result of guilt-shame-provoking sexual inhibitions experienced in past Programing. Sexual energy is a very powerful part of a person's psyche and chemistry that, if inhibited, will become negative, toxic power.

Masturbation as a Self-Control Pattern. Masturbation is an attempt to control an impulse or a need, and to prevent it from becoming an exploitative Pattern towards others. Masturbation can keep our communities safer. If masturbation was not so guilt-provoking by religion, it could create self-sufficiency and self-control in Patterns of sexual Imbalance and indulgence: Patterns that are among the most significant problems of our society.

Masturbation: Pattern of Prevention of crisis. We must recognize the harmlessness of masturbation, and its relevance for society's safety, and even its help in maintaining the peace between husband and wife, in situations where the person in need of sex must force someone, who becomes a victim (anyone that is not prepared or gets forced into a sexual act is a victim.) If one takes responsibility for one's own needs, the world will become a much safer and peaceful world, and few couples will feel alienated by one another.

Sexual intimacy becomes a choice, an act of love. Sexual intimacy must come from the intent of wanting to be with someone, instead of using another as the object of impulsive desire. An act of love is just that: without any forceful gestures, or for the purpose of satisfying one person's need at the cost of another. A true act of love involves the participation of two people at the same time for the purpose of getting close to each other, in which both agree to it equally.

End of sexual exploitation. Both a man who runs wild in the middle of the night to find someone to satisfy his need and a husband who feels frustrated because he has more passion than his wife and feels it is her duty to perform, are on their way to impose on and abuse someone else for their own unreasonable needs. However, if they take care of their own needs responsibly, they will both be in a position to be loved truly without the sabotage of personal needs.

Genuine and true sexuality arises. Because of the mere fact that they begin to look at their partner as someone to love and not as someone to be serviced by, that partner will begin to give with all the passion that any person has the capacity to experience. That's right. The need for sex and passion is not just limited to men; it is merely advertised as something that only men have experienced. Yet there are many healthy women, frustrated, for their sexual needs are unmet.

Loving for the sake of love, and with the intent to love. If those women also take responsibility for their own satisfaction, then the performance pressure felt by men will be reduced, and a higher level will develop in the relationship. Thus, space will be made for equal respect for each person involved, with care, consideration, compassion, joy and passion, willingly and lovingly.

Sexual Imbalances and Blocks. Sexuality is a natural, inherent Pattern of humanity. It is just as basic a Pattern as eating, sleeping and breathing, and its depravation will cause Imbalances and Blocks not only in Patterns of sexuality, but in other dimensions and functions. The Shame Patterns of being a bad person, the Fear Patterns of rejection by feeling sexuality, or exhibiting variations in Patterns of sexuality, and the mythical belief that purity and spirituality is antithetical to a sexual being, has caused individuals to neglect and thus create Imbalances and Blocks in their most significant Life Pattern: Sexuality.

Crime and violence by Imbalance in sexuality. Many other Imbalances occur as a result of Imbalance in sexuality. My Theory is that sexual Imbalance and inhibition has been a significant factor in the crime rate throughout the world. This is especially true in countries like the United States, where there is an abundance of sexual exposure and exhibitionism simultaneous with unspoken religious sexual inhibitions.

Pattern Change in Sexuality. Patterns of Sexuality develop and change by the significant influences, our Programers early on in life. Watching our Programers, as partners in life, either love or abuse and misuse one other, changes the patterns of love. A girl with a domineering mother rejects not only the aggression she feels from her, but also all of her as a woman. Likewise, a girl with a domineering, aggressive father and a passive, victimized mother chooses to become like the father because she does not want to live a life full of pain, as her mother did. Patterns of Sexuality, just like any patterns, have variations and types.

Sexual double-bind: exposure and inhibition. This Pattern is like the double-bind theory of family systems in schizophrenic families. The Pattern stems from mixed messages of our life Programers, like when a person says something and means another and the person on the other side does not get a congruent message. In the case of sexual double-bind, I am proposing the same connotation that the double-bind theory suggests. People who expose themselves sexually are usually not connected with their sexuality. They exaggerate their patterns on the outside to prove themselves to be something that they don't feel; much like the preachers or people who publicly pray and spend the time they could be truly spiritual by making a presentation of spirituality. The people on the other side get a mixed message of sexual or spiritual openness: a mere presentation that at the time of intimacy turns out as frigidity or, in the case of spiritual embrace, as punitive cruelty. This phenomenon had been called double-bind and is overwhelming for children too vulnerable to understand the Imbalances of others and personalize everything. In this case they feel something other than what the person is suggesting and it makes them doubt their own intuitive senses. A mother that yells at her daughter and tells her she loves her, or beats her up and tells her it is for her own good, is doing far more damage to her child than she will ever understand. The child may trust someday that she truly meant well, but she will have a hard time ever trusting herself.

Patterns of Sexual Inhibition. The inability or lack of choice to satisfy sexual urges and sexual desires and needs as they appear and develop within the body and the mind develops sexual tension and sexual Imbalance which, in turn, develops severe cognitive and emotional Imbalances.

Patterns of Self-Sexuality. Just as it is important to know thySelf before we can begin to know others, and as it is significant to know ourselves before we can expect anyone else to know us, in order to become healthy sexual individuals and have balanced sexual relationships with others, we need to understand self-sexuality.

Pattern of Sexual Self-Contentment. This Pattern is a part of the whole Pattern of self-contentment, which is contentment of Self freed from addictions and dependencies. Sexual contentment means contentment in regards to sexual satisfaction, which is far different from sexual intimacy. Sexual intimacy has been tainted, abused and neglected by the overwhelming need for sexual satisfaction and release at the cost of exploiting others' rights and boundaries. Sexual self-contentment is basically satisfying sexual needs with the safest methods existing today. Methods of Sexual Self-Contentment. These methods are:

1.) Sexual fasting and celibacy. This is a techniques where an individual learns, through Patterns of Excellence, to move towards purity and abstinence in a true sense, with the absence of feeling depravation or forced sexual inhibition that causes sexual Imbalance and Block. The strength that creates a pattern of excellence in this case is the development of a Universal Self and the development of Self-Expression that evolves from a universal self. When we have a Self larger than our body contains, and when we can see the world expanded outside of the boundary of our backyards or even our own community and society, we begin to develop and expand a self-expression pattern that will consume all of our power, our creative as well as sexual energy, thus giving us the choice of celibacy without feeling of depravation.

2.) Masturbation. Masturbation is the natural, inherent act of satisfying Self, which children discover in infancy before adult civilization inhibits them, causing them to build up tension that blocks a healthy growth not only in childhood, adolescence and adulthood, but also blocks the Patterns of a prolonged youth. This idea is explored in detail in my upcoming book *Patterns of Love*.

Disillusionment in Patterns of relating. A great deal of disillusionment in Patterns of relating has been because the intent for connecting has been self-satisfaction as opposed to the true treasure of connecting for the sake of connecting. In connections where one or both people involved feel no power in connection, it is because both are being used for self-satisfaction instead of for connection with who they are. Patterns of Imbalance are created because of a lack of sexual self-contentment, which stems from the religious and cultural myths of sin and dysfunction.

Sexual Self-Containment. Sexual exploitation, molestation, rape, family violence, teenage drug addiction, sexual abuse and sexual promiscuity, toxic control Patterns, and the lack of adequate sexual Patterns and tools for true intimacy all come from Imbalances and Blocks of choosing a natural, inherent flow of sexuality (according to my theory of Power Balance, which has sexual Power Balance included within it.)

Patterns of Excellence in Sexuality. A healthy and balanced choice of sexuality results in Patterns of Excellence, where a Power Balance of sexual, sensual and spiritual intimacy, where surrender and power is one and the same, and Power Balance can be reached with a soul mate through relinquishment of the physical self. At times, when the complete connection is not possible or chosen just having the free choice of sexuality without shame enables the individual to develop and maintain a self-disciplined Pattern of abstinence, long-term or short-term, at which time he or she chooses to remain celibate for purposes of mastery that need total devotion or selective separation for true connection and ecstasy.

Absence of Excellence Pattern of Self-Discipline. When we are inhibited sexually by intimidation, fear, and guilt, without developing Patterns of reasoning and self-discipline that create conscious and free choices of abstinence and a desire for purity, the toxic Imbalances and Blocks are seen as symptoms of the sexual inhibited.

10th Universal Law
Familiarity - Differentness

The Power Balance of Familiarity-Differentness is related to Patterns of Part-Wholeness. The *part*, which is us, is unique within Self, and universal within the *whole*. Our patterns abide by the same universal law. We have patterns that keep us unique while at the same time we grow and move towards universality. Patterns of harmony come from knowing that we are not alone even in the loneliest times of our lives. The Universal Powers of Wisdom and Nurturance, as compassionate parents, are always there for us. The requirement is only that we connect with our Universal Self. As we accept our own Patterns of Cognition and Emotion within, we begin to connect even more to the wisdom and nurturance, as available to us as the air we breathe; it is literally at our disposal.

Past Habitual and Repetitive Patterns. Some of the most primitive, destructive and Toxic Patterns that exist in today's society have continued only because of the *law of familiarity*. Oppression, victimization, fear, guilt, and many other Patterns that have paralyzed individuals and communities are surviving only because people do not have the knowledge or permission of Pattern Analysis, which is the basic questioning that shows us which Patterns we are still presenting for their mere familiarity, and which of these Patterns of the Past no longer serve a purpose in our lives, and need to be deleted by separation of Self from that which we have adopted without choice, in order to become independent beings.

Shared Core Commonalty. As mentioned earlier all individuals share, in core of their beings, an *inherent goodness*. At times, it is buried under Imbalance Programings of society. All individuals are born with inherent goodness and the ability to become the best of themselves. All other labels are what people themselves have invented in order to simplify life. Unfortunately, it has worked quite the opposite way. To learn how to stop acting on outdated

Programs will prevent us from creating further Blocks and Imbalances in the progression of humanity.

Shared differentness. Shared differentness is the pattern that makes us whole and unique in the midst of our sameness. Our differentness, however, should not come between us, but should only enhance and complement our togetherness. Like the pieces of a puzzle, we must strive to be different from one another in order to fit in and benefit from the multidimensional differences of each other. But what truly makes us different is not the place we live in or the color of our hair. Those are illusions of differentness pointed out to us, misleading us of our common cause, thus scattering our joint power. Our differences lie within the patterns in which we utilize our shared universal meaning and life purpose.

Home is where we are closest to ourSelf. The first five years of my life in the United States, and even a few years after I had become a full-fledged, legitimate citizen of this country, I packed my bags every summer and begged my husband to take me home. His wisdom, which I interpreted as insensitivity then, was to tell me that he would only take me when he knew that I would come back. I thought, "How selfish of him." He was denying me of my roots that I needed so badly to feel. Lost in the detached and cold arms of a giant melting pot, I felt I would die if I did not go back to where I once was known, to a place that was so familiar to me. I would write five letters a week to each member of my family and when I was through, the papers were wet from my tears of desire to be there, where I belonged and was loved. Here, I felt so unloved.

For an immigrant coming to America is a shock to the system: a condition that an unaware therapist, unfamiliar with the situational crisis of this sort, can call schizophrenia and refer to a psychiatrist, who might immediately take out his prescription pad and prescribe the legitimate drug that makes a zombie out of an intelligent person and who from then on, if not sophisticated enough, will be at the mercy of the diagnosis and labels written in a file. I did not go through this tragic process, but as a therapist, I have worked with many who spent half of their lives wandering in it. It is a painful process to leave familiarity and to search differentness; to leave what is already known to discover what is unknown.

But all those who leave the comfort of their homes and travel to unknown places, even if it is moving from one town to another do so with one mission; to find freedom; to move, grow and to progress. And almost all of those whom take the road less traveled as Scott peck described so eloquently, find that freedom is where home is, and home is within theirSelf. To search for the truth is to search for the Self within; it is the same process of painful honesty of letting go of the familiar to find the different and the analysis and discovery of not only who we are represented by our life patterns, but also our intent behind each and every pattern; not just those we present to our society, but those which we admit withinSelf.

Finding our true Self in a melting pot. There is a blessing and a reason for having a melting pot where all can come to a Balance. It is truly a blessing to live where the universe can meet and all its sacred patterns can exist next to one another; it all comes together, indeed in this land of freedom. People come from all parts of the world to find their true Self to a land that promises prosperity and opportunity to become the best of theirSelf. Only through learning about ourSelf do we come to our Power Balance and Excellence. It is also through observation and understanding of the process of others different from us that we can stretch our wings to fly to the ultimate of our own existence.

11th Universal Law
Universal Code of Ethics

The Power Balance of Universal Law and an Inner Code of Ethics is the ultimate law that has the power to bring back to communities and nations, not only peace, but prevention and excellence and restoration of humanity through advancement and progression.

Existential Clarity Program: the core. Underneath layers of justification, defense, rationalization, and mistakes, beyond hard shells shown to the outside world, I have found, deep inside, a powerful, Existential Clarity within every soul as I traveled with them on their windy, narrow, frightening, and difficult paths home, to inner peace. Over and over, the people who come to me while on their path to being freed up from pain, and even before that, on my own journey to find mySelf in the midst of the maddest crowd, I find no evil in the core of people, nor in the core of my own existence. The Blocks, Imbalances, helplessness, and even the manipulations of corrupt and toxic powers were caused by misleading signs on an unsafe path of life.

Universal Sign Program. Lost by misleading signs placed by people who claim to know better than us about what must happen in our lives, Blocks and Imbalances are created, and a legitimate lack of trust for the safety of the road is the result. We have been given too many instructions that not only fail in helping us reach our destination, but also lead us to the edge from which we fall. This is a natural Pattern that happens when we blindly obey and give permission to others to map out our lives and to program misleading and inaccurate signs to follow. What we really need are signs and languages based on universal knowledge and Knowledge of Self: signs that don't block us from connecting with all people existing side by side in the universe.

Inner Code of Ethics, beyond the societal laws. Anything forced upon people to obey blindly will be rebelled against, and will relinquish the inherent sense of responsibility and goodness, because people will look on it as something external and outside of Self. Inner spiritual ethics are beyond governmental laws, and must be taught in childhood by parents and teachers, or in adulthood by personal choice of Self Programs. Societal Patterns and Programs must be congruent with the expectations and needs of the individual, and not something dictated to them.

Universal Spiritual Ethics Program. People always say that laws are made to be broken. Laws and ethics that come from within, instilled developmentally and adopted by the individual's conscious choice and deductive reasoning, defending integrity and not fear, are laws that will not be broken and can become the foundation of an Excelled society.

Patterns of Ethics: an internal golden rule. In my theory and therapy of Pattern Change Programing and Power Balance, laws and ethics come only from within the individual and/or by Parental Programing during developmental years. Societal patterns and Programs must be congruent with the expectations and needs of the individual in order to prevent setting them up to break them, which would manifest another set of Imbalanced Patterns of guilt, shame, and anxiety stemming from the roots of unreasonable expectations of Societal Programers, as well as the absence of adequate Preventive and Universal Inner Ethics and Morality. Inner Codes of Ethics are the same as the Universal Laws of Power Balance because whomever has balance of the patterns wisdom and nurturance, well qualifies to be the judge of goodness within, or that of the other.

Universal Law and Universal Code of Ethics. My theories further challenge families, societies organizations, countries, and leaders of the world to take a look at their own Patterns and the intent of their actions towards their own people and others. We are too far advanced cognitively to manipulate the law and hide behind an influenced justice. Justice and fairness is not in the saying, but in the doing of what is right, ethically and morally, without selective bias, and even when others are not looking. Today, there is a great deal of rhetoric by those who use their positions of power about redefining civilization, the renewal of democracy and freedom, and the contract with America. The one contract America needs is the Knowledge of Self and the strengthening of the public means of the people's education. Education is the only institution that seems to threaten those leaders who say they want to educate the people in words, but in action are trying to keep them dependent to ignorance and the old order of blind obedience. Our societal leadership today consists of those who work hard to serve the people, and those who work hard to get the people to serve them. In order to distinguish between these two categories one must look within and search for their true intent by questioning their actions, not by blindly accepting their words of power play and intimidation.

Willow trees at the mercy of the intrusive wind. The television is packed with purchased hours of people who are selling us themselves, their ideas, their agendas and their product. In order to stay focused and not become a shaky willow tree bouncing back and forth by the intrusions of the wind, we must know our roots, and hold tightly to the ground.

Roots of our souls beyond the roots of our bodies. Our roots are not attached to a certain ground, nor are they nurtured by a certain food, nor will they grow by a certain sound. Only the sound of our own mind and heart will truly nurture the roots of our souls. Cultures, countries, languages, religions, families, relatives, friends and beliefs are all made to better serve us in our inherent and forever-processing journey towards Compassion and Excellence within Humanity.

Questioning blocks to the Self. For that matter, if anyone or anything stands in the way of the journey that requires us to become our true Selves while on our constant search for universal truth and the truth of others, then we must question the truth they claim to hold. If we don't, we have consciously bought into a collection of systems that have blocked our spiritual purpose.

We don't need Robin Hoods: we need guides. We no longer need Robin Hoods who hide in the woods to save us from the king's bandits. What we do need, more than ever, are people who can see and think clearly, and who will come forward, risk their comfortable positions and earnings, and explain the big picture to the rest of the world who is lost in the woods.

Walking in the dark, lost in the world. The world is full of people who are trusting and innocent, Programed not to question any authority. These people are walking in the dark as far as their rights and choices in life are concerned, unable to separate what is good for them from what others want them to believe. These lost people of the world are being robbed, daily, of their inherent rights, the power to choose, and the knowledge of healthy Patterns of Living.

Not enough Patterns of Courage and Sincerity. Is it because we don't have enough educated, intelligent, wise, and creative people in the world? Or do people forget their promises they make to themselves once they get to the top? I know that it is hard to remember the hardship of climbing once we make it to the top. But we must not forget that there are others who are still struggling on the bottom who may benefit from our sending a rope down.

Patterns of Forgiveness-Compassion. The golden rule of ethics has embedded within it forgiveness and universal non-selective compassion. Self-righteousness is only the denial of our own sins. But to forgive and to forget is the *doing* that comes with *being* a true person. Let us forgive and forget and begin our next moment with love and nurturance for Self as well as others, and recognize that there is always a day following the darkness of the night.

Six

Universal Patterns
of Success

Being and Doing

In order to succeed in anything we must have inner balance of our mind and emotion. Our inner patterns arc our most significant tools of our success. There is nothing we can't think of, handle or do, once we have our mind and emotion in control and in sync with our own purpose and mission. Balance Patterns are patterns of being that are consciously chosen by us after we search for our Universal Self and begin to polish our inner being. The absence of Patterns of anxiety, tension, procrastination and perfection which block our balance are indicate our growth and choice in our path of being. Some Balance Patterns are Patterns of Goal Orientation, Process Orientation, Strength, Vulnerability, Silence, Activity, Openness, Boundary, Cognition (patterns of the mind) and Emotion.

The Making of Successful Children

I had a session with a young man of nineteen years an hour ago. He is brilliant and a pleasure to work with. I have watched him come out of a life threatening crisis and patterns that were deteriorating his health, and move towards a sense of defined Self. Today he was eager to learn about Self-Discipline and a sense of direction. He had told me that he has no sense of direction because he has no need for it. He comes from a wealthy family and feels secure about his future no matter what he chooses to do. So he has no *motivation*. He also felt *"lazy,"* as he put it, and said that he is just like his father, which I translated to him as *fear* of success and *lack of Self-Discipline*. I had previously worked with him on his relationship with his father, and it was far too easy today to detect his remainder of lack of respect for his father, which had affected his image of himself. His image of his father has improved much since the first time we talked, thus changing their pattern of communication and expression of compassion not only between them but also for themselves. He didn't think his father, a man who has made a multi-million dollar empire based on perseverance and intelligence, was smart enough. But since his father comes from a different culture and his son was raised here, there is much for which his son feels superior. As I helped my client build the image of his father in his eyes, he began to feel better about himself. Our image of our parents are very significant in the direction of our life path: something neglected by many parents. No matter how competent they are and no matter how much they love their children, none such significant factors are discussed or demonstrated in the home environment. Fathers come home exhausted, and even if they have bought and sold the world, they retreat and, in their children's eyes, look like regressed children. Many children have never seen their parents in action when they are making things happen. Many parents are never complemented just for being who they are: two very significant patterns that will create success patterns in children.

I had sessions with the father present, where they were both able to communicate their love and affection without the fear of being used, which had previously been the case. They both had a notion that once they confessed their love to the other, they would be taken advantage of by being overburdened by the dependency of the other, which especially needed some work on the father's part. Indeed, the father had far too much invested in his son as a source of love and support. That was a reason for his son's rebellion and restlessness around him. When his father became more clear, the son began to feel calm, since he was more secure about his environment.

When my client searched within, he agreed that he always saw his father tired and rushed, and never truly understood the sweet taste of success. He had also been so critically raised that he second guesses anything he does he himself. But when I talked to him about many people whom I have witnessed lose all they have been inherited only because they did not know how to maintain their wealth, he became very interested. At my request to have him search to define himself, he kept telling me he didn't *do* anything in life, and that he has never done anything worthwhile to list as an accomplishment. As a result of such a perception of himself, he was much more comfortable pretending that he didn't want to do anything rather than face the fear that if he decided on a passion, he would fail. I had him write down a list of people he respected for who they are, not for what they do. He began to see the worth within himself, because he truly is a fine young man who just doesn't know what to *do*. But the lack of doing does not define his sense of being. He *is* a fine young man. He has changed many patterns of overindulgence, and has built patterns of patience and tolerance. He has grown from self-absorption to a larger domain of care and kindness. He is concerned about others and expresses thoughtful compassion. And from constantly wanting material things to prove to himself that he is loved, or as a measure of other people's love, he has become quite a content young man. He has calmed down, evolving from a person who could not sit still more than a moment to someone who has two hour sessions with me, and I am the one who ends them. As parents, when we focus on our children's doing rather than being, we raise them without self-confidence. And that was this young man's only problem. When he himself recognizes that he is more than just someone to *do* something and that he has already accomplished simply *being*, then he can change the patterns that can easily be altered in order to become goal-oriented and accomplish the dreams that he will no longer fear having. That is the requirement to become a successful person. The goal becomes clear when we feel worthy and confident of having a goal. And when we do, we have already gained what it takes to become a winner: a Self. A person with a Self will not fear to search and find what is needed to give one a sense of direction and what is needed to know one's path to self expression. Anything and everything becomes a challenge to unravel instead of a block to fear. For a person with a Self, the *goal* becomes clear.

I also reminded the young man that his father worked seventeen hours a day and if he seemed lazy it was only because he was exhausted by the end of the day. He was a bit convinced. But then he complained about his father's lack of wisdom when it came to women. He was concerned that they only wanted him for money. He felt much better about himself when I brought to his attention that his father truly was a good and wise person and the right woman would definitely be attracted to him for the right reason. He was relieved. He could now go on and think about his own success without having to become his father's caretaker or end up like his father, without the true love of a woman.

When leaving the session, he clearly and firmly said, "I am a leader just like my father. Just teach me how and I will make it. I don't want to lose what my father built and end up a loser." From someone who once had no motivation, the young man emerged as a leader who wanted to learn how to take charge of his mission. A lifetime of the illusion of not having any interest in life was suddenly transformed into a leadership vision. We all have within us the patterns of success we need in order to achieve anything we want in life. We only need to recognize them, take them off the shelf and polish them.

Patterns of Goal Orientation

For a goal-oriented individual, the Intent and Focus is the achievement of the goal in mind, often at the cost of denying the process. Goal Orientation has embedded within it the Patterns of motivation, dedication, willpower, Self-Control, focus, direction and ambition. Goal orientation is accompanied by a purpose and mission at higher levels of Excellence. Other Patterns may enter the Patterns of Goal Orientation, depending upon the individual's culture, thought patterns, vision, knowledge, and past pattern Programing, which are the strong foundations and the roots of Patterns.

Key Pattern for a self-directed life. In order to achieve anything, a person must have the Goal Orientation Pattern. Life and different Programers put in front of us many unchosen, unwanted or wanted options, especially in this enterprising country where every channel of media sells its products and ideas. Many things can distract us from our life goals; if we don't know where we are going, we will be at the mercy of enterprising, master manipulators who can convince anyone that their product is crucial to one's life. Competitive campaigning and promotion choose, unfortunately, many of our life paths, instead of being chosen by our own independent thoughts, actions and deductive reasoning that can omit unwanted life factors.

Creating Power Balance of Joy and Mastery. Having the Goal Orientation Pattern means having the ability to achieve a goal and Self-Disciplining oneself to not get distracted by the wonderful or not-so-wonderful pleasures that life offers us for the purpose of momentary indulgence. It means focusing on the substance that gives our lives meaning, living lives of both mastery and pleasure. This focus is extremely difficult for people who also have Process-Oriented Patterns and love life and what it offers. It is much easier for people who don't know how to enjoy life to focus energy on a goal. Sometimes, such individuals choose goals as Power Blocks to their Balance and happiness because they are afraid of experiencing life and prefer to pretend that they don't have time, or that their time is too noble a Pattern for experiencing the joy of life.

Choice creates Excellence. Until one has options to choose Life Patterns, the choices one makes are not sincere. Before having options, whatever one chooses is not necessarily one's preferred choice. One will never know if it truly was unless one has the option. Too often, the Patterns we choose are only used as avoidance, block, or denial of what could have been had we not filled up our itinerary. For example, one who has been hurt in love decides to fall into a goal and work so hard that there will be no time to feel the hurt. At the same time, any person who avoids the pain of love also deprives himself or herself of the joy of love.

Cultures and Goal Orientation. A Goal-Oriented person is not concerned about the process of getting there and the pleasure he should feel about anything he does; all that matters is getting there. Culturally, the Pattern of Goal Orientation has been attached to men; yet in history and in my own personal experiences and examining the lives of people who have worked with me, this is not an accurate assumption. Culture has, however, required men to be Goal-Oriented providers of the family. Recently, many men have rebelled against such expectations, choosing not to respond to this cultural demand.

On the other hand, culture has, in the past, looked down upon women with goal orientation and high ambition, calling them selfish, which, in religious beliefs, is a sin for anyone: especially for women, who are supposed to be providers of love and nurturance, and caretakers of others with no consideration of themselves.

Western culture. Many cultures look down upon the Patterns of Goal Orientation and see it as a material Pattern of living. In Western culture, however, goal orientation is a necessary survival Pattern. The competitive, industrial, and economical structure of Western societies, where people are not secure in their jobs unless they keep their performance level and productivity high enough, forces people to be goal-oriented.

Eastern culture. In Eastern societies, once a person gets a job, regardless of performance, security is provided by job stability: a culture shock for people who migrate to the United States and find themselves not only out in the cold in terms of being out of their own countries, but also out in the cold as far as having no promise of job stability.

Strength-Vulnerability of Western civilization. This is the drawback as well as the strength of Western civilization. Its strength comes from the competitive nature of industry, where everyone must perform their best. The drawback is that many people must constantly maintain survival values by focusing on basic needs, without time to further advance Patterns of Creativity, Prevention, Excellence and Humanity.

Process Orientation Pattern

Process Orientation is a Pattern that one must create within in order to enjoy life in joy and harmony. It is the ability to feel connected with the here and now of the waves of life, and the ability to become a part of the whole while remaining whole, in the experience of Self existing with universal harmony. Process Orientation bears the Patterns of Lightness, Innocence of the mind and the heart, like a child at play.

Cultural delegation of process orientation. This Pattern has culturally been given to women and in that, too, there is not much validity. During the past several years, many women have had to become goal-oriented. The characteristics embedded in their life natures of Process Orientation have taken a secondary position, even though it is extremely significant to have Power Balance in these two processes.

Gender does not determine Life Patterns. Gender does not determines the choice of Process Orientation Pattern, or any Pattern for that matter. It is, instead, the Pattern into which one falls, developing from a sense of security and satisfaction of basic needs; at that time only, one has the luxury to develop Process Orientation.

Ability to process life. The lack of Patterns of Goal Orientation, such as a lack of ambition, willpower, focus and direction, does not necessarily guarantee a Process Orientation, although it might facilitate it. Those who are truly life lovers can and will process life even in the midst of intense goals, and those who do not understand processing life will not be able to touch it even in the midst of having nothing to do.

For those who smell the roses, life is a garden. One who appreciates the environment, the flowers, the sunset, the sunrise, the ocean, the birds singing and the grace of the mountain; one who enjoys the aroma of a good tea or the joy of lovemaking in the breeze of an afternoon, will always be connected, in the constant process of incorporating its sense into life.

For non-believers, it is a senseless endeavor. Those whose lives are test rehearsals in an endless, ambivalent Power Struggle and Block of denial; those who don't believe that life is whole in and of itself; those who hide their own power in order to defy and deny the power of others who have influenced their lives: for those who withhold the love of life, love of themselves and love of others, life, with all its colors and adventures, becomes a boring and worthless battleground. Those who are afraid of life and its unfamiliar avenues and alleys, its different leaves, and its demand for Excellence before anyone can taste the sweetness of the fruit on its trees, are content with boredom: the fearful denial of the joy of life.

Process Orientation Pattern. Process Orientation means living in the here-and-now moments of life instead of thinking about the past or future. It means having the ability to stop and smell the roses, and not to watch the clock to make sure time was not wasted. Yes, women have in the past been given more freedom to develop this Pattern, as opposed to men, and at the same time were deprived of the opportunity for developing Goal Orientation Patterns, just as men did not have the opportunity for developing Process Orientation because of cultural expectations.

Goal-Process Power Balance

I mySelf come from a total Process-Oriented background, where in the summertime during my adolescence on my father's plantation, I had time to count the birds and the fruit on the tress, and run after my own pet deer all over the grape gardens and vineyards, and read a book all day, and at night stare at the stars long enough to see if one would speak to me. Yet as I began my college years, I became an organized computer who had planned her entire life, afraid of leaving an hour free for process: a word I had experienced too much of. It was not until I had my two children, who demanded process orientation from me, that I began to balance my wings on the two Life Patterns and began to plant and smell roses, while I planned to change my destiny. After that, I never again saw the two separate or conflicting, for I had made it my mission to bring the affairs of the heart closer to the affairs of my mind.

Relationship Imbalances. This is one of the most significant difficulties in relationships where one partner is Goal-Oriented and the other is Process-Oriented. It makes it difficult to meet each other in a meaningful way without frustration and Power Block. It also presents a problem when, based on cultural expectations and societal Programing, a sex who is Goal-Oriented is expected to be Process-Oriented and vice versa. An example of this is when a man wants to stay home, take care of the children, take them to the park, cook and watch cartoons with the children, while the wife works hard all day and gladly brings the bread home, and the money. Or a woman who likes to go to wall street, hassle the men out of their money, play power and chess games with the boys, and come home to a wonderful meal with her children and husband, in the midst of her Power Balance and Flexibility.

Power Struggle of the sexes: Societal Programing. The danger of buying into the cultural norms and stereotypes is that one oppresses and Blocks Patterns necessary to Power Balance, individuality and true Self: the keys to inner peace and harmony as well and relationship harmony with the absence of Power Struggle and animosity. Power Struggles within relationships originate when one person wants to become or do something that he or she cannot achieve, and envies the mate who can. This Power Struggle begins in adolescence with brothers and sisters who are given automatic privileges without considering preference and individuality, and continues in relationships where both sexes are victims of the Societal Programing of Power Struggle and hateful animosity.

Imbalances caused by society. Often, Process Orientation or Goal Orientation is not even developed within an individual only because of societal stereotypes and expectations. The significance of Preventive Patterns within families becomes evident when a collection of socially Oppressed and Blocked Patterns creates severe Imbalances, causing difficulties for the individual to express or experience Self fully. The individual then alienates from society only because of society's unreasonable rules and expectations, and is blamed by society's double standards.

Patterns of Strength

True Patterns of Strength rest upon the ability to be flexible and resilient in times of crisis and to accept life changes as part of an adventurous journey. It is the ability to feel solid enough not to fear the strength of another. Strength is in the Patterns of Silence of the mind and the silent participation of the body. Strength precludes the need for presentation; it is loud and clear in its unseen appearances. Strength is forgiveness, compassion, and thoughtful validation of others and validation of Self. Strength is calmness. Strength is softness and tenderness; it is Power Balance and harmony. According to my definition of strength, women have owned true strength, and fought for the false interpretation of it for decades. It is time that women come to accept and treasure what they own, and share it with the men they love who need it not only to survive, but to Excel.

Cultural Patterns of Strength. Patterns of Strength were culturally given to men. Men were supposed to not cry, to provide and take care of the family, to not bend easily in times of crisis, and to not panic or lose perspective generally. Strength was judged by body posture and muscles; whoever could lift heavy things and was big and strong was the preferred one. Obviously, men, with their biological physique that has since been challenged by some women who can also build muscles just as perfectly, won. Men were voted the strongest, looking honorable by society, feeling victimized inside.

At the work place. At work, too, men were the image of strength and women were the support system in background. Things have changed quite a bit; even men no longer prefer to be given such a heavy responsibility with no true gain. True strength cannot be bought by the stereotypes that society puts upon an individual. It is in being exactly who we are. For example, a woman that lives alone must take care of herself, lifting heavy things, working, and doing all that society once said only strong men were capable of doing. She must not limit herself in getting the job done. Yet she can still remain feminine, soft, and tender. The two are not in opposition, as we have been made to believe they are, so that we will remain helpless, powerless and needy for small leaders with large egos to feel their desired superiority.

Limitations of buying into societal rules. I mySelf have never allowed the limits that the society puts upon me handicap me in any way throughout my life. More often than not, I could only rely on my own strength to be there for me.

The cost: integrity and Power Balance. I was never willing to pay the price of my integrity by playing needy and powerless for a free ride. The pleasure one gets from carrying one's own load is a part of the process of building a solid Self that withstands everything.

Compromising fairness and humanity. I never felt it fair to treat others as object of my needs while I gave orders without having enough strength to be willing to stand side by side with others to carry them through.

I will never forget when I was pregnant and my husband worked very long hours. We were moving to a bigger house, and yet were unable to find movers who would do everything we needed. I felt bad that my husband would have to come home exhausted and help move things into place. So I did it all. Nine months pregnant with a four year old child following me, I even moved big stereos up flights of stairs. When my husband came home, I had showered, made fresh tea, and was ready to go out to dinner. I am a petite woman, very feminine and proud of my womanhood; yet I find it an insult to limit mySelf as a person or exploit others to prove my femininity. Whatever we feel the need to prove is not a genuine and real Pattern. For if it was, we would have no need to make presentations of its validity.

I grew up both as a tomboy and a dainty girl. The first seven years of my life, I was treated like a Persian princess with dainty clothes, dance lessons, and shoes with matching gloves. When my oldest sister, who was responsible for all the lessons in Patterns of Grace and Femininity, flew to England to go to college, my brother took over with lessons in sportsmanship. He was my best friend, and up to the time I became fourteen years old and he, too, left to Europe to study, I was treated as one of the boys in many circumstances. I played soccer right along with my brother and his friends, every day. In fact, I was the best goalie they could find. Later on I took up basketball, and sports of one kind or other became a consistent part of my life. For as long as I remember, in my upbringing I never felt I had to be a certain way to be who I am.

Power Balance of Masculine-Feminine Patterns. This Pattern will be discussed in detail in my upcoming book, *Love Patterns*. My life experiences exposed me to this Power Balance that is the key to my success in life: absence of societal stereotype limitations. Although my family had limitations imposed on them by cultural values and myths, they themselves were liberated at heart. I was allowed to utilize all of mySelf and was not limited to just what girls should do. I grew up developing all that I had to offer to mySelf and to life. There is strength and vulnerability in all of us that if imbalanced, we will not be whole, or nurtured.

Raising multidimensional children. This is how I have raised my daughter and my son. Unfortunately, many families stamp their children early in upbringing, damaging their Power Balance in life. I have worked with many women who are practically incapable of taking care of themselves just because they were *raised* to feel and act helpless and needy. I have worked with men who are totally out of touch with their personhood only because they are supposed to be "men," foreign to the tenderness and softness existing in every person's heart.

Buying cultural rules, remaining incomplete. For societally stereotyped women, pretenses of helplessness, neediness, and even brainlessness dominate their lives with much conviction, as a means to hold onto their men. They are frightened to show their power unless someone first promises them that if they show their power, they won't lose love. Unfortunately, on the other side of the Pendulum, their fear is realistic; there are many men who are frightened of seeing Power Balance between themselves and their women. Yet perhaps they have not seen a true balance of strength with softness, and have experienced in women the competitive imitation of what does not even work for men themselves: the pretense of being tough. Strength, like vulnerability, is among the Pattern that all human beings need and deserve to have in their repertoire of Patterns of Being human; it should not be a stamp for one gender or another, nor should any other Patterns of Life.

Patterns of Vulnerability

Vulnerability comes from innocent and childlike Patterns. It is the ability to trust others and to comfortably cry on anther's shoulders, to lean on another with the confidence that you will be emotionally taken care of. It is a precious quality that one can find in youth; enthusiasm and the lack of the need to control also accompany it. It is the ability to idealize another without the interference of reality in the picture we paint of that person. Idealization can harm, however; the knight in shining armor syndrome that most women have of their dream men, causes them to eventually feel cheated when they realize that these people are only human and are at times perhaps even more vulnerable than they are.

Vulnerability is a most significant Pattern in the ability for both men and women to love. In learning about Patterns of Excellence, we will find that in order to be an Excelled individual, one needs to be multidimensional and experience the Power Balance of Strength-Vulnerability. As wonderful as it is for a man to feel that his woman leans on him and trusts him to take care of things on some occasions, like in lovemaking and matters of finance or the heart, it is quite disappointing and lonely if a man is to be the strong one in the relationship at all times. In my upcoming book, *Love Patterns*, these issues will be discussed in detail since it is a very significant Power Balance Pattern between couples: one that can make or break a marriage if not taken seriously enough.

Patterns of Activity
Focus Outward

Activity is the door to the outside world and a tool for achieving connection with others. Activity wakes up the body as well as the mind. It is the way we materialize our dream world and make our desires, hopes, and life missions come to reality. It is the ability to awaken from our resting beds each morning, to get ready to get out of our cocoons, and be open to interactions of all kinds: distant and intimate alike.

Materializing dreams by tool of activity. If one can learn the games of socialization, which are quite different in each society, one can succeed in not only adjusting, but in getting ahead in any endeavor, whether it be professional or personal. In doing so, one can become a successful human being in an enterprising world that requires materializing our dreams into the world by our tool of activity.

Success creates choice for true spirituality. My theory is that until one becomes successful in society, or at least has the choice to be, the choice *not* to be involved is not a real choice, but only a pseudo-isolation that denies the choice to stay out, as a result of the lack of tools to be in, successfully. People who reject and condemn socialization are only expressing their inability to adjust and survive in it. Their rejection is not valid, since it does not comes from having had the choice and not choosing. A teenager who chooses not to get involved with his or her classmates and instead rejects them, only feels rejected and does not fit in. The man who chooses celibacy and labels sex as superficial and a cause to drift away from oneself, if he comes from failed relationships, his statement only results from the fear of intimacy and not from respect for celibacy.

Choice creates health and honesty. For that matter, a man who calls himself spiritual and feels that success in the material world blocks true spirituality, only says that as a result of not knowing how, or being unwilling to do, what it takes to become successful in society. Why do I say that? I, again, believe that true choice only comes from having different choices at our disposal and then making one clear choice, not merely rejecting that which we don't think we can have.

Experiencing dimensions of Self creates honesty. I believe in Abraham Maslow's theory of basic needs. Until basic needs are met, the individual is incapable of truly and genuinely moving to higher dimensions of Self. I have practiced and lived this theory with conviction in every step of my life process and have seen it in the lives of the people I have worked with. I add to this theory by affirming that when people miss the steps involved in making their own choices, wherever they are placed is not where they belong congruently. They are merely there because they have adopted others' Programing that says they belong there, or they want people to believe that is where they belong. We must experience what we believe, not repeat after others. And we must experience it by taking all the steps on the path that gets us there.

Patterns of Openness

To be open is to welcome all the input existing in life: to allow, sincerely, all output to be heard without the censorship that blocks openness, clarity and knowledge on both sides. To be open is to listen attentively and hear what is really being told. To be open is to say what you believe without fear, what you feel without shame, and what you desire without guilt. It is to express oneself only for the sake of being heard and not for any other purpose that deludes what is said out of pure openness of the mind and heart of one who, even if it is fearful, does not allow fear to stand in the way of being clear.

Openness tears down the walls of limitation. Openness pays no attention to the superficial rules that create distance. Openness moves ahead even if it is strapped in bolts and chains. Openness is a child greeting a friend with the desire to hear all that he knows and to tell him all that she knows, without a moment of hesitation, whether wrong or right, and without thinking of the best way to gain the most out of the transaction. Openness is being only for the sake of being, and giving only because it feels good, and receiving only because it is a natural and humanistic way to be with others.

Openness rocks the tower of authority. An open individual asks questions that are not supposed to be asked, and frowns on secrets, manipulations and intimidation of controlling persons, fear, shame-provoking systems and oppressive environments where things are censored, distorted and dictated. An open individual stirs up and rocks the boat of bureaucratic, man-made blocks and closed doors that set up the innocent. An open individual is a breath of fresh air to dictatorships and toxic entities that hold humanity and its movements in ransom with fear, guilt and the rejection of eternity.

Patterns of Boundary

Boundary is the responsibility that must accompany freedom. freedom without boundary becomes anarchy and a burden that infringes upon other people's right and freedom. Freedom without boundary becomes discriminatory where some exercise freedom at the cost of the freedom of others, and it is no longer freedom for all. Individuals who possess Boundary, are open, free, responsible, as conscious of their own freedom as of the freedom of others. Boundary is different from limitation or oppression.

Boundary: a frame of integrity-humanity around freedom. Boundary is not established by laws or rules of society, since that which is put upon us automatically becomes a limitation. It is what we learn as we become more Excelled beings; it is when other's right becomes just as important to us as the rights of our own. In a society where for decades we have been fighting to earn our own rights, once we have them in our hands it is natural that nothing else is important but the experience of those rights. It takes an Excelled individual to give just as much importance and thought to the impact and consequence of the rights of others.

Boundary is a limit in a limitless world. Boundary is even simpler than what we just described. It is the limit that everything needs in a limitless world, so that people can socialize with one another without being stepped on. In many cases, society rejects people with no boundary and stamps them as mentally ill because it cannot handle their intrusive and exploitative impact on others.

Boundaryless Society

The real acts of intrusion and exploitation are done by some of the inhumanc institutions and leaders of our society, and are being ignored by the enterprising nature of justice in our land of freedom and liberty. No one seems to be able to touch the boundaryless institutionalized corruption of this country, yet we can easily lock up the angry individuals who are fed up with the lack of boundary in society and don't have the power or the tools to deal with their justified anger constructively. Meanwhile, we let the real inhumane and boundaryless find their way to the voting booths, elect someone in to Senate, or better yet, go to Senate and vote on issues with complete conflict of interest, or even unconstitutional legitimacy.

Patterns of a Boundaryless Society. There seems to be no limitation to cheating the people's rights and voting with a conflict of interest in our free country. Soon we will have doctors, politicians, priests, and even the heads of the tobacco, drug, rifle and oil industry sitting in the Senate chairs, side by side, voting on health issues and religious matters, legalizing the enterprising products of this country, electing someone amongst themselves, who usually become giants by using people as objects in their multi-million dollar dynasties, as President of our democratic country, while the real people and their affairs stand patiently in the boundaryless line of hypocrisy. This is my definition of a Boundaryless Society.

Boundary tells us not to have sex with our own children. It tells us not to kill people, and it tells us not to seduce others as objects of our own dreams and fantasies. Boundary tells us not to steal others' belongings or rob others of their rights. Boundary tells us not to walk into a roomful of people naked! Boundary tells us not to put our hands in fire. One with boundary, just like one with ethics and morality, is aware of the consequences of acting on boundaryless desires.

Living in the jungle of societal anarchy. Boundary is a Pattern necessary for societal acceptance. It is in accord with interaction with others, defining true freedom and liberty for those who want to be more than animals living in the jungle of societal anarchy.

Boundaryless and limitless is the mind. The power of the mind and whatever individuals do with themselves is boundaryless in the privacy of their own space. Nothing needs boundary or limit that does not infringe upon others' rights or space. Dancing naked on the streets, making love to a lion or a beast, or anything that one's heart desires is free and without a boundary in the mind, the keeper of our true reality.

Mind-Body Imbalance

There are people who have been raised with imbalanced life patterns. Power Imbalance Patterns paralyze anyone experiencing them and anyone who happens to be around them. Just like the smoke of a cigarette that is as harmful to others as the person smoking it, Imbalance Patterns bring toxicity and oppression into environment harmful to everyone around. Children, who are vulnerable and do not have the power to question authority, are especially at the mercy of individuals who supervise and care for them. These Patterns are explored in detail in my book entitled *Pattern Change Programing; Creating Your Own Destiny* and

Beyond Patterns, which question mental health and societal labels while offering in-depth, brief observations and connections with the core of the person, within.

It is not God's injustice: it is our own neglect. It literally kills me inside when I see mothers smoking or drinking while pregnant or when parents have children. Their children sit on their laps and, at the age of three months, inhale poison that paralyze even two-hundred pound adults. Let alone the fact that they have all along been inhaling poisons and the traumatic Patterns that come with it during their entire life in the womb. When they are born deformed, they are angry at God or the society who has been the partner in crime. Such parents cannot stand to see a child who is the victim if their own neglect: the symptom of their Abusive Pattern of Toxic Denial.

Uncontrollable cruelties of Imbalance. In my practice, more often I have witnessed individuals who have been damaged as a result of toxic and Imbalanced teachers, parents and other Programers at early ages when they did not expect or understand the cruelties of a Power Imbalanced individual.

Any Pattern is changeable. The only wonderful thing about these Patterns, and all Life Patterns, is that they are indeed changeable if we are willing to see and acknowledge them as our own. Yet the ten percent who lack morality and conscience, seeing people as objects to use and then throw away, have no willingness to change their Patterns. They are the toxic and destructive elements of society, and we must become aware of them and refuse to give them power. They are too far gone, devoid of a soul, and their return is nothing they would wish, and therefore would do.

Those without a soul. Those whose souls have been sold by others by the long-term, addictive paralyzation of drugs, or those who have sold their souls to the golden devil of profit, the yellow grains of greed, and the toxic authoritarianism of corrupt power, are almost beyond help. Yet I have made it my challenge to bring back those people, and have been successful only when there was still a glimmer of motivation within them, when they wanted to understand the gains of decency, and when they wanted to change. The rest of the people have within them an inherent capacity and potential to become the best of who they can be. The rest are capable of Excelling, and making a difference in the Patterns of Humanity.

Whenever there is Intent, there is Change. For those individuals, their Power Imbalance Patterns are as temporary parts of them as the food they didn't want and ate the night before. We all have Patterns that we possess merely from being around other Programers who have had power over us and have been significant in some way or another in our lives. As children, we were all very vulnerable to the love, approval, and acceptance of the people whom we idealized as our saviors.

As children, we did anything for love. We did anything they asked, and even when they did not ask, in order to please them. We even imitated them in order to feel closer, even if we disliked what they were doing. Sometimes they imposed their Patterns on us, and we accepted it just to make peace. At times, we picked up Patterns just to protect ourselves from the cruelty and pain we felt when we were victimized and abused by the very people we loved, under the name of goodness, which confused us even more.

Doubting our own feelings. We began to doubt our own feelings, to doubt the justice and humanity on earth, or at least in our own homes: the sacred place that should have been the safest and most nurturing and loving place for all for us.

Adopting other people's Patterns. Picking up Patterns for one justified reason or another left us with a repertoire of Patterns: some wonderful, some good, some not so bad, and some that we simply did not care for, yet were stuck with. Even professionals of mental health and the wise men of psychology, who knew everything, told us that all the characteristics we picked up from ages one to five will stay with us forever, and we have no choice but to accept them as our doom. No wonder there exists the common, unquestioned belief that people are not changeable, or if they do change, it won't last and it will be fake. The fact is, people are changeable, and people want to change. It is just that there is no one to guide them and teach them how.

Pseudo-Patterns. My belief is that Patterns (which are shades and series of characteristics that come together to form behavior) which people own without their own choice, are Pseudo-Patterns, and easily changeable if people so desire. I feel if these Patterns were truly the person's real set of characteristics, then people would not be so miserable, and would instead be very happy and content with them. For instance, many people who have Patterns that don't seem acceptable by some are happy with those Patterns, and in that case they should think twice about changing them, unless those Patterns in the long run do damage to the person's health and personhood as a whole.

Change is deep if chosen clearly. Recognizing, accepting and understanding these Patterns and the ideology and purpose they have served enables individuals to be in a position to change these Patterns if desired, and become clear in both consciousness and in the subconscious world. This change will not be temporary or superficial if the Patterns are looked at and dealt with deeply. This change is done by personal choice, for the person and no one else, towards the best of who they want to be and beyond.

Seven

Universal Spiritual Excellence

Universal Spirituality

Psycho-Universal Spirituality Power Balance. The Power Balance Patterns of Universal Spirituality embraces a universal spiritual health and discipline, and a spiritual connection of a Universal Self with Universal Wisdom and Nurturance. Among the Psycho-Universal Spiritual Patterns are spiritual boundary, spiritual grace, morality, inner ethics, respect for the differentness of others, spiritual understanding, kindness, universally spiritual peacemaking, and compassion with absence of selectivity (where only a chosen few are included and masses are alienated and discriminated against by their own kind.) Universal Spirituality tears down the walls of discrimination and allows Universal Unity: the failed mission and purpose that religion was organized to accomplish.

Universal Spirituality. Human beings have an inherent capacity and desire for spirituality. Unfortunately, spirituality has only been related to religion, which has always demonstrated selective compassion. Selective compassion occurs when people justify feeling connected with a select group of people, hence alienating and discriminating against others who may not fit into their box of approval. Universal Spirituality is compassion for people without discrimination of any kind.

True spirituality. True spirituality must not be in conflict with non-selective compassion and kindness for all. Otherwise, there is no truth in it. For people of clarity, that factor will become the test of truth in claims of spirituality. If I can love a black brother, a Christian brother, a Jewish brother, a Moslem brother or sister, equally, I have truly and spiritually loved humanity.

Ultimate Universal Parental Power. The connection of the Excelled Self with the environment taps into the ultimate power of light and energy: pure energy and power that is capable of anything the mind can focus on. It is the reflection of the power of beings, the power of the mind, and the power of collective Universal Patterns.

Where ignorance breathes, spirituality dies. In today's world there has been a tremendous abuse and unethical use of the word "spirituality," especially in places where people so desperately seek spirituality, kindness, compassion, and a sense of connection with themselves and others. Unfortunately, people end up losing their Self and are forced to alienate other perfectly fine human beings only to please the limited and biased minds of the masters of pseudo-spirituality.

Nothing good expects to be accepted blindly. For many, it has been so long since they have been in touch with the true sense of spirituality that they have no questions to ask even if given the opportunity. Everything existing on our planet and the planets around us is for our existence in harmony. And that is why nothing good expects to be accepted blindly; anything good expects to be chosen, freely, intelligently, consciously.

Patterns of Compassion

Compassion is kindness for the sake of kindness. It includes softness and tenderness for Self, for another, and for all beings. It is in the tenderness of the words, it is in the softness of the voice, it is in the sacredness of the silence, the attentiveness, and the focus. It is in the forgiveness of the posture, and it is in the generosity of the invitation into one's space, to one's key to prosperity, to one's world. Compassion is the power of healing with love: healing oneself, another, and the world.

Compassion is in our voice and in our eyes. It is in the mannerisms, the intents and good thoughts of a person about all beings, not just a select few.

Compassion is free to all beings regardless of color, race, gender and preferred belief systems, as long as they don't hurt other beings, and are harmless to themselves and others, especially their loved ones. We must begin to recognize, in this age in which we are conquering space, that differentness is not a sin, and anyone who advocates its sinfulness is neither a spiritual being nor a worldly individual. The world can be interpreted as a place of sameness through tunnel vision and limited eyes. Compassion means to love Self without condition, only to become prepared to love others as you love yourself, with compassion and without selectivity.

Having a inner sense of morality. An inner sense of morality is achieved in silence of the mind, privately. It means not saying what you know will hurt someone if it does not help. It means stopping yourself from saying what would hurt anyone if you can feel it ahead of time. It means having "good intent" in everything you do, say, or think. It means being constructive to yourself and others, thus aiding the survival of humanity.

Patterns of Morality

Morality is a Pattern of inner strength and discipline created by being alone in silence with Self. Solitude, silence and introspection develops humanity and morality. Morality is being one's own judge even when others are not looking. Morality is believing that all human beings are born with equal rights and deserving equal respect. Morality is not doing anything that feels wrong, even if it seems right to others. As long as you know what you do will hurt others, that is enough to not do it. The real judge that sees everything, and knows the truth, is watching from the inside, not from without.

Moral Freedom. To be so right as to make others wrong is a dogma that becomes limited with its own prejudice. To sees others as right in their differentness creates moral freedom. True compassion and morality is when the intent is the growth of oneself and others, without one being at the cost of the other. And that is the moral responsibility that nurtures moral freedom. Any Pattern of Freedom is not a true Pattern if it does not stem from the Pattern of Responsibility.

Morality is in thought and action. Not every act to free oneself from inhibitions is immoral. Only that which hurts others, directly or indirectly, is immoral. What people do in their own space in order to grow, or even to satisfy basic needs, is not immoral. Immorality begins when there are other people involved in the picture, not in the sacred and free dimensions of individual mind and body.

The Roots of Moral Values. Moral values are learned best in childhood. Kohlberg's Stages of Morality, regarding childhood moral stages and moralization, Carol Gilligan's disputes on Kohlberg's findings in "in a different voice," and Piaget's "moral realism," give invaluable information about the development of morality during childhood and throughout the individual's life. Children learn morality, which means knowing right from wrong, through the consequences they experience, and through the system of reward and punishment that we, or the life consequences, inflict upon them. For example, if they touch the stove and burn, they will never touch the stove again. If they do something wrong and get sent to their rooms, they will eventually learn not to repeat that behavior.

Damages of punishment. Punishment of any kind has never been successful in the discipline of children. On the contrary, it is the most degrading and inhumane act of immorality imposed upon the innocent bodies and minds of our loved ones: an act supported by fanatics of different religions, an act of violence inflicted upon the body of an innocent child by the people that supposedly love the child. Most often children get punished only because of the adult's lack of control of their anger, or lack of control of their subconscious, inhibited sexual or toxic impulses that burdens them in feelings of guilt. They punish a child who has stirred such impulses within them; children thus pay the price of Uncontrolled Patterns of their adults Programers.

Wounds, seen or unseen, of bodies and minds. Research has continually indicated the negative impact of punishment on children. In therapy, we are always dealing with the negative impact of punishment on children long after they have left home. To begin with, children tend to rebel against authoritarian orders that they must obey, and do not respond to the blind inhibitions of their need and desires. The punishment that follows their rebellion to blind obedience will have no impact except affecting their self-esteem, self-worth, self-trust and trust of the people who love them.

Development of Patterns of Morality. We must be moral beings in order to teach morality. We must let our children and our adults develop their own sense of morality: morality that they don't want to rebel against because it is their own decision. We can teach morality by teaching them how to recognize what's right and what's wrong by the way they think and feel about it. And we can teach our youngsters morality by the way we act upon the choices in our lives. If they have done something that they feel is wrong, they should do something about it. If they feel they have done the right thing, they should feel proud, and their reward is how they end up feeling about themselves, right here on earth.

Focus of Responsibility on the individual goes even beyond the laws and rules that beings make in order to break. It is a golden rule that according to Kohlberg, who classified the degrees of morality only a small percentage of highly regarded individuals would be able to reach. My question is, why must such stage of morality be a privilege of the few? After all, we are all inherently capable of Excellence and heightened spirituality.

In Excellence, being Immoral is not an option. I truly believe, with confidence, that if we become the best of ourselves, and are given responsibility of our actions, we, too, will take pride in our existence. In doing so, being immoral is no longer an option. In fact, Excellence is in Non-Selective Compassion and Universal Patterns of Spirituality.

To polish our souls, we need training. As with everything good in life, we need training and motivation to do it. Yet this we can learn also. For example, someone who is born with the talent to play the piano will still need to sit behind the piano and train. Someone who is athletically inclined still needs a coach and a trainer in order to successfully perform the inherent Pattern and materialize it in reality.

Patterns of Excellence are Transferable. All we need to do is to study the five percent of people in the world who are Excellence Programers. These people are not pushing their own product and purpose onto anyone, they are merely sharing them with those who are interested in growth. As a result, they may be silent beings, busily writing, discovering, reading, or doing any other function helpful to humanity. When we Program quality Patterns, and use them in silence, in introspection, in thought, in action, and create our own Cognitive-Emotional Power Balance, then we become a great deal more capable of recognizing and appreciating the Excellence in others. By the mere acceptance of Patterns of Excellence, they become transferable to us.

A key Pattern to Guidance. Only if we have already engaged in the active participation of finding our true Self and transcending our own soul, will we be able to guide others. A clear soul is capable of not only receiving Patterns of Excellence, but also transcending and transferring them onto others. And that is the significant ingredient and key Pattern of Guidance and becoming Programers of Excellence.

Self Search creates independence of thought-action. Focusing and searching for Self, and finding answers that create clarity within, is an attempt to create the power balance of thought and action. In doing so, we learn to become responsible for our own wrongdoings, and accept the consequences of our actions. At the same time, we recognize our individual power and capacity, and create a positive self-image and self-worth, thus preventing future Imbalances.

Pattern of Kindness

Kindness is another universally spiritual Pattern. Kindness, when its roots have penetrated the heart of an individual, cannot become selective. It can be withheld, temporarily, only from those who see it as weakness and want to use it to exploit others, but it cannot remain selective.

Kindness is a Pattern of softness and tenderness of the heart and actions towards those whom the person knows and loves, and those he or she knows not and loves not. It is not weakness, though in its softness there is an absence of a righteous rush to condemn others, or to reject others for who they are. Although a kind person can seem, at times, Existentially Angry for the injustice inflicted upon the innocent, the anger does not go beyond the words to educate the vulnerable and the victim. The kind individual will always see the bully and the victim on the same side of the Pendulum, victimized by ignorance and denial, waiting to be saved by the courageous voice of truth that wakes them up and gives them the opportunity to be, once again, human.

A kind person would not dream of hurting another, even if the law does not catch it. Unless, of course, it is to scare away the untamed and toxic wolf that is eating the chickens. The kind person has respect for himself or herself and respect for others, and would treasure and protect someone else's properties as if they were his or her own.

Patterns of Decency

Decency is another ethical Pattern. Good and decent people are safe for themselves and everyone around them. They do good, say good and everyone around them will benefit from them just because they are who they are. They are helpful whenever possible, harmless and responsible. They do their part without anyone having to tell them because their own conscience guides them at all times. They are their own judge and jury and have a clear and fair vision of what is just and what is not, objectively and honestly.

Decent people expect nothing from anyone, and whatever they do for others is only because it makes them feel good. They feel it their responsibility to help a fellow neighbor, or friend, or even a stranger. Decent people don't use, abuse or misuse others, and blame no one for their mishaps. They have a firm boundary and never cross the boundary of others without having been invited. Decent people don't play games and are consistent in their thoughts and actions. They do not need to control others and do not enjoy power struggles or power plays. They have goals and missions in life and above all, it is important to them to be good human beings and bring happiness to themselves and to the lives of others.

Decency and turning the other cheek. Decency is *not* turning the other cheek if someone slaps you. People with Patterns of Toxicity and Anti-Humanity who are labeled as sociopaths in psychology, equate decency with stupidity and an inability to defend oneself. That is why, when someone is inhumane to the point of emotionally or physically slapping another person, true kindness is not to reward the Toxic Pattern or to allow the slapped person to feel the loss.

Decency without Self-Respect will turn to anger. The decent individual cannot remain decent for long if he or she takes whatever is thrown at him or her unjustly. A decent individual is very aware of his or her rights, and defends and protects them as well as being sensitive to those of others.

Decent individuals make peace. Decent individuals are peacemakers, but they do not make peace at the cost of principles and their integrity. In cases where there are power struggles, misunderstandings, and hurt feelings, and yet the intent of the person is obviously a good one, the decent person puts himself or herself above and beyond the situation and brings forth peace and harmony. For an anti-humane person, one must come from the position of strength, since these people only operate with force and exploitation, and will get more aggressive and abusive with the presentation of Kindness and Decency.

Decent people of our time. All of the universally decent people of the world, who do not compromise their principles and stand by the purpose of protecting humanity, must, and do, present their strength just as equally as their compassion for the world. This is especially true in today's sensitive and Power Imbalanced world with its universal crisis. The world needs to understand that kindness, decency, and humanity does not mean weakness and an inability to prevent people with Patterns of toxicity and imbalance from materializing the intent of destroying one's dignity.

The Power Balance of Strength with Decency allows us to maintain our level of Compassion without bitterness, resentment, anger, or disillusionment in humanity. Among the Patterns of Decency are also the ability to respect and appreciate those who dedicate their life to the progression of humanity against all odds of political competitive rivalry and the pressure for votes of popularity. We must change the Pattern of Glorification of the dead and burying the alive: it is the only way we can encourage decent people to continue their efforts towards the mission of universal peace and prosperity.

Patterns of Excellence

Evo-revolution of becoming a person. It is only by accepting ourself that we can find peace within and begin to move in the direction we choose, becoming the people we want to become. And that is what life is all about: the challenge to Excel in the evolving progression of becoming a Universal Self, at the revolutionary risk of being multidimensional and different.

Success-Spirituality is one dimension of the Self in harmony. The collective Power Balance of dimensions of the Self existing in harmony creates excellence both within Self and in environment.

Collective power balance of patterns of psycho-physicality universal spirituality, socio-environment and cognition-emotion within an individual breathing in harmony into all dimensions of Self creates a Program of individual Excellence. When one is connected fully with all dimensions, the flow of power becomes unlimited. Patterns of Excellence are the ultimate Programing in being. They are Patterns acquired by choice.

The Nature of Excellence

Excellence is a Pattern of existence that can be created after the person has gained multidimensional Power Balance. An individual who can be whole and experience all dimensions of Self, which consists of all the Power Balance Patterns mentioned above, has reached the ongoing process of Excellence. Patterns of Excellence, embedded in Programs of Excellence where all the multidimensions of Power Balance Patterns exist side by side regardless of their polarity or similarity.

Absence of mind-body distortions. An individual with Patterns of Excellence possesses no mind-body distortions or addictions of food, love, religion, drugs, tobacco, gambling, or material distractions that keep the individual needy and separate from the Excelled Self.

Collective Progression. The process of Collective Progression is progressing, moving forward and towards the future consistently, in all dimensions: emotion-cognitively, psycho-physiologically, environmentally and Universal-Spiritually, throughout your life. This is the path to Excellence. Excellence is not an end, not a goal, not a predetermined entity or being. Excellence just *is*. Excellence is arriving at the end, it is a beginning; and is an end of a beginning.

Excellence is not Perfection. Excellence is different than the need for perfection that some of us were raised with, like the image of the perfect child with perfect clothes required from a mother who wanted to be seen as perfect. This child grows up wanting himself or herself to be so perfect that he or she spends half of his or her energy paying attention to the appearances of perfection, and fully misses the path to Excellence. In order to be on the Path of Excellence one has no time for pseudo-perfection.

Patterns of Excellence Types

Collective Universal Power Balance. The Collective Universal Power Balance is the connection of universal Power Balance with individual Power Balance that stem from the Universal Self. Universal Power Balance is reflection of individual power, the power of the mind, the power of the collective consciousness of the universe, and the power that this connection creates. The universe's collective consciousness is the universal Parental Pattern of Wisdom and Nurturance that surround us all. When an individual feels in harmony within Self, with others and with the environment, in mind, body and spirit, then she or he has obtained Patterns of Excellence.

Patterns of Self-Discipline

Discipline in mind and body is an Excellence Pattern. The self-disciplined individual has a built-in chaos-order control and built-in golden rules. Actions follow the body, the body follows the mind, and the mind gives rise to intuitive emotions and an spiritual connection that the mind may not be able to explain, momentarily, but one that it will catch up to. The ability to slow ourselves down: our minds, our bodies, and our actions, is as equally powerful a Pattern of Discipline as is speeding ourselves up. Any choice that comes from a clear mind and a conscious decision is a Disciplined Pattern. Some choices are merely harder than others and require more practice. Self-discipline includes the pattern of tolerance for delay of gratification, the impulse control pattern, pain tolerance and avoidance of seduction and temptation. It is a Pattern of Purpose and Mission, giving the ability to see the larger picture, beyond the appearances and the presentations of perfection.

Disciplined Self breathes true relationships. Ridding ourselves of the chain of our addictions that were brought on by Adopted Patterns is a life adventure and challenge for those of us who treasure having independent Selves. It is only from a self-disciplined mind and body that we can receive a true connection, a long-lasting commitment, and a prosperous partnership without any external expectations.

In Patterns of Self-Discipline. Mental exercise, just like physical exercise, must be practiced daily and consistently in order to build a self-disciplined mind. No matter how genius a mind, if it is not self-disciplined, meaning that it is not able to produce what we want it to produce at the time we want it to, it will break and will not survive with the stringent and rigid rules and rapid changes of today's society. A clear map and the underlining of where to go and how to go about it is needed in order to not get lost on the roads others have contracted out for us, leading to where they want us to go, to be an object for accomplishing their plan in life .

The disillusioned are those who know it all and know it better than others, and yet their arrogance makes them neglect the fact that speed is not everything. Since they are hollow inside because of a lack of Self-Discipline and Self-Control, like the rabbit who is sure of being fast, they took a few shortcuts that will cost them not only their fame and fortune and everything that came with all that, but their lives and their dignity as well. I am talking about those whose success has become a nightmare to themselves and to others, because of their lack of having a solid Self. They climbed the ladder without looking within, they ignored the scars and the pain in the hopes that the color of money would brighten it all and make them forget that they hurt. It never does. They either must face their Inner Self, or neither they nor the world will be safe.

Success of undisciplined is just a short dream. Self-Discipline stems from having looked within, from having faced Self, and from having healed the scars of the deprived child who is alone in the biggest crowd. Self-Discipline is created from the moments of delay of gratification, moments of absence of self-indulgence, and moments when the Self is strong enough not to adhere to the hymns of the facade, tastes of the denial, smiles of the corrupt.

Slow but sure, is a jargon we take for granted which is another essential key in life; it comes from the Self-Discipline gained from exercise. It is very valuable to know that being fast is much easier than taking one's time and slowing down to see, feel, and think the process through while enjoying life, instead of getting there without truly knowing how.

Not incurable, just out of control. I have been able to successfully help individuals gain control of some Patterns that came only from lack of Self-Control, and the symptoms of those Patterns that were for decades labeled as incurable, such as schizophrenia and manic depression.

Patterns of Self-Control

An individual without Self-Control experiences chaos that in turn creates the life crisis. Patterns of self-control have embedded within them patterns of flexibility which allow one to change easily as needed, preventing Patterns of Rigidity that create instability. Individuals with patterns of Self-control understand their feelings, thoughts, and actions behind them, and therefore do not easily lose control over sudden experiences in their lives. If someone who is an annoyance approaches them, they can either walk away or, by using logic, calmly point out to the person that he or she is out of line. Their demeanor does not allow others to intrude on their boundary, nor will they intrude on the boundary of others. Calmness, in self-controlled individuals with an absence of block patterns of pseudo-cheerfulness and friendliness that is usually Blocking underlying anger, creates harmony within the environment as well as harmony within the Self. The assertion of self-controlled individuals with the absence of aggression allows others to respect their rights and determine the boundaries for their Imbalance and block patterns floating on the surface. Self-controlled individuals possess Pattern of Responsibility-Freedom, and consciously lack exploitative Patterns that are developed from Patterns of Freedom without boundary.

Patterns of Silence

Silence (Focus Inward), is the ability to be alone with oneself and to hear one's inner voice. It is the ability to communicate with oneself and to respect and treasure one's feelings, intuition and inner peace. It enables one to consistently become more aware of one's inner strength and to expand on one's spiritual strength: qualities that can only be strengthened by silence and the inward focus onto Self. The process of exercising the mind is, to begin with, silence. Daily silence is not only necessary for the mind, but also crucial for body health and healing. The mere exercise of silence with a blank screen before our eyes will enhance the slowing down of mind activity, causing it to heal and increasing its capacity to function. No organ, if worked full time, will function at its best forever. Even in our sleep, we don't turn off the power of our mind. It goes on and on, and they say that it will go on even after we die. Such a mind needs breaks so that it can reprogram, reorganize and re-energize.

Silence with a blank screen is the best break for an overactive mind. Be all that brings you power, flexibility and diversity. The next tool to be used for exercise of the mind is to ask it to imagine being things, places, and people with as much clarity as possible. The most effective exercise for me is to think about the ocean, the mountains, the desert, the jungle, and to become all of these.

To think and feel with our outer eyes closed, and seeing everything with our inner eyes, is the ability to be everywhere anytime we want to be. This is another tool to Self-Discipline the mind. The ability to consistently become whatever we want to become in our minds, and each time with a shorter preparation, will enable us to feel, think, and consequently materialize whatever we want.

In Silence, one can focus on oneself. One can be alone with oneself. In that aloneness, one can be attentive to what goes on inside, which is most important to one's spirit and life. Getting in touch with, and traveling within, the inner world can be the most adventurous, exciting and at the same time fearsome adventure. The fear comes from discovering the unknown with anticipation that the unknown will be corrupt. People think that what they don't know is best kept unknown. The Programing of curiosity and questioning as "sinful" has kept many away from traveling inside. Focusing on the inner Self and learning the self-disciplined act of silence has been down-played in the Western world and replaced by a compulsion to socialize and talk loudly.

Silenced movement of the mind. Even at the health clubs that open-minded people frequent in order to grow and develop their bodies and minds, there is a constant need to talk. This tendency is seen in the locker room and even on the machines, where one needs to connect the movement of the body with the silenced movement of the mind. Whenever I exercise at my health club, I go into a state of meditation, offending people who, as soon as they see me, want to ask frivolous questions that take them and me away from what is gained by the connection of the silenced mind with the body: the body that reincarnates through activity.

Unseen Success Patterns. Creativity, vision, and all of the unseen successes can only be gained in Silence: a pattern much neglected and downplayed by Western civilization.

In silence, we travel paths less traveled. It is only in silence that beings can travel the less traveled road to their higher Selves, becoming the best they can become, and understanding their own human qualities. Whatever we find out about ourselves in silence has always been there and, good or bad, we have been affected by it. It is a myth that if we don't open Pandora's Box we are better off. The box, if closed, still contains the poisonous snake of our troubled minds. Yet if we bring out this snake, we can transform it into an innocent rope that pulls us out of the dungeon of self-doubt.

Forever at the mercy of the unknown Self. We are forever at the mercy of what we don't know about ourselves until we make directs attempt to know what we carry unquestionably, accepting it as a part of us, and choosing to change or delete it if we so desire. Until we acknowledge and accept what is already there, we cannot change the position or its impact our life patterns or our lives. Just as we cannot drink water out of a glass unless we acknowledge that there is indeed water in the glass, we cannot change what we don't know; nor do we have any control over what we hide.

In Silence, there is music. When I go on long walks on the beach and engage in my mind-body-spirit prayer, I become aware of a world that does not exist during my daily activity; a world that takes me away from mySelf into an external reality that only exists within me; a world of dance, laughter and music that speaks not only to my joy but also my sorrow and gives me peace.

Silence is boring or painful only in absence of Self. Being alone with oneself is reported to be boring. We are bored, in my opinion, only when it is scary to do something. Boredom is a Power Block of Denial: a denial of fear of what is inside of us. Once we become honest with ourselves and look inward, and once we give our inner feelings a voice and allow them to come out, we immediately realize the universality of our problems of being human, of not being exactly as perfect and complete and whole and holy as we want ourselves to be. Then we can take a deep breath as we allow all of who we are, our true Selves, to come out.

Silence speaks to inner crisis and chaos. Silence not only teaches us about ourselves, but it also speaks to our inner crisis and chaos, becoming a healing instrument. While it tells us about the screams and nightmares in the dark; the passion and love; the fears of abandonment and rejection, it allows us to evaluate, analyze, and examine the roots of those fears, and to heal from the pain that has kept us isolated and lonely inside.

In silence we hear the voice of our soul. When we are silent, and when we can picture a blank screen in front of our closed eyes and think about nothing, we can hear the voice of our souls: the voice that has had no chance to speak to us while we were too busy negotiating with outside world, leaving ourselves alone inside.

Establishing connection with ourselves. It is just as crucial to our well-being to have time to ourselves in a true sense, as it is to establish ties and connections out in our communities and society. The more complicated and socially clever our outside world becomes, the more we need equal time with ourselves and our souls, so that we don't become what the outside world demands us to become for the purpose of bringing order and profit to society at the cost of our individuality and integrity.

Silence and Western religion. Silence is used to get close to God in most religions through the ritual of prayer, and yet many enlightened people know that until we get close to ourselves, our closeness to any other entity is but a surface, Adopted Pattern we choose to believe as the commandment of our destiny.

Externalization of power and responsibility. The Pattern of focusing on an outside image, even in silence, which is the door to the soul, must change before human beings can understand and accept themselves, and grow as responsible and free individuals with independent minds the way they were born to be: free, with connections they themselves choose. Freedom of mind and action must replace the strings, ties and ropes around their throats that only benefit systems that treat people like mindless slaves, using them against each other to keep them limited, dictating to them what will be.

Silence can liberate us. Silence, if used appropriately, is a Pattern that saves humanity from slavery and from forever being at the mercy of super-powers that see people only as numbers on a board, for or against their own profit in their competitive games of rivalry. Anyone proclaiming that he will be their representative to prosperity has only found a way to riches through the naiveté of souls in search of the truth outside of their own mind and body. The truth is that only each person can be his or her connection with the Universal Power. And only Silence heals and sews this Connection that is created from our own clarity.

Patterns of Flexibility

Flexibility is an Excellence Pattern. It means being without rigidity which comes from the Block of Power Balance. It means having gone through the pain of growing and having become comfortable with oneself with sincerity, honesty and openness.

Flexibility. Flexibility is the ability to cry at our own foibles. It means allowing feelings to penetrate our soul to the point where our body and heart hurts deeply enough to bring tears from our eyes. Flexibility is to be clear of Power Blocks that we develop in order to protect ourselves from being hurt, for those Blocks also prevent us from feeling loved. Flexibility is the ability to fly high and still be connected to the earth, both metaphorically and literally. Flexibility means being practical and logical, and yet creative and emotional. Being flexible means being real, without the clouds that we see around the people who reject living because they are afraid. They reject everything and everyone around them just to assure that they will remain the same as yesterday and the day before: without mistakes, without change, without love and without life.

Flexibility means having healthy connections. It means having a healthy mind-body connection and healthy relationships that can endure any hardship. Flexibility means having healthy families and children who have never experienced not being loved just because they were different, broke the rules or did not keep up with the pace.

Flexible people

Flexible individuals go with the flow without compromising principles, because they see the picture beyond that which is often presenting the conflict. They are clear about who they are, and therefore are not afraid to let others be who they are. They know what they want and yet are willing to try what others recommend. They know where they are going and that is why they are curious to try out different routes. They will not break easily in times of crisis, for they are flexible.

They will not give up their rights to those who insist on taking them, just to get out of the way. They stand tall and proud, and yet humble, because they truly are beautiful beings on the inside. They do not have friends who are unwilling to grow; they listen to others without being preoccupied with changing the minds of others. They respect all beings, and are not afraid of different beliefs. They do not respect rigidity or close-mindedness which represents an unwillingness to grow, to love and to be loved. It is from flexibility that we can have healing relationships that protect us from regression and abusive environments that promote rigidity: environments in which people are chained to restrictions of hate and discrimination too rigid and harsh for a healthy, flexible mind. Flexibility means having appropriate boundary and ability to change, as opposed to rigid boundary, which has no room for differentness, playfulness and freedom of action and thought. In every genuinely democratic mind, you will see freedom, openness, and respect for other beings that non-democratic minds would never understand because of their lack of flexibility and rigid boundary. That is why people who abuse power are rigid and advocate rigidity; they cannot convince a flexible mind to accept slavery and the hatred of other beings. It is only from rigid minds that sickness arises and spreads. Flexibility is a sign of health, joy, prosperity, compassion, and love.

Patterns of Responsibility

Responsibility is the most significant Pattern necessary for both success in society and for Excellence in humanity. Responsibility includes responsibility for ourselves, for the welfare of the people we love, and for the rights of others. Responsibility and freedom are two sides of a coin: something people often misunderstand. Responsibility means that no one else has to worry about your welfare and their own safety. When we are children at play, we need not be responsible. It is the only time of our life when we don't need a balance of joy with a sense of responsibility. Only during that limited time of our life are others responsible for us. Yet children have no freedom, either. They are told by their caretakers what to do, where to go, when to come back and when to sleep. With the absence of responsibility, there is also, always, the absence of freedom. It is wonderful to preserve our childlike qualities and to also balance them with our adult responsibilities.

When adults become children. But when we become adults and demand and exercise our precious freedom, there also appears freedom's mate: responsibility. When adults pretend that they don't have to take responsibility, when they literally become children and deny their share of responsibility, everyone involved, including themselves, gets hurt.

An addict is a danger to society. Addiction creates a false impression in adults of being carefree. When an individual is struggling with addiction, he or she suffers from the consequences of a distorted reality. Yet when an addict is involved with others in relationships or is a parent to innocent and vulnerable children, he or she is playing Russian Roulette with other people's lives and is a danger to him/herself, others and society. The freedom of one person becomes meaningless in a civilized society if the freedom of others is being endangered by it. Holding other's safety, health and happiness ransom becomes a crime of neglect and denial for the lawmakers of society.

Patterns of Freedom

Freedom is the right to be. Freedom without responsibility creates confusion and chaos that only looks like freedom. The beauty of freedom is in its walls of responsibility for oneself and for others. I have not met a person that is not responsible and has true sense of freedom: the freedom of thought and action, and a soul with appropriate boundaries. Freedom without responsibility is pseudo-freedom. A free being is a responsible being.

Freedom of this country is in hands of its justice. Ruth Bader Ginsberg, while being elected as the Supreme Justice of the United States of America (the most democratic country whose freedom is most felt by other countries), in answer to a question about freedom, she said that she was not sure of the extent of freedom in this country, and would have to think about it. When she sees that the freedom of speech on some college campuses, for example, causes pain, hurt, and, in many circumstances, hatred for others, she must think about when freedom stops being freedom and begins being the abuse of others.

We must free up the chained freedom. I would concur. Yes, she must think about this issue, and think quickly. Both world peace and the survival of humanity depends on redefinition of the meaning of freedom and its boundaries. I have always had problems with unlimited freedom that does not consider others' rights. The primary abuse of power in the world, and especially in our democratic and humanistic country, has been done under the name of freedom without considering the right of others. Unfortunately, if something is not done about it during our current governmental administration, which is comprised of the most humanistic group in decades, I see no hope for true freedom in the future of America.

Patterns of Ethics

Ethics surpass societal laws that, to most people, are nothing but laws made to be broken. Ethics are the inner laws and golden rules that Excelled individuals establish for themselves without consideration of what others think about them. Ethics are far from the laws made by the society or government. Social laws were made because people are not Excelled enough to establish their own ethics. Ethics are the golden rules of individuals who not only care about their own Self-Respect and integrity, but also are their own judge and jury about what's right and what's wrong in regards to humanity. Whether others see it or not, they must do the right thing, according to their own books: even if it seems wrong to others whom are not clearly informed.

Patterns of Ethics. Honesty is the key ethical Pattern in individuals, couples, families, cultures, and the world. Honesty with self and others, being true to one's convictions, sincerely and truthfully having good intentions, and coming from the truth within Self, are the keys to ethical boundary and the survival of humanity.

Ethical people do not need society to define rules, and yet they comply to them, for the rules don't seem difficult or unreasonable to abide by, since they consciously choose to respect them in a deeper sense, seeing them as necessary for a developing humanity. Yet they might many times break societal rules when they are in conflict with ethical decisions that come forth unique to the situation; inner ethics surpass any law made by society. Inner ethics are covers we put on our desires, taming them with the power of Self-Discipline, for the sake of becoming the best of who we can become, in the race of humanity. But it is a conscious personal choice to tame desires, one that if proposed as a rule, will only create rebellion and Imbalanced promiscuity.

Redefinition of Ethics. We must redefine ethics in all cultures throughout the world. The second half of my life, since age twenty, has been spent in the United States as an American. This second half has been the most important part of my life, since all my training and major life experiences have taken place during that time. In fact, I had a rebirth stemming from my growth in this country. In the first half of my life, there were many Patterns that were considered ethical and virtuous in my homeland. The same Patterns later on, in the West, were seen as weaknesses.

Example. For instance, being shy and not looking into men's eyes, but instead looking down when talking to men, for women was a virtuous Pattern; it was interpreted as having noble character of purity, innocence, and femininity. Western health professionals label such virtue as schizophrenia. In the West, it is crucial to stare into people's eyes while talking. It indicates honesty, assertion and clarity of the mind. I mySelf think although there are many shades of gray to any cultural interpretation, the intent of any cultural rule and interpretation must be questioned and examined.

Cultural misinterpretations. Interpreting assertion as vulgar in Eastern culture handicapped Eastern women, a price they had to bear to keep men protected from the anxiety stemming from fear of loss, rejection, fear of their own impulses, and possessive patterns of being. It is obvious that, by the nature of looking down while talking to someone one automatically feels inferior. Perhaps it was also men's preventive attempt to curb feeling passion for the women they were not married to, at the cost of the women's integrity.

Religion Programing and its limitations. Most of sanctions and limitations put upon women, globally, are done by unreasonable and Imbalanced Religious Programing. Religious myths and rules are set up to protect men who set such rules without consideration for the women's rights or dignity. It has done nothing but planting the seeds of inequality between men and women. Although it has made men feel superior towards women, at the cost of women's self-esteem and equality, the Power Imbalance has cost the men as well, by feelings of lack of support of having true partners in life and feeling lonely.

Misinterpretations of Patterns of Ethics. Ethics, as they have been presented to-date, can be interpreted as something even more oppressive for people in general, and not just for women, if we examine their definition. The interpretation of ethics is not to question authority, not to say what's on your mind if it shocks others or is different (which leads our young people to lie.) Ethics means the inhibition of thought and action, creating rebellion in our young people.

Patterns of Ethics should be taught by parents. I believe that ethics, too, must be Patterns that each individual takes pride in practicing, and not forced by Cultural or Religious Programing. While raising children with Patterns of Prevention and Excellence we must focus on ethics-building. Unfortunately most of the precious and valuable time of parenting is spent on survival Patterns and establishing control in Imbalanced ways. Yet by merely role-modeling ethics for our children, we will be planting seeds. One of most important ethical Patterns, to me, is Honesty.

Patterns of Honesty

Being truthful to oneSelf and others is a Pattern of Honesty. An honest person who has this Pattern ingrained no longer needs rules and laws to force him or her not to steal, lie or be dishonest to Self and others. This, although it seems to be a simple fact, is difficult to recognize and practice for many people as a Habitual Pattern. We are born to rebel, because before we have a chance to understand who we are and what we are all about, we are told what to do and what to believe. Every thinking being will rebel against what he or she is supposed to believe, supposed to think and supposed to abide by, unless that individual has learned to analyze right from wrong, and to make a choice based on what he or she understands. That will develop an honest land.

Living a lie is not an easy Pattern. Many people who come to therapy just begin to become honest with themselves, let alone others. After fifty or sixty precious years have already gone by, they realize the pressure and the price they have been paying as a result of not exercising the truth.

Living in the closet of our own minds. Feeling dishonest and unworthy as a result of lying, and being stressed out constantly so we don't get caught (for dishonesty creates memory failure), does not support a life of leisure. If we don't have honesty, we have nothing: not even ourselves.

Honesty is a stress-free Pattern. Honest people have no stress and pressure in their faces and bodies, since they don't have to lie to themselves and get confused all the time. They don't have to try to remember what different stories they have fabricated.

Honesty for preservation of integrity. Many people, however, prefer to lie. Culturally Programed into them, they think that the truth will be either unacceptable or more difficult to tell. In some cases, it may be. But we don't choose our Life Patterns just to have an easy life. We choose them to be congruent with our true Self and to be able to respect ourselves and preserve our integrity.

Honesty: a liberating experience. As painful as the truth is most of the time, it is the most liberating experience anybody could ever have. People constantly tell me that the truth has set them free. It makes life less complicated and more honorable. It brings a world of credibility to the people and will win them the world if they choose to have it. But most of all, it will give them their Self.

Honesty gives us our Selves. Honesty furthermore brings the individual closer to Self, to loved ones, and to anyone else that looks at the individual's honest face. Honesty causes a glow that nothing else can match. And it is catching. Dishonest people can pretend to be honest for a while, yet their actions will inevitably prove them wrong.

Honesty: root of the Pattern of Trust. With honesty, parents will never need to worry about their children lying to them; even if a child has a hard time telling them about something, the child will find a way to be honest. People appreciate honesty, and honesty is the basis for the establishment of trust. Of course, honesty is quite different from being cruel to others by hurting people's feelings and being obnoxious under the disguise of honesty. We will always know whether we are being honest or are trying to hurt people's feelings.

Eight

Programing
Universal Success

Path to Success

Success, like any path of direction, needs a map: a map that you yourself have drawn, for you alone know the direction. At times it may look like everybody else knows more than you do about yourself. They may be wise in guidance and be able to help you recognize that you are you own true maker of your path.

A. *Define yourSelf*. Define the being and the doing of your essence, both the patterns that govern your life at present and the patterns imposed upon you that seem to have confined you in a pseudo-existence.

B. *Define your goal and direction*. Recognize where you are coming from, where you are now and where you want to be in one, two, three, four, five, six, seven, eight, nine and ten years. And then break it down to months, days and hours of your existence. Ever since I began to plan my life to the tee every single day, I have gained true freedom. When we plan our work and when we plan our joy then we know that we know what we are doing, and just because we find ourselves at times walking on the beach for five hours it is not because we are lost. It is all planned. And it is better that we acknowledge this rather than going through life wondering how it will begin and how it will end.

C. *Recognize your Blocks*. When we are walking on a new path that has many obstacles and bumps, no matter how exciting and beautiful the road, we still look for the blocks and the rocks that seem to be planted before of us.

***Realistic blocks*.** It is the same with the road we choose in our life. We must look and find a way that does not compromise the adventure and the scenery and yet does not lead us to dangerous zones or throw us over the cliff. In life there are two types of block patterns: realistic and unrealistic. Realistic patterns of block are those that truly exist on our way to achieve happiness. For example, a person is blind and wants to see. A blind person can feel, hear and touch as if the world is a movie screen before her eyes, far more vivid than any eye can see.

Unrealistic blocks are those we put in front of ourSelf because we fear success. Those blocks can be personal, environmental, societal, familial and economical. Those blocks are there only because we are not yet ready to begin our journey. On the day we are ready, the road becomes clear. Our readiness is directly related to the degree of the groundwork for success we are willing to accomplish: the process I have discussed later in this chapter. The bottom line is if we have a Self, we have already packed and can get on with our journey up the exciting road we have planned to travel. In my seminars on success and spiritual excellence, I witness that all the blocks that people plant ahead of them soon disappear as they search and find the source of why they are intentionally pausing to delay.

D. *Recognize your Strength*. To focus only on our fear is to plan our defeat and not our life victory. Waking up daily with the mind-body prayer of embracing our strength and allowing our vulnerabilities to surface so that we can nurture them and turn them into blessings to have near, are the keys to a strong mind, body and spirit of a successful life cavalier.

E. *Nurture your process*. No goal or mission in life will mean anything if we neglect the process to which we must adhere. To reach a goal without sensitivity to its process is like bearing a child and giving it away. I have never experienced that pain, but I have heard that the pain is intolerable and there is no reward in the end.

F. Keep your balance of mind-body-spirit guidance. The Power Balance of mind-body-spirit is a law above any law of the universe. Without such balance we will always be at the mercy of others. Without such a connection we are not only incomplete but our eyes see distortions, delusions and illusions as reality.

G. Intuitive feelings and the power of the mind. The balance of feeling and thinking is just as significant as the balance of the goal and process. The thinking gets us there by telling us how to go. The feeling tells us where to go.

Mind Control for Success

Thought control and focus is the master plan of a successful mind. To learn how to focus is an art we must practice.

Focus. Focus is everything in creating healthy and Excelling Thought Patterns, just as it is everything in life. Scientifically, everything has more power and energy if it is directed and focused. Mental focus is like the laser, the latest discovery in light; its power comes from the light energy being focused and, as a result, intensified. The same rule applies for increasing the intensity and power of thought (Cognitive Power and Balance.)

Timeless activities of mind create Self-Discipline. In order to focus intensely, one must either learn from role models who have spent their lifetimes disciplining their minds, or begin to perform self-disciplined tasks that require mind focus. Self-disciplined tasks must be repeated in order to develop and create Habitual Patterns. It is easy to choose a task, since everything requires focus. The task merely needs to be something the person enjoys, since in order to focus, one must stay at one task for literally eight or nine straight hours. For example, my son catches me when I am so focused on writing that I am lost mySelf in my computer screen; at times, he walks into my room and turns on the light. I get so engulfed in writing that I completely forget about the passage of time. Many times, I would have missed appointments if I had not had anyone around to remind me of them. My body becomes weightless, and I feel as though I am in a trance. Even the quality and clarity of my writing changes, depending on whether or not I have complete focus.

Thought Control. It is crucial to learn Thought Control for not only time-effectiveness, but also for quality, constructiveness, and productivity control. thoughts can be programed in many different directions; we can focus to the right and become process-oriented, or we can focus to the left, and become goal-oriented, we can program our thoughts to save, to delete, to move, and to copy patterns positively, destructively, constructively, progressively, repressively and in many dimensions existing within us, through our thoughts. The power that exists within must be utilized in one way or another. If it does not get utilized in a positive direction by our choice, it will be utilized negatively. Energy unused becomes toxic energy that not only creates Imbalance, causing physical and emotional pain, but also explodes and creates Imbalance without, in the world.

Our destiny depends on the direction of our mind. Our life direction depends on the direction in which we control our thoughts, or the direction in which our thoughts run without our control. That is why it is so important to learn how to control them. As long as we have not learned how to control our own thought directions by our own choices, we are at the mercy of Habitual Thought Patterns.

How are Habitual Thought Patterns formed? By growing up as a result of identification with or rebellion against a Programer, we choose Patterns that over the years become habitual without our awareness or conscious choice. At times, the Causal Patterns, meaning those which current Patterns stem from, are our survival and decisionmaking Patterns. Many times, unfortunately, Patterns are created as a result of the reward or punishment of different directions we chose, and not by trial and error, or the freedom of creative thinking, which is the process of learning and gaining Self-Control.

Fear of rejection of who we are. Children experience that every time they cry, play helpless or feel low and negative about themselves, and claim that no one loves them, the mother runs to them and rewards them for that Pattern of Helplessness. And when they take creative risks and challenge their parents' old Thought Patterns, they get punished. Therefore, many children learn to play victimized and weak in order to gain love and feel secure and safe from their parents' anger: anger that only appears when they express independence of thought and action.

Ambivalence existing amongst young generation. The ambivalence tearing society apart, beginning in adolescence amongst young people, is not from a lack of intelligence or motivation. It is not even a lack of desire to become an active participant in the community. It is only the result of the fear of being themselves and of having their own minds. In fact, the generation gap and rebellion we see amongst our teenagers are not true demonstrations of their identity; they are a rebellion against conformity and blind obedience, and at the same time expression of the fear of being who they really are.

The root of Patterns we adopt without choice. If the young people, who have been rejected for expressing independence in mind and action at home by the people they love, ever challenge their own thoughts in adulthood, they will develop stress and anxiety from the anticipation of rejection by those whom they love. And that will become an experience which a Pattern is born from: a Causal Pattern of the formation of Cognitive Patterns that become habitual over the passage of time. Many Life Patterns develop their roots by such adaptations of rebellions against or reactions towards Patterns of other Programers.

Creating distance between parents and children. Religion is a powerful Programer often used by parents to impose the most unreasonable expectations upon their children without any explanation, adequate information or education. The parents, likewise, were never given explanations, and therefore don't know the reasons behind many things they hand down to their children.

The lack of knowledge or ability to teach their children what they expect of them, or at least role-model what they preach, causes children to lose respect for their parents and engage in a Power Struggle with the very people they love.

Root of Patterns of Rebellion. The parents' inability to reason with their children, and at times forcing them to believe in rules they themselves did not abide by or believe as youngsters, also creates an environment of double-bind and hypocrisy that creates thought confusion for the children, making them doubt their parents and their own truth and deductive reasoning. Parents become another authority to rebel against, and children can even go as far as rebelling against their own good, for authority in their eyes is no longer in a position of reason, fairness or even justice: something the American people are feeling today about their more extended parents: their democratic leadership.

Progressive and creative Thought Patterns. Progression and creativity are driven from the freedom to experiment without being punished. Children must be encouraged to think creatively for themselves and must not be humiliated or punished for their mistakes. They instead should be encouraged to analyze and interpret their thoughts step-by-step and find solutions for the problems that led them to errors in the thinking process.

Let children create their own thought processes. Children with positive Thought Patterns are taught that they matter, and so do their thoughts and ideas, no matter how different. They are listened to, no matter how raw the process of learning is. People don't just awaken one day and think clearly. The times when our children's ideas and patterns of thinking are so painfully different from ours are times that will measure the fairness and maturity of our parenthood skills. When we are able to sit down and carefully and objectively listen to our children, not fearing the differentness we feel from them, no matter how drastic and, at times, no matter how wrong, is when we must be proud of ourselves. In doing this, we can be sure that our children will definitely be all right.

Developing independent minds. The process of objectively listening to our children establishes their trust in our love and, most importantly, their trust in their own competence and the power of their own minds. They deserve and must have time to think about their own mistakes and discover answers for themselves. It gives them a sense of pride and self-esteem; it is the only way they can develop their own Patterns of Cognition and Independence. Parents who think for their children and brainwash them with their own beliefs, needs and desires, are only planning to create clones of themselves and do not want to raise children who will grow up having their own minds. By doing that, they have taken away another individual's right to his or her own life with a choice of her or his own identity, creating handicapped individuals who will always need to have decisions made for them and will always depend upon the parents; even when the parents are long gone, they will need to find others like them to depend on.

The roots of family crisis and broken homes. It is these children who wake up one day and their lives feel as empty as their hearts. They wonder with all their effort why they are not happy in their lives. No matter how good a life they were given, they do not feel it belongs to them. They don't fit in, and their life they did not choose. They resent and rebel against their life, like anything that is forced upon individuals. Many people come to me who are rebelling against themselves continuously. They are out of control; rebellion has become a Habitual Pattern that they began as children to go against their parents or religion: two authorities that dictated to them when they were vulnerable.

Patterns of a meaningless life. Many people come to me with divorce papers in their hands, confessing that they awakened one day and realized the life they were living was not their own. They did not choose their life. The degree was from what father wanted them to pursue, the job was the family business, and the wife was chosen by the mother. Even if the parents knew nothing about their influence on their children, the fact that they dictated their beliefs to them all their lives is enough to cause their children to follow their footprints in all aspects, or even rebel for the sake of rebelling; yet after years of hard work they find themselves, regardless, in a meaningless life. It is time that every authoritarian system, from parenthood to religion to the government, realizes the inadequacy of their forced system against the right and choice of the individual. It is time they learn to treat individuals with respect and dignity and recognize their personal power.

Thought Patterns in parenthood. Parents need to role model positive thinking Patterns and enthusiasm for life for their children. To teach positive techniques and to coach constructively is a task that every parent must prepare themselves for or learn alongside their children, for both the sake of their children and themselves.

Cognitive Pattern Change in adulthood. If you are already an adult and in the process of Pattern Change from negative to positive:

a. Recognize the negative Thought Patterns.

b. Accept them as Patterns that you have adopted in the past without conscious choice.

c. Examine their root and purpose with a trained Pattern Change Programer.

d. Recognize that you no longer need your old Patterns.

e. Recognize your own positive Thought Patterns. Learn Patterns of Self-Discipline, Silence, Meditation, and other Balance Patterns that will assist you in deleting unwanted Pattern.

f. Delete and let go of the negative Patterns you did not choose to begin with.

g. Create an environment where you are supported in continuing positive Patterns, and stay away from the seductions of negative Patterns.

h. Remember that you are not your parents. You will not be a bad person if you try to be yourself. The guilt you may feel because you will have a better and a more successful life than your parents, because you will automatically be smarter than them (you know what they knew and much more), and recognize your right far more clearly than they did, is a natural Pattern for every child raised in an oppressive environment.

i. Know that your parents, too, were better and different from their own parents. They may have forgotten their own fight for independence of thought and action and their process of becoming true to themselves, but deep in their hearts, they are on your side. Remind them of that, instead of getting into a fight.

J. Remember that even if your parents have forgotten, they worked very hard so you could have a better chance at life and at being yourself than they had.

Roots of Success

Self-Validation. The first step to any Pattern Change from our past programing is the development of *Self-Validation.* Remembering what we have missed as children, being validated for who we are, and nurturing that need to ourselves is not only a path to success but it is also a process of rebirth. To be validated is a prerequisite of validating oneself. So, for one who has not been validated, it might sound foreign when someone says, "Validate yourself."

Creating Patterns of Self-Validation. How do we validate ourselves? First and foremost, it raises the questions of: who am I? Who is this person that I must validate? Years and years of being the person in tears behind the facade of a polite, successful, entertaining or funny face, has blocked us from the true feelings we once had, and the feelings of fulfillment that we felt worthy of validation. Perhaps we have never truly understood the meaning or the feeling behind the world "validation." But we cannot afford to spend another thirteen years to find out about it. Good!

The short-cut to get the air we so desperately need is to begin breathing right this moment, and to begin validating whatever we say we are and whatever we think we feel. Believe me, it is a start on the right Pattern.

To love all of who we are: second step to Pattern Change from Past Programing. To validate ourselves as we are at this moment, and to accept and love that person with all the passion and compassion we have missed feeling towards ourselves, is the process of re-birth, Reprograming and Re-Patterning from the bottom up. In this process, we can be guided by our children, or the child within ourselves, once we claim her or him again. Loving unconditionally, and accepting without critical eyes, are gifts that only children possess naturally and without training. Once we become adults, we have already been through the process of not being good enough by other's standards and expectations, and that is how we see ourselves, our world and others: not good enough.

Acceptance Patterns create path to Excellence. Self-Acceptance opens the path to change towards Excellence, within ourselves and in our world. Acceptance of Self, if genuine, creates acceptance of others, for the people we reject are the people who remind us of a part of ourselves that we have not yet accepted.

In order to get past our present situation we must accept and acknowledge where we are at this moment. It is only then that we can choose a new destination. If we feel not good enough right now, all our power and energy goes to hiding ourSelf, denying who we are, and finding fault with the rest of the world. But if we can see ourselves, accept who we are, and then begin to love, nurture and validate our Self, the true Self will emerge. The Self that emerges will be a Self without blocks and without imbalance. Self-Validation polishes the soul and the Self.

Self-Program for Change: Self-Validation. Sometimes that's all it takes; the love and validation we give to ourselves is the Master Program for healing wounds, rebuilding the soul, and creating Power Balance and Excellence, given we have the knowledge of Self to free ourselves from what is not a part of who we are, and from uninvited intrusions of Past Programers.

Loving Self: reflection of a stand-still moment. Some people ask, "But how do I know who I am? How do I trust mySelf? How do I know how to love mySelf?" The answer is: just begin to love who you think you are and validate who you feel you are. By just accepting who you are in the moment, you are loving yourself. No phony smiles to pretend who you are so that you will be loved. No rushes of greed so you can have more to gain more respect. No lies so that you can be more interesting to love. And no regrets of what you missed out on. Nothing but a clear and pure recognition, appreciation, and contentment of your reflection in the stand-still moment of time.

Imagine the beauty and clarity of that and capture the feeling for a moment with your eyes closed. Throw away all thoughts of past and future. Think about nothing. Nothing could make you any happier than the peace you can feel this moment. Imagine sitting in a rocking chair, rocking forward and back, with no thoughts about anything but being right in the middle.

Stop the Swing of Pendulum, right in the middle. Stay in the middle, where everything stops calmly and quietly, free from the rush of moving back and forth, back and forth, just like the grandfather's clock that kept me up at nights with thoughts of what to do. And when it stopped in the middle, I fell asleep peacefully, and felt so rested when I awoke in the morning that I could look forward to the day ahead. I remember that my days were packed with things I had to do, like homework that never seemed finished. But after the good night's sleep from when my grandfather's clock stopped right in the middle, I was not afraid of anything, and nothing made me tired.

Right in the middle, you will feel at peace. If you stop right in the middle as you are going back and forth on the Patterns of your rocking chair, you will feel at peace with all the changes you have to make later, because you will feel at peace with yourself, right in the middle, inside: now. That's excellent. I know how you feel if you did this exercise with me, as I am sure you did.

Understanding those who walk the same path. You wouldn't have come with me so far if you didn't want to be adventurous and travel with me in my search for the truth, because I feel wonderful and feel that you and I, if you have stuck with me so far, are understanding each other. And therefore, we are going to understand many other things that arrive from that understanding. For to understand a person, it means that we have traveled the same path with them. And even though we don't quite know each other, we know of one another, and we can better copy the Patterns, for it is as if they are our own.

To feel what it means to be validated. I want you to imagine yourself still a child, and your parents are taking turns holding you, loving you, kissing you, caressing you and playing with you. You can do nothing wrong in their eyes, and there is nothing that you cannot do. Imagine a place where you remember being loved and nurtured, or a place where you feel nurtured and loved when you are there.

Imagine how you love and nurture someone you love the most, whomever it is, and how you express your love to that person. Now begin to transfer all of that love you have for them onto another person: you, yourSelf. The people I mentioned are you. And you deserve love from yourself and everyone else around you. Begin to show them what it means to be loved and begin to feel loved and validated by all of you. Excellent.

Now, I want you to imagine that you are doing a task that you are good at or that you wished you were good at. I want you to really get into imagining this scene happening in front of you, because as we have discussed earlier, thought is everything, and everything we think will materialize if we take steps towards these thoughts. Now I want you to take some very small steps towards this person you are imagining doing something that she does or likes to do very well. That's right.

It is you doing something very successfully. Get closer and closer, so that you can see every detail of how you look and how you feel successfully doing a task you do well or would like to do very well. Now see yourself doing this task in front of a big crowd. I am somewhere among this crowd, and we are all admiring and applauding you, and are very proud of you. Feel the warmth from that sense of being validated for who you are being at your best at that moment, whatever that best is, and you will know it easily by focusing on your feelings and the way you are being at the moment. Think about that moment and stop right in the middle, right in the middle, where you feel the peace and contentment of just that moment. Nothing in the past, nothing in the future, can stop how you feel right now. Excellent. Now tell me if you feel validated and if you know what it means to be validated. I know I do, so you must, too.

Creating your own fantasies. Now what would be fun and educational, is to make up your own fantasies that give you feelings of validation, contentment, appreciation, self-acceptance and love in the moment. I would very much appreciate it if you shared your ideas with me. It teaches me a great deal about you and maybe I can be of a lot more help to you in my next book. That is, after I use what I have learned to further enhance my own Patterns towards Excellence, my friend.

Person-to-person: beneath the pages. I hope you don't mind my attempts at talking directly to you and getting as close to you as I can, from behind this cold, square and lifeless computer screen. For someone who loves the true and direct connection with people, and wants to finally accomplish her mission of putting her words onto paper and spreading them farther than she can reach in her comfortable and cozy office, this is my attempt to feel the connection as I am accomplishing my mission. I hope that I can finish this task soon, and come back to the one-on-one, face-to-face, person-to-person connection.

Power Balance of personal beliefs and objectivity. Meanwhile, we can feel the person-to-person connection through my efforts of creating it by trying to make a deep connection with you from the surface and in-between the cold and blind pages of this book. I, mySelf, truly appreciate being able to do that; it makes the process more personal and joyful for me than just writing for no one in the hope that a number of people will read this. It creates personal subjectivity, understanding and unbiased compassion, and understanding one needs in order to connect with the world of another person. It is this same kind of personal subjectivity we need when we read about a murder, or watch on television someone who has been accused of murder, or when we are the person creating the news of any kind about anyone, or try to attach someone's character. If we always keep our personal subjectivity pattern turned on, it actually enhances the power balance of our pattern of objectivity, which comes from unbiased openness to new knowledge and creativity. Do you understand what I am trying to portray here?

Validate yourself, fully! You might truly understand me, or you might think to yourself: at least she is brave enough to pour all of this out onto the white sheets of paper that are becoming a book for millions of people to read and judge her by. That's right. If you understand me and the pictures I am trying to portray here, you are already the Programer of your own Patterns. You are an unafraid, willing to see the vision I am communicating with you, searching for not only Patterns of Validation of any kind within yourself and others, but also entering the path to Excellence by a mere openness to life and what it has to offer at its best. Once we are willing to accept the responsibility that comes with freedom, we become free beings.

Stuck? Unable to get beyond differentness? If you are lost in my words, stuck in your pattern of rejection of differentness, afraid to open the door and see the other side, and are complimenting me on my courage to risk my credibility, my friend, try it sometime. It truly is liberating to dare to be yourself and to live the passion that stirs within you! Validate yourself, and live truly and fully.

One person's fantasy: answer to humanity. History has proven to us that what we have rejected at its time of creation has always been the next generation's answer to the most complicated life questions. It probably won't be me. I am just content and grateful that you are reading my thoughts, even if it ends at just that. Believe me. I am not looking for a miracle more fascinating and powerful than that. But what about you?

Write until you lose track of time. Have you ever given yourself the validation and the liberty to be creative even if it seems to you not very serious or genius? If you haven't, start this moment. Sit down and get a piece of paper and a pencil. (You might get the paper and the pencil before you sit down.) Excellent! Now, write. Pick a subject, it can be anything. But since we need to learn about Self, write about yourself. Start a life story. Put feelings into it; don't merely report it. Write as quickly as you can. Don't stop to make any meaning out of it. Write for as long as you can until you have lost track of time. It is only then that the magic begins to take place and, as you let go of the control that has kept you blocked, you will begin to feel a true sense of Self-Control, and your thoughts will pour out onto the paper as never before.

Life is a chess game: to win, analyze the moves. Think about nothing. Just write. Believe me. That's exactly what I am doing. At this point, I have either truly proven to you that you can change your Patterns easily and work towards Excellence, or I might have lost you altogether. What will it be, my friend? Life is a chess game. In order to win you must analyze the Patterns to move. If you don't calculate your Patterns, others will, and you will find yourself check-mated out of your own life. But if you can, there are many options to choose from.

Self-Control: letting go of Pseudo-Control. Tell me what you wrote. By the way, you can do this exercise with other movements, like dancing and talking to yourself into a tape recorder, or while flying, or while giving a speech in front of thousands of people. By writing or talking to yourself into a tape recorder, you not only will learn Self-Control, but you will also have communicated something that can be read or heard easily by you and others later. However, it is the same thing with dancing, acting, painting and other artistic movements if others can read that subject as well as you. Communicating in any way with yourself and others while letting go of surface control of the environment will bring out Self-Control and a real connection with yourself and others that validates all concerned.

In the drama of life, far different from the theatre, in order to succeed, you must play you. In theatre, a good actor forgets himself, thinks about the motivation of the role he is playing and then plays that, without controlling the environment, but with Self-Control, spontaneously and creatively. In the drama of life, you must play you, without the need to control the environment so that you can gain Self-Control. You then need clear motivation, good intention, creativity spontaneity and courage to be the best you can be. Once you let go of the imbalance pattern of control, you will gain Self-Control: a phenomenon that philosophers, artists, scientists, spiritual leaders and successful people of any profession know very well. All it takes is self-trust, validation and a courage to be.

Balance Pattern Recognition. Changing the Patterns of Imbalance and Block first requires the ability to recognize, acknowledge and validate the Balance Patterns existing within. This acknowledgment, validation and recognition of positive powers further enables the person to recognize his or her inherent ability to have Power Balance and Excellence. This recognition will further increase the self-worth and respect that the individual needs in order to want to change, and to be able to change, the Imbalances and Blocks within.

Patterns of Subconscious. Recognition and focus on our other dimension, the subconscious world, is vital. Patterns of Subconscious are Patterns from which we separate ourselves: Patterns that have not been accepted by our judgment, our approval, or the stamp which we have borrowed from our society. The different, the brave, the outrageous, the genuine, the colorful: the subconscious.

The shadow Pattern: the child within. The child within is our neglected shadow: the other side of the Pendulum that has not been swung to. The child within is the person behind the bars of our Imbalance and Block Patterns of inhibition, judgment, criticism and neglect, just as it was done to us in the past. The subconscious self is the other half, the other dimension of Self: the shadow, the forgotten child within, the Subconscious Patterns of our lives in which we see the exaggerated presentations without our own control, the parts we often don't even question or want to know about. The vulnerable, the hurt, the afraid, the shy, the abused, the neglected, the inhibited, the forbidden, the victim, the perpetrator, the innocent, the naive, the guilty, the hidden Patterns within: our Subconscious Patterns of our multidimensional mind. Everything about us not recognized, acknowledged, validated or loved, openly, becomes the Subconscious Patterns determining our lives and controlling our every move, simply because we have not accepted these Patterns as our own. Rejection has that power in everything and everyone. The rejected one rebels and comes out on top, most often at the most inappropriate and unexpected times. Just like the virus in a computer, the unwanted Patterns of our lives become enlarged and take over our entire destiny unless we hold up the white flag of acceptance, validation, respect, peace, and harmony.

Unaccepted Patterns: Subconscious Patterns. Based on what you know by now, after having gone through many Programers to get to where you are, and having Blocked many Patterns as a result of the Programing you received, it is not surprising that at least half of you exist in your subconscious, only. When our Patterns that belong to us are punished, oppressed and blocked, they don't go anywhere. They remain within us, placed in our subconscious.

Subconscious Patterns can become destructive. The nature of Subconscious Patterns is that they control us because we hide and deny them. As I stated earlier, whatever we hide not only cannot be changed, but will also get the best of us; it will control us, and we will be at its mercy. The power of that which is denied and hidden may even become destructive because of its intensity and because of our frustration stemming from a lack of validity that every living species needs to function in health.

Our other half is within ourselves, not in others. We must, therefore, acknowledge and bring out of the closet that part of us that we have hidden or that has been hiding from us. As we bring our Subconscious Self out in the open, at least to ourselves, we begin to balance our power and move towards a more complete Self. We all need our other half, and our unhealthy and indirect attempt to find it in others, especially our mates, is proof of that fact. Finding our other half through others has been a common practice that even mental health professional have agreed to. Freud calls it role complimentary, and argues that it is a natural tendency for people to find their better half because they themselves are incomplete.

Completed by others, stays incomplete. This notion is one of the biggest mistakes of the centuries, and has kept the people who have adhered to it blind and incomplete, compromising their potential by hiding behind someone else's. Almost all married couples make a lifetime decision of connection and commitment based on this wrong and temporary notion that they have found their better half, and are left disillusioned after a few years of investment because of a lack of strong balance between their logic and emotions. A true connection is a connection of two whole people, for the purpose of liking and loving each other for who they truly are, and not to use each other as Blocks to growth. I will explore this in detail in my upcoming book, *Patterns of Love*.

The better half we must create, inside. The true mistake lies in the fact that once people get involved with their partner who owns the Patterns they are missing, they become content, hide behind their partner, and remain incomplete. The real tragedy occurs when the partner changes. The person feels empty and decides that he or she no longer has any use for the partner, or blames feelings of emptiness on the relationship. Until we own all of ourselves and change by choice, we are not safe partners in relationships, for we tend to unload the responsibility of our success and happiness onto them. No one can find true love in such a lopsided, distorted and unspoken contract, for the intent is not to love the person for who they are, but to hire them to be what we ourselves are not willing to face and create, from within.

The Merger. The Subconscious Self merging with Conscious Self creates Power Balance and Excellence that would otherwise be Blocked. If the Subconscious Self continues to remain hidden and unexpressed, the effect is reversed; it develops further and becomes a more severe Power Imbalance and Block.

Subconscious Self: Subconscious Patterns. Subconscious patterns are almost always the other side of the conscious patterns we experience in our lives. There is always forgotten aggressive subconscious pattern for a passive patterned person. There is always a subconscious cognitive pattern for a emotional patterned person. There is always subconscious silent pattern for an active patterned person.

Power Balance. To the degree that we can expand by recognizing and expressing all that is within us, subconsciously and consciously, to that degree we have moved towards Power Balance, where we can express Patterns as we choose to express them, and not as they choose to come out without our control over them. Obtaining Self-Control instead of controlling others is nothing but the process of gaining Power Balance.

Born Free. Bringing out the subconscious, forgotten child is the process of owning the inherent gifts we were born with: ourselves as spontaneous, free, and primitive: the part that is unfamiliar with Societal Programing.

Pattern Change of Past Programing: remembering what we were born with, the way we inherently think and feel. What we are born with is taken for granted and minimized by our Past Programers, our parents. They can't wait to change us. They think they are actually helping us. Yet there is an inherent wisdom within us when we are born. Magically, like the incredible way our bodies work, our minds, from the very beginning, work wonders. And emotions, although unpolished, are so clear that they could be used as lie detectors.

Power Balance of Wisdom and Spontaneity. We lose all of that magic during our process of maturation and civilization; not because it is natural to lose it, but because of the incorrect Programing of our most significant Programers: our parents. We lose the way we question everything as a child; we lose waking up with great big question marks in front of our noses, seeing everything as a puzzle that we must immediately solve. It is the most remarkable stage of life; a stage when all of our answers must be given to us in a loving and patient manner, as if we were the most important scientists whose questions are a matter of life or death.

The child within: not to be seen and not to be heard. We are constantly told to be quiet, to mind our own business, and the biggest error of all: "Don't question authority." Since as children we are the most absorbent beings, we absorb the unsafe feeling that we create whenever we ask questions. We learn, quickly and clearly, that it is not okay to ask questions because it "rocks the boat" and is therefore a "no, no." We learn that asking questions makes people notice us in a negative way, not with happy faces.

Patterns of Curiosity means: alive and living. When we grow up with a lack of motivation to learn anything at all, our parents are disappointed and tell us that we are not functioning with our full capacity, while our teachers write in our report cards, "does not function to his best potential." What an amazing discovery for the very people who have created the condition! It is not as if they themselves are functioning to their fullest capacity. Well, everyone has had parents and teachers and preachers. We can at least understand each other and empathize with each other's pains of growing.

Make Your Own Mistakes

To question and to disagree does not mean to be critical or impolite. Nor does it mean to be mistrusting or suspicious. It simply means to learn, develop and utilize the inherent capacity of curiosity, to ask questions, and to question the intent of every authority. Human mistakes don't know any ranks that we humans give to ourselves. Everyone makes mistakes. The only hope is that the more we learn and experience, the more we learn from our mistakes and learn not to repeat them. That's all. Authority, too, makes mistakes, especially when it comes to determining what's good for somebody else.

Remember your childhood Patterns. Imagine yourself as a child, when you were a little girl or a little boy. Try to remember as far back as you can, focusing on the earliest times of your life. Remember the way you saw the world, and the way you felt in it, before you were Programed to be who you are now, or who you had been before you became who you really are.

Remember how you laughed. Remember how trusting you were, and how wonderful it was to just be. Doing nothing was fun, and fun was doing nothing. If you can, remember way back, to some point in your life, when you felt taken care of, loved and protected. Remember the close connection you had with nature. All children are so very amused and absorbed by what nature has to offer them, and they treasure it with respect.

Remember how curious you were. Questioning everything was the Habitual Pattern you were born with. Being full of love for life and anticipation for its adventures is what woke you up every day, and wouldn't let you sleep at night. Remember that you never took things at face value; you always wanted to know the intent. And you intuitively backed off when what was said to you was different from what you truly felt.

Remember your Patterns of Pain, then let go. If you can, remember the times when you were alone and could play for hours, as if you had many friends around; or when you had your little friends around you and everything and everywhere was an adventure and mystery ready to be discovered. Go back and try to remember the child that you were. If these memories are too painful to remember, stop right here. And if you like, you can remember them in the presence of a trained individual so that you can be guided to benefit by remembering and then being able to let go, instead of having these memories hurt you by preoccupying you and inhibiting your daily tasks. Just remember, anything you allow to surface, any Patterns of Pain you have had, you can let go of, and can delete the control they have had on your life. Once you accept that they exist within you, you gain control over them, and can either utilize them positively or delete them from your Patterns of Choice.

Recall of Past Patterns. To free ourselves of Past Programing and the pain it has created for us which has caused our Patterns to go in directions that we have had no control of, is the process of Recall of Past Patterns. During the process of recalling a past that is very painful, it is better to be gradual, and to first become extremely relaxed by thinking a great deal of good thoughts about the places that give you an extra state of relaxation. Once relaxed, you can gradually think about the painful past. Relaxation and anxiety are too opposing Patterns. Once relaxed, anxiety cannot preside; the body is free of tension, and one can go back further into the past.

Merging Patterns of Joy with Patterns of Pain. One woman always froze during lovemaking with her husband because the situation reminded her of when she was raped. This was a very lengthy case and there was a great deal involved, but one technique used to reduce the woman's intensity and fear of the situation was for her to think, while making love with her husband, about other situations, with or without her husband, that brought her joy, relaxation and peace. She felt a lot more capable of enjoying her husband by doing this process. She was also able to confront her husband's Aggressive Patterns of lovemaking that had triggered the recall of her past experience.

Patterns Children Teach

Patterns of Curiosity	*Patterns of Joy*
Patterns of Spontaneity	*Patterns of Love*
Patterns of Honesty	*Patterns of Acceptance*

Patterns of Simplicity	***Patterns of Nurturance***
Patterns of Vulnerability	***Patterns of Flexibility***
Patterns of Intuition	***Patterns of Forgiveness***
Patterns of Trust	***Patterns of openness***

We must search within and find the forgotten Self. Life puts special assignments and paths before us in order to give us as many choices and opportunities as possible in order to become whole within our Self. If we trust life and if we accept the universal laws of existence, we grow and excel. But we must be willing to painfully and honesty search within, and to find the patterns that have blocked our transcendence. Before I began my mission of writing nine books in January of 1993 so that I could gain a credible enough a voice to represent the masses of voiceless people and to embrace the injured and the slashed out humanity, I thought I was whole. I knew we never truly arrive but with all my humble pride I thought I was pretty much there. But since then I have learned that I have much further to go. What writing nine books in one year and this mission has done for me is miraculous. I thought I was on a mission to help humanity. I did not know that humanity had given me a mission to heal my own wounded mind and body and my much scared trust, from the pain of witnessing human brutality. But when I wrote day and night and then night and day, and then began to reach out to the masses with the hope that they would receive and hear me, I began to trust. Perhaps because there came a time when I had no other choice left to me. In a moment of anguish and fear of pssibility of causing my children danger or pain, fear of exposing myself and them to the darkness and toxicity of the ignorance I was trying to fight, I saw a guiding light. I began to not be concerned about being hurt or even being received or heard. All that truly mattered was that I was making an attempt to reach out. The miracle was that by beggining to trust myself and my destiny, I began to trust others. Instead of the fear of getting hurt, I began to dream of finding out that indeed there is far more spirit and love on this earth than we have had the courage to demonstrate, or the spirit, to see. I felt elated by the thought of finding that even may be I am widely mistaken. I felt the trust within me because I realize that my mission was not about proving that I was right, but to try to bring together what *was*. From that moment on, I was clearly walking on air. My mission was already fulfilled. Because if I could find the final challenge for the truth within mySelf, then I surely could find it out there. Even if it was the final challenge for just a passing moment, I had no more fear. The part has within it all the patterns of the *whole;* and the whole had embraced all the patterns of the *part.*

Our parents built America through change of patterns. This country, with all its limitations, is the greatest country in the world. Our fathers and our mothers were no longer willing to accept the bureaucracy, authoritarianism, dictatorship, elective compassion and privileges that brought oppression, abuse, and the lack of validation and respect for all unique beings.

They questioned status quo of ignorance. They left their countries and came to America to create a free country of their own. They exemplified patterns of independence and courage, bravery and creativity. And you certainly are a product of that peace-patterned evo-revolution. You certainly can be inspired by their efforts, even if they have long forgotten and are preoccupied with repeating what is safe and comfortable.

Your parents made sacrifices: it is your turn. They made their sacrifices, and it is now your turn to take charge and do your share of demanding your rights. It is your turn to develop more extensive levels of liberation, responsibility, compassion, and progression than your fathers ever dreamed of when they started this land of freedom.

Following footsteps of choice. If they stand in front of your progression because of their own fears, and cannot accept your differentness, just hold them in your arms and tell them how much you appreciate what they have done for you, and that you find it your responsibility to follow their footsteps in continuing the mission they, or their fathers, left their security and comfort for:

the mission of progression and not giving in to regression and stagnation; challenging the comfort zones of Habitual Patterns; questioning authority as they did at a time more frightening for individuality and uniqueness than now.

Fear: the gap between parent and child. At a time when it was less acceptable to be different, your parents exercised their own courage of being different. It is not only unreasonable to expect you not to exercise the power they have handed down to you; it is a denial of their own power and independence of mind. That denial stems from a fear instilled within them: a fear larger than their own courage, a fear uncontrolled. The fear of a sinful Self: a fear injected into them that they would go to hell if not obedient to ignorance, and if not obediently and blindly chained to Patterns of Regression.

Delete imposed Patterns of Fear. Fear of Self, fear of what is within one's core: this fear is a seed of self-doubt planted in the minds of innocent children and parents by those who fear the power of Self and the power of individuals combined, collected, towards the common and inherent dream of all beings: the dream of progression.

Only a self-directed life deletes toxicity. Throughout my practice of working with people, I have never found someone who searched within Self and found evil inside. The evils of our lives are hiding outside to catch us and take us to their own domain where they can suck our fresh blood in which an inherent knowingness flows, and replace our wisdom with doubt, fear, and guilt if we don't guide ourselves.

To be pure is not to be blind. A directed Self is an intuitive, thinking, feeling, analyzing, questioning, loving, compassionate, kind, strong, vulnerable, forgiving Self and encompassing all that is necessary to be Power Balanced. A directed Self is not attached to dogma of the old: dogma that pulls one down and creates doubt within the soul, predetermined and pre-defined, singing that in order to be pure, one must be blind.

Question the handed-down myths. Many successful people, during my practice as a psychotherapist, have come to me disillusioned about their lives. They, like most people, have worked hard for the American dream of being successful and happy in life. They, too, were born with the inherent quality and capacity for fully functioning in body and mind; they, too, did everything necessary to pay their dues of education, experience, responsibility, family, providing and playing all the rules and roles there were to play. But somewhere down the line, usually in the ages of thirty-five to fifty-five, and older, they realize that although they have the pretty picture, they find themselves all alone behind it: alone, sad, unhappy, and disillusioned. Why?

A predetermined life. They, too, did not examine or question what was handed down to them to see if it fit in with their unique being. They spent their lives trying to make their parents happy or society proud, or to prove they could do it just like others. In some cases, they were stuck with other people's Programs and did not know that they could change and become themselves, live their own lives, and plan their own golden dreams: the dreams preached to them as children, and yet no one showed them how or truly allowed them to find out for themselves.

Our parents, our most significant role models, were so drowned in survival and providing security for us, that they failed to show us how wonderful it was to be a person with a mind unique and individual from others. Father came home, perhaps from a very dynamic day at work out there in the world, but he was so tired that had no energy to share his adventures with us. Mother was so busy being a good mother by washing and cooking and cleaning that she had no moment free to enjoy us as her children and make us feel how wonderful it is to be an alive being, and how joyful it is to live connected, loved and in harmony.

Teachers who teach guilt and shame. Half the time, things were so hard that they even forgot that the purpose of their efforts really was that children would grow up healthy and happy. We, as children, were the first ones, and the safest ones, to be the target of their frustrations on their path of trying to create a life for us that we did not choose. The intentions were noble, but the actions were colloquial. They had never been taught how to be the best parents they could be. Some of their teachers were too busy making them feel guilty, worthless, and powerless, so that they could collect from the fruit of their hard work. No one had in mind to teach patterns of progression, health, peace and harmony to a family.

Becoming the parents' protectors. We found ourselves seeking safety consistently, from the webs of our saviors' temperaments and lack of control. Instead of moving away from the Imbalances and crises they were supposed to protect us from, we ended up accommodating, protecting, and creating safety and calm for them. Instead of them parenting us, we became their parents and protectors from their ignorance.

Healthy development, advanced progression. We did all that at the cost of our own healthy development and establishment of our own unique identity. Since we were born with the inherent capacity to think and to learn, we soon learned that at times we must identify with parents to survive their toxicity. At other times, we must rebel or there would be nothing left of us. We did all that so well that by the time we were on our own, and free to choose, we could not figure out who the real us, our true Self, truly was, or what we wanted to choose. Many people ask me, "Who is the real me? What do I want? And how do I know that this isn't my mother or father or teacher talking?"

First step to Pattern Change: question. Questioning will lead us to the answers. It will keep our brain fluids stimulated and running. It will take us away from a predetermined destiny, and towards choices made by ourselves. Yet it is always difficult to question and to rock the tower of authority of our Life Patterns and destiny.

To penetrate the thick wall of denial. At times, it requires a bit of exaggeration in order to penetrate society's thick wall of denial. But throughout history, only by stepping out of line and announcing the uniqueness of Self has there been any change on the path of progression of humanity.

All destinations require the same Patterns. If my purpose seems too arrogant and global, if people truly see it, hear it, and feel it, they will see no difference in the patterns, paths and directions towards achieving purposes much smaller in quality. Success and Excellence for a person, for love relationships, for family affairs, and for societal harmony, are all Patterned and achieved in the same manner: by creating Balance in the Powers that lead towards the finish line of destiny.

Nine

Universal Excellence

Mind-Body-Spirit Movement

Step by step: Universal Mind-Body Programing. This path is a limitless Mind-Body-Spirit Programing. The limitations that we have put on ourselves as a result of our handed down blocks and imbalances will disappear when we live excelled lives. We begin to observe this in the freshness and ongoing youthfulness in our bodies and minds. It is only the stagnant that deteriorates, grows old and becomes outdated.

Pattern Choice. For change of patterns towards Power Balance and Excellence, we utilize Pattern Search, Pattern Observation and Pattern Analysis, and through Deductive Reasoning we will gain Balance, Power Balance and then Excellence Patterns and Programing that can change our lives. Pattern Choice is a process in which we consciously choose our Life Patterns instead of remaining at the mercy of what has been handed down to us.

Program Choice. Deleting patterns of imbalance, adding and saving patterns of balance, power balance and excellence to our repertoire of our program of choice, of our life and of our destiny, is not a dream, or magic, or a miracle that is created or granted to us by any other entity other than our own focus, self-control, and self-discipline: patterns that offer us the choice to the direction of our life.

Motivation and Clarity facilitates change. *Self-validation, pattern recognition, balance pattern validation, Universal Mind-Body Prayer, silence, fasting of mind, body, and spirit, and* *focus within*, will enable a balance patterned individual to take on power balance and wxcellence patterns. Although it is more difficult to add power balance and excellence patterns than to change imbalance and block patterns, the motivation and clarity of choice, and the groundwork prepared, will enhance the process.

Pattern of Aggrandizement. Aggrandizement is enlargement: the ability to see the bigger picture; it is the global nature of the Patterns. It is our link to universality. Through a Universal Self we can enlarge our vision, our purpose, our hopes and our mission for not only our Self and our family, but also for our extended family: humanity. It is through the eyes of a Universal Self that we see the world with a great deal of commonality, while we can accept its multidimensionality. And it is through the enlargement of our eyes, our hearts and our soul, that we can come to values that have universality. It is very important to see oneself as a global person: a being who can be anywhere and everywhere without the prejudice and bias of just belonging in one place, one piece of dirt, one particular language, one religion, one political party, one flag, one color, one solution; what cannot be the desired answer for everyone. It is no longer the people of one tribe that need to be reached, or only certain people that deserve to be saved. No law written in stone supersedes the engraved universal law of humanity. Knowledge of this truth is a sign that one has reached Excellence: an inner polished soul that has gained the Power Balance of all dimensions existing within, from mind to emotion, and from body to spirit: a pattern of aggrandizement.

Physical Fasting. Physical fasting was mentioned earlier in this chapter. The more habitual our power balance patterns become, the more flexible and the more excelling beings we will become.

Mental Fasting. Mental fasting means having long periods of silence (Sokoot) and going through the process of clearing the screen (clear mind), for the development of a mind free from any distortions, such as addictions to drugs or alcohol, mind-body distortions such as psychosomatic or eating disorders stemming from cognitive-emotional Imbalances and distractions such as the labeled "incurable disease" of schizophrenia, a thought disorder in the Diagnostic Statistical Manual of Mental Disorders.

Focus in Silence: Self-Discipline Control technique. Focus in Silence creates awareness and recognition of not only the moment, but of exactly what is occurring in the moment within Self. Only with this Pattern of Awareness and recognition can we develop Self-Control. To gain control of anything, we must have it in the palm of our hands. In the absence of recognizing the present moment, we lack the knowledge of what is going on within ourselves and with our surroundings; in effect, we lose control. I am not referring to Imbalanced Control: the need to control others. I am only referring to the Pattern of Self-Control, the kind that makes us safe for both ourselves and others.

Feeling our breath in the palm of our hand. With Focus in Silence, we can begin to breathe fully, calmly and calculatively, as if our breath is a part of our own creation; its control, we are holding in the palm of our hand. In Focus in Silence, we begin to notice what goes on around us, beside us, below us, beneath us, and inside us. In Focus in Silence, we can begin to feel what has been latent for years, perhaps decades. Only in Silence do we consciously allow the truth of our being to peacefully exist. Only in Focus in Silence are we are able to closely look at the impulsive reactions of our mind-body connection, and through the Universal Mind-Body Prayer, teach ourselves to slow down, to speed up, not to stay, not to jump, and not to rush: in essence, Patterns of Self-Control and Self-Discipline.

Patterns of Silence. The Pattern of Silence, performed alone, is a cleansing of the mind, essential for maintaining its capacity; it is a prerequisite for Silence Within.

Focus Within. Focus Within is a Pattern of Silence with the focus on Self: an essential key to power balance and excellence. All Eastern techniques of meditation are helpful tools for increasing the capacity of the mind and for the development of Cognition-Emotion Power Balance and Excellence. Religious prayers were used initially for this purpose: to bring human beings closer to themselves and to enhance human quality.

New Patterns blossom from Focus Within. This break will enable us to relax our mind from the rush of the day, and from the long periods of restless time when all we do is to think about things we can do something about, as well as things we cannot do anything about; it will provide room for new and significant thoughts about that which we most definitely can do and change, like our Life Patterns, our Programs and, ultimately, our destiny.

Meditation. Meditation is to focus within and become aware of inner feelings and the inner being, beyond and above all labels and Patterns. All forms of meditation are helpful and, if the person is raised with one or another, the familiarity can be nurturing in bringing one back to one's roots. All prayer is meditation, useful for getting close to the Self and for creating Patterns of Mind-Body Self-Discipline. No meditation or prayer is better or more superior to another. The quality lies in the person's focus within.

Fasting is a spiritual experience. The Ramezan month of religious fasting for Persian Moslems, during which they eat very little at dawn and very little at supper, fasting in-between and praying most of the time, is another tool that brings spirituality and inner focus to people who at the time were outward and addicted to indulgences of lavish lives. Likewise, when Moses, Jesus and Mohammed gave message of humanity and spirituality to their people, the focus towards such patterns was absent and people were distracted with indulgences that took them further away from getting close to themselves and to others.

Universal Mind-Body-Prayer

The Universal Mind-Body Prayer is the movement of the body to the hymn of the mind, motivated by the soul in harmony. When we make music in silence and dance, not by the sound of unknown external music, but by what is inspired within our soul and by our spirit, we have engaged in a Universal Mind-Body Prayer that moves us to not only a solid seal of compassion and connection with our Self, but with all godlike children of humanity and with the parental power of the universe: the paternal wisdom and maternal nurturance. There is no rule for this exercise of unity; what is commanded from within takes on the nature and pattern of the movement. To hear the hymns of the inner voice, to feel the movements directed from within, we must use aggrandizement, a larger picture, a stronger focus to bring together all the forces and *power balance patterns* of the mind as well as the spirit to the surface so that it materializes in our body, in the flesh. The flow is a dance; a song; an exercise; a movement; a prayer to awaken all the patterns of being, to enhance all the patterns of doing, to embrace all the patterns of existence and all of life's meaning. It is a purpose, a cause and an effect. The Universal Mind-Body Prayer is freedom from anything that holds back from the liberty of existence.

Thinking and feeling in the present. How you feel in the moment is very important to your sense of Self, to your congruity and to your joy in life. What it mean to you to feel the way you feel: the purpose of the feeling and the intent, is also significant. Without a purpose, you are left at the mercy of feelings without meaning, over which you have no Self-Control, unable to move towards life's mastery. Being spontaneous and living in the present does not mean having no control of your faculties and losing Power Balance. It means having the courage to own all that there is to yourself, so that you can experience a true sense of Self-Control.

Patterns of Self-Control. Only the wisdom and experience of the Excellence Pattern of Self-Control will enable us to feel life, to be a part of it and to have it as part of ourselves, without getting lost and losing ourselves. Only with Self-Control will we have true courage, instead of naiveté and lack of control, to become a part of everything in life without Blocks of fear and the panic of losing ourselves.

Flowing Patterns of Chaos create Self-Control. To have Patterns of Self-Control, we must let go of the pseudo-external control that we pretend to have, on the outside, and allow the chaos that flows from the powers within us in each direction, on the inside. Feeling out of control is the beginning for development of Patterns of Self-Control.

Fear of chaos Blocks order and true control. The fear of chaos disables us from living and being a true partner to everything that exits, everything that makes a difference to us, and everything that we make a difference to. In order to lose the Power Block of fear and panic, we must gain something more powerful inside. Focus Within will enable us to gain that powerful phenomenon: the Excellence Pattern of Self-Control.

We focus on the effect instead of the cause. When we pay more attention to the disease, we get more diseased. When we pay more attention to health, we find more health. It is not anything magical. It is quite scientific and matter-of-fact that anything we focus on will gain the benefit of better light, meaning that it will grow and become stronger. It is only unfortunate that we know this, and yet habitually focus only on the symptoms, the results, and the effects, instead of focusing on the cause of it all: ourselves.

Far past moon, yet so far from the light, inside. A result of this is both our technological advancement and our human regression when it comes to ourselves and our relationships with others. Human beings have always been very proud and conscious of their props in life: that which proves to others that they are indeed progressive and mighty. And yet, while we are proud of reaching abroad, the child within and the children at home are neglected and ignored. We are habitually preoccupied with the presentations and appearances, while we ignore the real thing and the key to it all: our Inner Self.

Awards for good intent, not good action. We need more encouragement for being people of good intent. We need to get away from the toys and distractions of our minds, and get into the focus of our beings. We need more people who like people for who they are and not for what they have created, made or provided. We need a people-focused society instead of a product- and object-focused society. And believe me, it will make a difference.

Pattern of Altruism is not created in anonymity. It is in the nature of our Habitual Patterns that anything or anyone anonymous will lose the motivation and intent to be altruistic. This has been experimented and proven in cities such as New York, where people lose their altruism because of the anonymous nature of existing in such crowded cities. This was my first experiment at California State University of Long Beach during my undergraduate studies with Dr. Robert Thayer, a teacher from whom I learned cognitive balance, who proved to me first-hand that people, including mySelf, lost their conscious responsibility when they were put in a position of anonymity and thought no one knew them.

There is no magic, only the miracle of Self. I ask all people who come to see me for Pattern Change Programing to begin a daily exercise. It changes their chemical Imbalance immediately and some get rid of their depression by the first session. Our bodies and minds only function the way we allow them. If we want to change their Patterns, it is we who must do so. There is no magic.

Nothing outside of Self creates power within. The Excellence Pattern of Self-Responsibility will bring the spiritual morality we need in order to be altruistic even when anonymous, because what will matter is no longer what others think, but what we ourselves think. The focus will be on individual responsibility and not on something outside of ourselves to be in charge: a concept missing in religious teachings today.

True wholeness, not just a perfect presentation. All parts must be recognized and acknowledged equally, their significance validated and taken seriously, for the whole to be balanced and whole in the true sense of wholeness. We can always have perfect presentations and maintain them for long periods of time. The imbalances of our patterns, however, will catch up to us sooner or later, at times when we think we have it all. They will take us off-guard if we go on pretending and not recognizing that the truth will come out sooner or later.

Pattern Change Therapy
Scientific Method for Excellence

Pattern Search (Root Search.) The ability to find Repetitive Patterns. To listen to present Life Patterns, and to then go back to the past, match Patterns and explore the experiences that have created the Power Imbalance and Block Patterns disabling the person now. This short-cut eliminates years of therapy.

Pattern Observation (Root Observation.) The objective but passive observation of patterns in order to recognize their root and intent of activity. It is much like the passive process of psychoanalysis, but far shorter in duration.

Passive therapists. Although there is a time to passively observe and interpret, for the most part, a guide must lead a person through short-cuts that enhance the search for Patterns in the most time-effective ways. Therapists who still follow Freud, the genius psychiatrist who taught us a great deal and yet did not have enough time to discover everything, are far too inefficient. Some of us remain regressed while time, creativity and science pass us by, and we still do not realize that we can use our new experiences and knowledge and can stop following a dead man's techniques. If science was as much of a follower as we are in mental health, and if it had not kept trying, where would we be technologically? Pattern Search or Root Search is directly related to the therapist's experience, clarity, and absence of cognitive and emotional Blocks that inhibit the ability to Pattern Search in the Selves of others.

Pattern Analysis (Root Analysis.) Pattern or Root Analysis is the analysis of Repetitive Patterns in the person's Programing. It is also the analysis of Causal and Effect Patterns, meaning the reasons behind their existence, and their impact on the person's Life Program. The ability to find the control Patterns, their cause and effect on the person's life, and the degree of impact and severity, are significant skills of a Pattern Change Programer developed only from the experience and knowledge gained by working with people with curiosity and faith in their power to heal themselves.

Pattern Analysis

Analyzing Patterns that have dominated our lives is extremely significant for the process of Pattern Change. The natural tendency of people is to not question why they are behaving the way they are, why are they living the kind of life they live, and why are they where they are in their life and not somewhere else. Some never even question the reason behind their lack of motivation in life, or the apathy they feel every time they enter their home and spend time with their family. They just take what is given to them by other influences in their lives only because they themselves are not willing to become the strong force behind their fate. Pattern Analysis consists of the following:

Analysis of the Past

Recall of Past Programers. Recall of parents and teachers who have made a significant impact on you. Those for whom you have had a great deal of love, respect, hate, or anger.

Recognition and Recall of Past Patterns.
Recall of all past Emotional Patterns.
Recall of all past Cognitive Patterns.
Collection (writing down) of Repetitive Patterns
Recall of all Past Programers' Patterns.

Deductive Reasoning Of The Present

Recognition and logging of all Present Patterns. Repetitive Imbalance, Block, Balance and Excellence Patterns, if recognized and logged, can help gain knowledge of inner Self.

Scientific Pattern Elimination or Addition. When we become clear of our past Success and Error Patterns, and when we recognize the roots of those Patterns and the Programers behind them, then we can use deductive reasoning and the scientific process of elimination or addition of our Patterns. It is truly that scientific to gain Self-Control and the control of our own destiny.

Communication techniques: with Self and others. Learning how to communicate with ourselves will help us connect with our inner Self, creating Power Balance within. Silence is the powerful tool for connecting with our inner Self. Learning to communicate with others will connect us in harmony with the outside world, creating Power Balance without. Inner Power Balance becomes our tool for connecting with others and for creating Power Balance within our environment. In order to understand, respect, accept and love others, we must first learn to understand, respect, accept and love ourselves.

Pattern Recognition. Recognizing the Pattern by feelings of pain and loss. In Preventive Pattern Change where we are doing Preventive work, one goes through Pattern Analysis by choice in order to recognize the Patterns that in the future might cause crisis in life. In crisis intervention, the Pattern is automatically recognized by overwhelming feelings of pain and loss and through searching for the source of the feeling.

Balance Pattern Recognition. In order to change the Patterns of Imbalance and Block, we must first be able to recognize the Balance Patterns existing within us.

Balance Pattern Validation. After recognizing our balance patterns we must acknowledge and validate them. This validation, acknowledgment and recognition of positive powers already flowing within will further enable us to recognize our inherent capacity and ability to have power balance and excellence. This recognition will further increase the self-worth and respect that we need in order to desire change and to be able to change the imbalances and blocks we hold within.

Pattern purpose (Intent.) Determining the purpose of the pattern consists of the following:

a) Past Purpose (Intent): if the Pattern has had a purpose that it has served in the past.

b) Present Purpose (Intent): if the Pattern is serving a purpose now.

c) Future Purpose (Intent): if the Pattern has a future purpose that it will be serving.

Pattern Perspective. According to the purpose of the pattern, and the purpose it will be serving, it will be put in perspective. Patterns that have already served their purpose and no longer seem useful or seem, indeed, damaging, will be omitted.

Pattern Change. Pattern Change occurs as a result of going through the process of this collective work. And yet Pattern Change can also occur instantly in a given moment. There are experiences in life that create a short-cut in our process of making conscious choices from the unconscious collection of Patterns existing within.

The Final Analysis

The result stemming from the collective work above consists of the following:

Deductive Reasoning: process of Elimination. When we analyze and recognize all Patterns past and present, where they stem from, who their Programers are, and how they have affected our lives; by taking all that into account, when we consciously choose to copy, save, add or delete a Pattern, then we have engaged in scientific, deductive reasoning and a process of elimination. This is much like the process one goes through in discovering problems or upgrading computers.

Pattern Addition, Copy and Save. Patterns necessary to Add, in order to gain additional strength for Pattern Change, can at anytime of life be added. Patterns that we want to copy from those whom we find appropriate role models, and Patterns that we want to Save by our own choice for future use, are all Patterns of Choice that we have, with scientific and deductive reasoning, incorporated in the Programing of our own choice.

Pattern Deletion. Patterns that have served their purpose and are no longer useful, or that create Imbalance or Block within our Programing, will be Deleted by the process of deductive reasoning and scientific elimination.

Pattern Merge: subconscious self merging with conscious self. The Patterns that have been blocked in the subconscious will be recognized and will join the Conscious Patterns so that the individual can develop the Power Balance that was otherwise Blocked.

The Excelled Individual

The Excelled, by the nature of her or his existing Life Patterns is an ever-growing being in a constant process of rebirth, regeneration, and redefinition, unaffected by the limitations of a stagnant society or system. The Excelled lives by the rules of her/his private inner world which is shared by those possessing the same nature in their Patterns in an unlimited Universal Boundary of mind.

Paths, traces, and Programs of being Excelled: The path of an excelled is not a common path, it is a unique path chosen by those who find their Universal Self and follow the directions of the Power Balance of their bodies, their hearts, their minds and their souls. When we reach excellence we will feel, think, hear and see, differently, but amongst those whose road to excellence is a way of life, there is always patterns of commonality.

The lightness we feel when we wake up in the morning, awakening each day as if it is the first and last day of our lives:

treasured and fresh, like a flower that has been watered and nurtured all night. Like a prayer, blessed by the holly and wise.

The depth we feel as if we were born light years ago, when nothing had simply one dimension, nor did anything of quality ever seem alike. Like the depth of the ocean that deceives us with its lightness when we have only looked from the top. Only when we dare to experience do we realize that its depth can drown us within if we do not move with it, and become alike.

The curiosity, enthusiasm, and joy we feel about our day and how we will spend it; it feels as if we have been imprisoned all of our lives, and this is the first day of freedom to live, and to be alive.

Feeling with our outer eyes closed, and seeing everything with our inner eyes, is the ability to be everywhere anytime we want to be. This is another tool of Self-Discipline of the mind. The ability to consistently become whatever we want to become in our minds, and each time with a shorter preparation, will enable us to feel, think, and consequently materialize whatever we want.

The wisdom of the old, of those who have been flying free all of their lives, with the knowledge of all their rights and privileges as persons of honor and integrity, even in the midst of insanity. The clarity of their souls spreads non-selective compassion, placing them amongst the outnumbered members of humanity.

Clear, clean, holy, and human, we take every step as if the child and wise person within are hand-in-hand, sharing every decision and every experience that comes from that decision.

Power Balance of Cognition-Emotion. Recognizing that we don't have to be a stranger to our emotions if we are wise, and that we certainly can run wild with our emotions while holding them gently in our mind's sight, is the Power Balance of Cognition-Emotion.

Life is a treasured choice and not a burden. Life is a gift, and not a cheap, taken-for-granted burden we can do away with or waste in indulgences, addictions, and appearances of a living facade. It is a choice for living for that which is meaningful, and dying, when we have come to the end of our journey on this side of the pendulum, and have made a choice to move along.

Teaching not what we say, but what we feel, what we think and what we do, in harmony with what we think, what we feel, and what we do, unto ourselves and to others, equally. It is living by our own experiences, the consequences of those experiences, and the acceptance of those consequences as our own doing and no one else's.

Golden rules operate inside of you and you are not guided by rebellious obedience to the signs made by others, outside. Only the inner signs do you follow: the signs that will become the universal, cross-cultural, leading signs of humanity.

Freedom from preoccupation with details, and moving towards the expansion of your mind to a larger, bigger awareness, towards an openness of time, space and perception of what is real, freeing yourself from the facade, the pretense, and the societal agreed-upon appearance of reality.

Freedom from having to be free, from connections and obligations that bring honor. Freedom from the carelessness and lack of humanity, freedom from the pretense of being free to hurt others with pseudo-freedom, abusively untamed and without boundary.

A Universal Connection. It is the liberty to be at home anywhere, and to feel at home anywhere. With no need to have roots to verify your worth or to feel connected or clear.

Self-Discipline and Self-Motivation. It is the ability to work without needing authority to tell you what to do or push you to do it. What you do is directed from within; you are the authority, you are the motivation and it is you in the lead.

The ability to remain objective throughout both joyful and painful moments of a day, and to treasure all moments equally. There is a joy in pain that one will never find in mere joy that lacks the power to delay gratification, and have tolerance for pain. It is from pain that joy is created; without it there will be no gain.

Inner Ethics and Morality. It is going to bed with a clear and clean conscience every night, and having the ability to fall asleep quickly because you have done nothing wrong to leave you fearful of what will be.

Universal Spirituality. It is to love with compassion without selectivity, it is to honor all the children of humanity, it is to be a stranger to hate, and a friend to kindness and decency. And it is to be all that not just for the promise of chocolate, milk, and honey, nor for the fear of being punished and thrown out of the kingdom of supremacy. Doing anything out of fear deserves no reward, nor does it grant legacy. Universal Spirituality is to want to be kind and decent just for the sake of decency. It is to be color-blind; it is resistance to blind obedience to any authority.

Excellence: initiating Paths to create destiny. I believe that ninety percent of the people can help themselves avoid crisis and Excel in life. The other ten percent, who have either waited too long, or their cognitive and emotional abilities have been taken away from them by being abused or numbed by drugs, must get help from professionals. I believe that you are among the ninety percent. I believe in not only the intrinsic growth ability of anyone who is willing to search for his or her own truth, but also in the inner healing ability that is generated from such Patterns of Flexibility. You picked up this book. That makes you amongst those who will always initiate Patterns and Programs to become their own Programers and to create their own destiny.

Patterns of Change
Purifying the Spirit

Imagine. You are standing on the warm sands of an island. On each side of the island, you see forests and mountains and the unlimited blue color of the ocean. Above, the sun shines white and healing rays on your head and shoulders, going through you and filling your body with warmth. You feel weightless: one with the sand, one with the sun, one with the mountains, one with the forests, one with the ocean, and one with the person standing on the sand. Strong, vulnerable, clear, mysterious, thinking, feeling, caring, and loving, with an open mind and heart. Yes, imagine all that in this creative moment of togetherness with yourself and each other and everything and everyone and every thought and all knowledge that is out there for us to grab in an instant of need for another's shoulder, guidance, love, or nurturance.

Imagine. You are right alongside me as I take your hand into the chest of time where you can find everything there has been, everything there is, and everything there will be, all at your disposal. Can you tell me what you see and what you would grab to take with you to keep? Be assured that it is just that easy, my friend, to gain what you need from the collective unconscious and conscious, the Universal Power of Wisdom, Nurturance and Wholeness. Just pick up all that you need from the bag of time. Now close your eyes, take a deep breath, and imagine that you are as large as all that there is around you, above you, and below you. You are as grand as the magnificent grand, so grand that you can't see the beginning or the end. You can see, in your path of destiny, it is written: this is the path of my existence. Tell me, what do you see? And that, my friend, is the substantial sign to the path, the laws, and the facts. What we can see all of is too small and unchallenging for our unlimited mind that is only fulfilled and fed from the challenge of questions, of answers, and of the challenge of discovery.

Imagine, and in fact you might tape record this journey so that you can hear your voice in my words, so we can both close our eyes and travel lighter, much lighter, even lighter than we had intended to become, so we can feel more and see more of what was missing before in our back and front view, of the vehicle that is guiding us through the path, the channels of discovery. Just like all other vehicles of time, advanced by technology, we are moving rapidly and quickly. Isn't that wonderful? Know that we live in a country that has offered us the tools, the technology, the organization, the opportunity. Know that we have the freedom to leap beyond the restrictions imposed upon us by the rigid limitations of ignorance and hypocrisy.

Now, I want you, just like me, to go into the forest on your left hand side. Go right in. Get into the feel of the leaves underneath you and the **smell** of freshness and the noise of the birds and the look of the animals around you. You are, indeed, in a forest and so close that you all of a sudden might feel that you *are* the forest, with its magic and mystery and magnificence and yet down-to-earth, simple existence and presence. Feel...

Feel the forest, feel to be a forest and feel...how does it feel to be...a forest. This will give you a better feeling about a part of yourself that you have not discovered before. Every man and every woman has a forest within them that is undiscovered. Only searching, only questioning, only trying to find the mystic parts of the forest, will take us deep into ourselves. This is your chance to discover your forest. Get deeper and deeper into this experience.

Think about it. What have you got to lose except **hearing** some dead leaves around the edges as you find your way towards the light at the end, the far end of the forest? You can see the light and you can further progress towards the edgeless, limitless, endless body, mind, spirit of your own destiny.

Know. Did you ever know that you can be so open and so imaginative and creative with an experience like this? Or are you an old pro and find this exercise good only for amateurs? Either way, it will work perfectly for you. If you have not done this before, it will be the first of many better and deeper experiences. If this is simple for you, then move right into it; bring your past experiences right in and feel at home. Excellence is for those to reach who have already begun their journey. You are one who has chosen to be a part of the whole process of choosing your own path, molding your own clay and creating your own destiny.

Now, I would like you to put the image to your left, the image of the forest, to rest for a very short while until the next time you want to experience it by easily and purposefully looking to your left. Now, I would like you and I, as a joint experience, to look to your front; where you can see the mountains. Stand tall and feel the hard sand on the ground and look up right in front of you; the mountains are so magnificent. So powerful and so peaceful and so stable. Stand tall and feel the mountains around you, above you, under you and within you: solid and full, just the way you are and how you feel right now. It is wonderful flexibility that you are exhibiting by allowing yourself to take control.

Feel whatever you have ever wondered a mountain feels like. Expand your wings and get wide and even wider than you ever imagined you could get. I feel like I am trying to struggle to catch up to you. You, in silence, are reading my thoughts and the thoughts of others. You have the control of staying with me or leaving me without even rejecting me, without even letting me know. You do things so much smoother than I, and that motivates me to try harder to be able to fly with you. You are a good teacher and a good learner and I am happy that you are on this journey with me, my friend. Aloneness is a magnificent thing to feel. But loneliness, for you and I, has had its final time. I know that it has for me, and I see you with me right alongside, if not even further ahead, and that helps me to assess where you are.

This is quite serious for me and I assure you I didn't need to take any drugs, or drink anything, to get there, just as I know you don't have to. Distortion of the mind will only inhibit the boundaryless act of flying with natural wings, just like the eagles who fly farther than any bird. They can reach the top of the mountains and nest there until the day they die. For an eagle that has traveled to the top of the mountain, coming down, is not an option.

Now, look to your right for a moment and experience the ocean. The blue and clear water is clearer than our thoughts. Isn't it? Dive into the ocean and feel the cool and cleansing nature of this baptism of our mind and heart and being born into the different dimension of energy, thought, vision, and time. Be the water, be the sea, be the ocean. Move like the waves and make waves; yes, make waves. What is it, my friend? Are you wondering if you heard right? Had they told you, too, all of your life, "Don't make waves"? Well, we did say a new birth to a different time and energy and Patterns of thinking and Programing, of a new life, a new world, a new picture: a larger one with an ability to expand more and more, as much as we desire, and it is all up to us, each one of us. And isn't that wonderful?

Now, look above you and be the sun as you feel her shining all over you and be the rays that heat up and bring color to everything you touch and be all that you can and want to be right now because, my friend, this is your chance for today, and tomorrow, and the day after. This becomes much easier each time as you open your eyes to the world in the morning and close your eyes at night. Almost clock-like, you can count and repeat it all and repeat every new things that you want and add to this special experience. Even when you are watching television on a senseless and meaningless screen, or walking on the beach, or any experience that you are having at the time, you can become all of that and more as your eyes and mind expand to new dimensions of time and energy. More power to you, and more balance. Just remember, life is not only what you see out there. Life is what you feel and create inside, and then bring out for others to see; this you have seen and known, all along

Paths
to Power Balance

If one is selfless, what does one have to give? Those who are "selfless" have demanding, empty Selves who want others to fill their void, and hand them their souls. I will only trust one who has a Self and cares about that Self, for then he or she knows how to truly care for the Self in me. Besides, who would enjoy the burden of filling the empty vacuum of a selfless identity? I cannot accept responsibility for making another person happy; I can only promise to be happy with one who is able to be happy with me.

That is the toughest promise one can make, a promise only possible with the presence of an ever-existing and present Self.

When only one gives: Pattern of Imbalance. The splendor of love is when two people can love each other, and the moments we choose to love one, temporarily, over the other. Or when we choose to compromise, not the core of who we are, but the choice of paths that we would have crossed faster if we were not connected. And yet the process of sharing life with another, giving life to another, compromising the choices of paths we temporarily walk on, and doing so without losing ourselves, is what confirms our flexibility, our strength, and our individuality.

Everyone loves to give as well as receive. Only giving and never allowing ourselves to receive love denies the right of the other person to give equally. I know many people who have left relationships only because they did not have a chance to love the other. It is the most selfish and sabotaging act to deny another from loving us just as much as we love them. It is just as pleasurable to sing someone to sleep or give a back-rub, as it is to receive such indulgences of the heart. It is just as fulfilling to be seductive and to initiate lovemaking as it is to be seduced and made love to. It is as gratifying to compromise what is meaningful to us, as it is to know that there is a person in our life who would compromise the same for us. It is just as wonderful and comforting a sensation to be a mother to a child, as it is to be a child who is mothered.

Balance of inner silence and activity. We must balance our busy time spent in activity with our quiet time, meditating in inner silence. Just as it is significant to spend time in activities, it is just as important to meditate in an inner silence, alone. Silence is the quiet and unseen activity of the mind. What one can achieve in silence can never be achieved in activity. The paths of activity are chosen in silence.

The blessing of Patterns of Silence. Individual power lies in the ability to be alone and introspective with the Self: the silent mind, the all-knowing and quiet. The truth of every individual's existence can be seen in the nature of the silence that he or she is able to achieve. The closer we are to our true Selves, the more we become at peace, the more wisdom we cross, and the wider and clearer the paths we walk on. Only in the presence of silence can we have enough light to see the path we want to take. The purpose of activity is only to share our path with others.

One who avoids silence fears Self. When we have not faced ourselves, the thought of confrontation can be quite frightening. When we finally do confront ourselves in Silence, we become capable of confronting the world, with a voice.

Blessing of Silence, Blessing of Voice. That is why people who don't grant themselves the blessing of silence find themselves lost even in familiar paths, looking like they are moving forward, and yet going around a vicious cycle of life without knowing their destination or intent. An those who don't grant themselves the blessing of having a voice, will become a pawn to those who can shout loud and say nothing.

Ten

Tales
of Universal Excellence

The Power Balance

The tale of the lonely couple. A couple who looked as if life had left them long ago, came to see me. They were only going through the motions. Communication had stopped, both with themselves and with each other. They had stopped caring.

Life had lost its colors. Hope was felt only through the little envelope of donations they sent out every month to charity. I asked both of them what life was like for them. They both answered at the same time: "It is lonely." They had not felt the presence of themselves or each other for years. I gently said, "Your lives seems empty." They both nodded their heads, while trying to keep the tears that had appeared in their eyes from coming down their faces.

The process of Pattern Change. I asked them both in detail what it was like to have an empty life, and to tell me if they wanted to go on living the way they had been: dying. I asked them if they were planning to leave each other, and if they were thinking that without one another they would have a happier life. They were not sure, but knew that they were in pain. She was more ready to blame him for everything and leave. I told them both that unless they changed first from the inside, no matter where they went and who they went with, they would be lonely and empty. So they might as well give it a try with each other. In a two-hour session, that couple found what they had been missing for twenty-five years: their Selves.

Back to where he once felt joy. I asked him if he remembered anything that at some point in his life gave him joy. He could not remember easily, so I asked him to go back to his childhood. He saw himself at age seven, sitting on a bench playing guitar. I asked him how long had passed since he had played. He said, "Since I got married. She doesn't like it. It reminds her of her father who got drunk every time he played his guitar."

Recognition of Past Programing. I helped her to go back to her Past Programing and remember the pain she felt as a child, while never again forgetting that she was no longer a helpless child. The tears, the anger, the loss, and the release were all a part of the half-hour process of stepping back to the painful remembrances of childhood with the strength of an adult.

Going back in order to move forward. It is significant to go back for two reasons. On one hand, it is to leave the pain behind in the past, where it belongs, for others handed it to us by mistake. On the other hand, it is to bring back the joy we left behind as a result of numbing ourselves to the pain.

Children don't have selective-screening. Children cannot decide to leave the pain and take the joy, but adults who go back to the past with their inner child the second time around, can.

Selective path to her past. It is not necessary to go through tedious analysis half of our lives as I know many intelligent and creative people have, in order to find the root to the adopted or borrowed Patterns that we have dragged with us to our own lives. It takes a skilled coach, a guide, a Programer, and a Pattern Change creator to hold your hands, to lead you through the map, and to help you land right where you need, to pay another short, brief visit and say your final good-byes.

Key Pattern connecting her past to present. For her, it was the pain of having felt abandoned by her father, who had basically tuned the world out while letting her mother dominate her life. She felt the shame, embarrassment, guilt and abandonment common in children of alcoholics. She also felt betrayed because he let her mother take it all out on her. Her husband's guitar playing was to her the key Pattern that triggered all of her past, painful remembrances of her father and his pastime of playing his guitar and passing out drunk on the couch.

Back to where she once felt joy. I turned to her and asked her the same question: "When was the last time you felt joy?" She answered, "Our last dance at our wedding. We danced all night. I love dancing, but he has a bad leg and can't dance. He is always limping, and that goes for making love as well."

Selective path to his past. I asked him about his relationship with his mother. Experience had already taught me the shortcuts to the mystery of solving the sexual Imbalance Patterns of men. The root always goes back to the relationship with the mother, just as the root to sexual Imbalance Patterns of women can lead us to the father.

Key Pattern connecting his past to present. He remembered his mother as a domineering woman who overshadowed his passive and quiet father. He remembered that she always dragged his father and him to all the events and places they did not want to be involved in. More than anything, he remembered that when his father was absent, he would always feel a great deal of responsibility around the house. In ways, not conscious to him, he felt like he took his father's place when father was gone, even in matters that he was not capable of fulfilling.

Removing the dark shadows of the past. His mother was a very flirtatious woman, and flirted with him even more than she did with his father. He also remembered that she was against him having any girls in the house, and in one way or another they were never good enough. He felt tremendous guilt, and did not know where it came from. But when he married his wife and found her to be another domineering woman/mother, he could no longer go to bed and get excited without feeling the guilt of having sex with his own mother. That was how their sex life was carefully put on a shelf until they dealt with their past and removed its dark shadows out of their life.

Sometimes a cigar is just a cigar. Aside from all that, who would truly want to make love to a tyrant? Reality becomes clearer, and the people involved can communicate and Program the Patterns of their lives, once the shadows of Past Patterns disappear and let them see the light.

New Patterns of connecting. We focused on Communication Patterns, next, during which time I taught them the art and science of the Power Balance Patterns of connecting. How to talk to each other so they could be heard, how to look at each other so they could be seen, how to touch each other so they could be felt, and how to Program the time of their communication and loving relations so that they could both be ready for it. All of these will be discussed in detail in my upcoming book, *Patterns of Love.*

Compassion and passion: Power Balance of love. When people involved in relationships recognize that neither one are evil or at fault, and that they both have been victimized by the limitations of their Past Programing, they begin to relax and see each other as who they truly are. The anger, blame and Imbalance Patterns that once Blocked the Power they could give in loving each other disappears, and in its place comes a second chance to love. They begin to not only feel empathy for each other, but to feel once more, with all the power they felt in the past, their love for each other. When we have chosen our Patterns of relating consciously and freely, then the power of giving and receiving never ends, but circulates and regenerates itself each time we love.

The consciousness of our Patterns. I asked him if he could tolerate the pain of dancing if he could sit down and play guitar for half an hour before he danced with her. He was willing to try. They have been dancing at cafes all over the world, where he sometimes gets a chance to play his guitar. Their life, they say, "has had a new beginning," while they themselves feel as though they have been born anew.

Key to joy: having Self to celebrate with others. We feel the joy of life when we have ourselves to celebrate with others. He also admitted to me later on that he was afraid of losing her because she was so pretty and he always felt less than her. She, too, admitted the exact same fear. They both laughed at their own wild imaginations, while they learned how to utilize them for a more creative, intimate, everlasting and joyful life.

We fear being alone when we lack Self, within. Victor Frankel was a known Jewish writer and philosopher during the Holocaust. He was stripped of everything he had: his family, his security, his clothing, and his social dignity. He survived it all because, he wrote to the world, "They could not take my Self away from me." And it was having that Self, or the lack of it, that determined the destiny of the millions of people of a bright and intelligent race who were manipulated by the toxic, ignorant and distorted mind of their leader. No one can truly dominate us if we have a directed, consciously-Programed Self.

Disconnected and Imbalanced Self. Even in the midst of success and happiness borrowed from the pictures in popular magazines, when the Self we are inside is different from the Self we show to others, we are indeed alone.

Magic wand of true Self. I have had the privilege of meeting many people with their masks off; in those sacred moments, many have shared with me how frantically they went about life with the purpose of making money: enough money to be able to buy everyone. But the best moments of their lives were when someone financially down stayed around anyway for the sheer joy of seeing their true heart. After years of living a lonely life, with all the heads they had bought to serve them, one person was able to touch them with the magic wand of "true Self."The most powerful tool, far beyond any gimmicks and techniques, is the sheer presence of two wholly naked souls, without guilt, shame, or the need to justify the passion that flows like the magical dance of fire between them.

Tale of a successful man who had nothing

A man came to me who was successful by any standard. He was an extremely respected physician, married to homecoming queen of his high school. They had two beautiful children, lived on a mansion on a hill, and were invited to all the elite gatherings in town. His wife had sent him to my office because she felt he had not been himself since his best friend died a year ago of a stroke at forty-one, and it had begun to affect their sex life. This man was forty-five. He agreed that his friend's death had affected him severely. He kept saying: "And he had just started his life." He told me that his friend had just divorced his wife, liquidated his company, and was going sailing around the world. Just when he had it all, it was all taken away from him. Tears shed for others are for our own lost life. When I told this man that it was obvious to me that he was mourning his own lost life, after ten minutes of denial and sarcasm, he burst into tears. He told me his father had chosen his profession, he chose his wife to please his mother, he was a stranger to his children and he had a lover who was threatening to sue him and go to his wife if he didn't get a divorce and marry her. A lost soul has everything but the Self. Alienated from everyone, including himself, he had begun to abuse alcohol, which had started complicating the profession he had worked so hard to build. He was indeed a lost soul in the midst of success. He could not even begin to know who he was. After his friend died, he began a love affair that he didn't even enjoy. All he could see was a wasted life, and at that point, he was willing to lose it all in order to have a fresh start. He was too afraid to deal with his problems and was taking the easy way out. Unfortunately, the easy way always becomes the most costly in the long run.

Nothing good comes easily in life. Only bad deals are wrapped in silk stockings, being sold for a smile. It is never too late to change our lives. We must be prepared to pay the price for our mistakes as well as our successes. We need to recognize, analyze, take responsibility for our mistakes and choose change, before we can move forward. Mistakes are changeable. If we wait too long sometimes the consequences are not.

We need our true Selves in order to live true lives. Although the mistake of not developing his Self did not belong to him and was somebody else's mistake, he and the people he loved were paying for it. When we blindly go through life accepting other people's Programing as gospel, there will always be a time when we must come back to ourselves and begin again. We must come back with a clear and true Self: a Self that knows who we are and where we are going.

Others suffer when we don't have our Selves. This man's children had suffered emotionally from a great deal of sadness and confusion. Feeling like the family's situation was their fault, it had left them with a great deal of guilt too overwhelming for little children to handle. Their schoolwork suffered and they did not identify with other children because they were not as happy-go-lucky as children should be. They felt betrayed by both parents who seemed too burdened by their own soul-searching to be good adult parents. Just when they were beginning a life that should promise them joy and prosperity, they felt it was painful and unfair. Power Balance of Patterns of giving-receiving. Patterns of giving are only half of being a whole Self: the other half is within the Patterns of receiving. After a brief separation, during which time he and his wife dated while he spent his time understanding himself, he was able to reestablish a meaningful relationship with his wife. He discovered that he had a Self which enjoyed both giving and receiving.

Individual Power Balance and Excellence. After he was able to look at his Past Patterns and recognize the Addictive Patterns that from early-on in his life stemmed from a lack of adequate nurturance and deprivation of the love he needed, he was able to commit to Patterns of Prevention and Excellence that provided

Self-Discipline and freed him from indulgences that buried him in denial.

Family Power Balance and Excellence. Together, the couple reevaluated their roles, priorities and purposes in life, and looked at the Patterns of Relating they had developed with each other as a result of the handed-down belief systems that were no longer working for them. They spent time with their children to help them understand that what was happening was not their fault, and to help them feel loved and secure. Since my client had his own Self to share with his loved ones, there was much to identify with, to understand and to love.

The miracle of life. A miracle had taken place. He was able to salvage what he had lost in his endless efforts to make a person happy whom he did not even know: himself. The man behind the title of Chief of Staff, a title which meant nothing to him since he did not like or believe in his career until it was he who decided to remain as a doctor; the man who did not own the passion he truly felt for his wife; and the man who felt so neglected inside that he did not know how to love the inner souls of his own children. This man was given a second chance at a new life.

Rebirth: a second chance at a new life. He began a new life based on his true Self: a Self he himself Programed by making clear choices in his Patterns of Relating. He became a Self separated from the past mistakes of others, committed to the responsibility of a life of freedom and joy. Today, he is living happily with his two children and wife, who has also undergone her own process of Pattern Change to meet him halfway, in a path of Power Balance with joy and mastery.

Tale of a woman
who feared her power

One of my interns turned her client over to me and told me that she had been seeing this woman for two years and just could not do anything for her. The client, I was told, had no problems, and her life was perfect.

Physical problems become secondary gains. She did however, have Chronic Fatigue Syndrome previously known as Epstein Barr. An athlete who had always played tennis, she now could barely walk or have enough energy to do anything. Life had become colorless and she felt very empty and sad. Her poor husband was a bit more nurturing towards her and was coming home from work early to take over so she could rest.

When a guide must be whole. My intern could not possibly help this young woman for one reason. She herself was in denial of a marriage that she was very angry about, and a Self she was very frightened to feel. She too, experienced arm pains every time she talked about a divorce that was on the way. And she, too, was terrified of not looking perfect.

Repeating a safe story. When I saw my new client, it was the same story at first: a perfect life with everything she could dream of, yet she felt energyless, depressed and paralyzed. She spoke highly of her husband, her parents, her child, her house and their dog. She just complained that she missed playing tennis, and had neither the energy nor the strength in her legs to even walk.

Numbing the symptom. She felt that it was all her fault that her relationship had become troublesome. She was on all kinds of medication from her doctors and was on antidepressants from her psychiatrist who, other than refilling her prescription, hardly talked to her. It was not easy. Every time she came to see me, it seemed like she had no power left to talk. I couldn't blame her. Even an elephant would fall into a deep sleep if given all those drugs.

Breaking the denial. I told her that things she had told me didn't add up but that I respected her perception of her life. History had shown me that anytime there is such a handicap for an individual, the rest of the family not only suffers from the pain involved, but they also share, equally, the problem.

Permission to feel the Suppressed Patterns. I told her that there must be something or someone she feels a great deal of anger towards other than herself. I told her that almost everyone I know who is paralyzed in one way or another has a great deal of suppressed anger inside. I gave her permission to feel something that was obviously frightening to her. Yet she didn't think my analysis applied to her.

Acknowledging Patterns of Strength. I play a bit of tennis for the pure joy of it. So I began talking to her about the times that she played tennis and the joy and energy that was created in her by just showing up with her tennis clothes at the court. Her face lit up and, for the first time in the two years that my intern had seen her, her voice lost its monotonous pattern of saying little with no feelings attached.

Remembering her power. She began to describe to me how she played, and how wonderful she felt after each game, having so much energy that she would swim hours afterwards. But she felt that those times were over.

Finding cues to remind her of her lost strength. I asked her to start swimming. The next time she came in, she had swam and had a bit more energy. I told her it was time she grew up and face her anger so that she could become a better wife, mother and, once again, the wonderful person she used to be. Her fear had lessened.

Recognizing Past Patterns and their Programers. She started with her mother, whose dominance had cast a shadow over her life, and her father, who would not support her or save her from her mother's cruelty.

Connecting Patterns of Cognition to pain. After some work towards getting her anger out of her body and into the story that belonged to her past, she began telling me about her husband's affair three years ago and the devastating impact on her feelings about herself and their relationship.

Habitual Repetition of Past Programing. She had lost trust of herself and her husband, and had begun to backlash her mother's negative messages of her worthlessness and the fact that no one would love her. When her husband began having an affair as a result of her withdrawal from marriage and preoccupation with social friends, she had proven her self-fulfilling prophecy; she was truly not lovable.

Tearing down for the purpose of rebuilding. She confronted her husband, who was more than happy to have an angry wife rather than a dead wife, and they began to rebuild on a stronger foundation; a foundation that had two clear and strong Selves as the pillars of their lives.

Power Balance. Their child, who was hyperactive because he carried all the denied emotions of the family, began to calm down. She began to help her husband at their company, and helped him get used to the idea of having a powerful wife who was a partner instead of a burden he had to carry. He himself had a problem with this until he, too, confronted his own past Patterns of being intimidated by his domineering mother, resulting in him trying to dehumanize his wife and make sure she would not hurt him; to do so, he hadn't let her be a part of the company and, on top of that, had an affair.

Towards Spiritual Excellence; Universal Law of Mind-Body. She was no longer in any kind of physical pain or handicap, and had begun playing tennis once a week with her friends and on the weekends with her husband. They sold their lucrative business and moved to their hometown because they no longer needed the glitter of the big city of Los Angeles. All they seemed to care about was their love and compassion for each other that flourished all over again, and for providing a peaceful life for their children.

Instant Forest
amidst maddening crowd

A client came to me the other day, confused and restless. She immediately told me: "I am lost. I am so lost in this crowded and confusing world. I want to get away. I want to run away where there is no one." I felt her pain and confusion. I had nothing to tell her in denial of her reality, for it was real to her. In a way, the world out there, the crazy cars and the crazy drivers, the drunken people coming out of the bars, and the whole scene even in the respectful city of Newport Beach I live in, the town of conservatism and family values, just did not seem like anything to brag about. So, her reality, in fact, was a reality of mine, except that I was able to see the beauty and the wonders of life amidst the maddening crowd. All she needed was the tools, to do the same. I looked around the room. I needed to calm her down. And yet just telling her that, or even in a superficial manner having her close her eyes and count down from ten, has never been my style. I always have many fresh flowers in my office to keep me sane. I looked to the flowers and stared at them. I waited long enough to distract her attention from her frustration with the rush of traffic and her heart that was still beating quickly and noticeably. She looked in the direction of my eyes, and she too, stared at the flowers. And I began to calmly talk to her as we stared at the flowers, together. "See these flowers? Aren't they beautiful? Look at all the colors you see in just one bunch. Smell the fragrance of the roses and the tropical flowers that have filled the room with their essence. These flowers are my cue to remember the forest that I am at the moment so far away from, only in vision. But in reality, it is right here in this room with us. For a *part* of something has the qualities of the *whole*. These flowers are the wildlife we treasure every day of our lives. They are the little forest within this room, and in all of us. Pay attention to each petal, to each color, to each thorn, and to each leaf; aren't they the forest you want to run away to, coming to you in a different form? Pay attention: you will see what you want to see. The picture of the forest is already in your mind and heart; your mind and heart is that forest that you want to travel to, and that you are away from. Pay attention to each flower, to each petal, to each leaf, every time you miss the forest you have inside is that you are looking so far away for: the forest that you are never truly away from. Pay attention."

To read is an adventure, I have found, far more adventurous than to travel. When we read, we can see things from so many perspectives different from our own. I never forget when I was eleven and read the *Adventures of Oliver Twist*. We can learn so much by focusing within. And we can learn even more, by observing and reading about the evolving change of patterns in others, their joinery to places we have never been; where someone else leads the way to search and to find Self, there are many dimensions of Self we can begin to find within, just by traveling between the lines, and read the unwritten chapters, creating our own adventurous page.

Tale of the woman who slept with the devil

I looked to my client. She was calm and peaceful, deep into the forest pictured in her mind. She is very dear to me, for she has returned from sleeping with the devil, and she has brought with herself a pair of wings to fly. When she began to see me, it was forced by her husband who was in a great deal of pain. He watched his beloved wife stay out every night dancing nude in bars and coming home several hours later than even the street sweepers who woke him up just in time to wipe his tears before his wife showed up.

Pattern Search, Observation, Analysis. She would sit in her chair and tell me: "Make me change, no one can." I was much younger then, more arrogant in thinking I could change the world by reaching the families, the nucleus of the society one by one, and had far more energy to waste on someone who did not want to change, and did not believe in change. She was to become "the madam of neighborhood and make a lot of money." And I did not stop her. I believed that if I did not guide her to have the choice of becoming who she wanted to become, then any choice she would make in life would not be genuine. I told her I would help her get what she wanted and succeed without having to sell her soul. She laughed. To her, everything was up for sale to the highest better.

She swung the pendulum from being a low class go-go dancer to having the opportunity to become a high class businesswoman, and she turned it down. For she also had learned, through her process of the *Change of Patterns,* that the inner core of her existence was a beautiful flower; the thorns were only there so that others would not hurt her or take away her chance to bloom.

She had been victimized in childhood, having been taken away from her country in the middle of the war, and having been given an instant family with a father whom she felt intruded upon by, a real father who left her mother, a mother who was cold as ice, and no root to her existence but what she could dig up. Her husband had directed her towards becoming a dancer in bars, setting her up to challenge his own evil, or innocence. He had told her it would either make or break their relationship. Having come from an abusive family, he had his own mountains to climb.

Sexual Ambivalence leads to Patterns of domestic violence. He was ambivalent, sexually, and as the shades of this pattern, chose promiscuity. But nonetheless he was possessive and passionate towards his bride. We have seen many of the kind in the news where their fear of intimacy turns to anger towards women becoming the causal effect of treating them as objects, turning to uncontrollable patterns of relating. He was lucky, he unveiled his, and changed the toxic patterns that lead to destruction of one or the other in many relationships. Many deny it until it is too late. He was also able to utilize the toxic power in its power balance of creativity and Self-Expression. Gaining a more clear self, he let go of many patterns of the past, prospered financially and emotionally, in a mind-body spirit connection.

Patterns of Imbalance and Block. You name it, she had it. Resistance, denials, rebellion towards her own happiness and health and a mean streak that wanted to corrupt everyone and take them down right along with herself. She was promiscuous, but felt frigid inside. She was beautiful, but anyone who touched her, including her husband, had to pay a heavy price. She hated her husband, but was intimidated by him. She felt victimized by him, but ran after him with a knife. At times, she did not know if she was a man or a woman. She was not sure if she was feeling victimized or if the bullies were her victims: the oppressed dimension within her. She felt suicidal, full of guilt and self-hatred, but she was splashing it onto others, for she felt that everyone in the world, including me, was a fraud.

Teaching her boundary, self-worth, and self-love. Working with her and just surviving her toxicity was the toughest challenge I have ever had, and I have had many challenges in my life. She later admitted to me how hard she had tried to make me feel miserable and bring me down from the pedestal she herself had put me. Being flexible enough to create Pattern Transference on both sides so that I could transfer Patterns of Morality, Decency, Ethics, Responsibility, and Boundary to her, and at the same time allow her to transfer all her Patterns of Projection, Anger, and Self-Hate onto me, without losing the grace of relating, was scientific mastery, not just an art.

Pattern Change: a rebirth. I have guided many clients to gain power and wealth beyond their beliefs. Even her husband has gained much success, although he was once a frightened child with outstanding ambition, tremendous creativity and talent, and a thick shell of denial and fear. But she has not earned much fame or money. In fact, she has turned down lucrative jobs, for she is on a special journey of self-discovery.

Beneath layers of pain turned into anger, is a pure flower. Today, she looks back at her past corruptions and cannot recognize the Patterns of Inhumanity that seemed so ingrained within her. She has been learning many other techniques of cleansing her soul, and plans to polish herself even more in order to become a healing entity. And for me, it was all worth it the day that she told me she was so happy that I was as strong as I was. For it was my persona, strength and boundary that were the keys to her Pattern Change Programing. She proved to me, once more, that beneath all the layers of pain turned into anger and hate, there is always a flower ready to blossom, a flower inherently good and pure.

Glossary

Balance Patterns: Patterns of being that honor and value the multidimensional nature of the universe. Examples of Balance Patterns are Patterns of Process and Goal Orientation, Patterns of Cognition - Emotion, Patterns of Strength and Vulnerability.

Block Patterns: Equivalent to denial. Patterns that interfere with the flow of power between two Balance Patterns, between a Pattern and the core of individual, between individuals, between individual and society, or between leaderships, globally. These include Power Blocks, Power Abuse, Power Jam and Power Neglect.

Chain Effect: A series of patterns that is caused by power struggle in the patterns of the mind and body. The mind is chained to the past and to outdated rules, while the body pulls away to be free.

Chain Theory: When an individual is chained to the past with outdated myths and inhibiting patterns of thinking, the body pulls away to set free. This creates the boundaryless society: a Chain Effect Pattern of the mind-body.

Change Agents: Either the individuals or the environment they create within and around themselves that provides the necessary tools for Pattern Change to occur.

Evo-revolution: *The evolutionary process of power balance and wholeness in being with the revolutionary tools of a scientific mind Pattern Change Programing and Power Balance Therapy, science(the advancement of the mind) and wisdom (the oldness* *of the spirit) work together in creating harmony within and without.*

Excellence: A way of being in the world that connects with the multidimensions of our humanity and the harmony and clarity of our Self that comes from living in Patterns of Power Balance and beyond.

Existential Patterns: Patterns of existence inherent within all individuals. A common core of knowledge embedded within our Self from birth which include Existential Power, health, clarity and the existential reality. Included are: Existential anger, existential reality.

Imbalance Patterns: Patterns of being that are not in harmony with the core of the individual. These are Patterns that can paralyze a person from functioning fully or living fulfilling lives. Examples include Procrastination, Jealousy, Envy, Perfection and Need to Control.

Inhumane Patterns: Patterns that harm others, and society.

Mirror Effect: Projection (mirroring)of our thoughts onto others.

Multidimensionality: The essence of Power Balance Theory. The knowledge, appreciation and celebration of humanity as a multifaceted being made up of the interconnectedness of science, philosophy, psychology, enviro-psychology, psycho-physiology, Universal Spirituality (humanity).

Patterns: A series of processes and movements existing within an individual that create the presentation of the behavior we ***observe.***

Pattern Change Programing: The method of creating Power Balance and Excellence based on the principles of Power Balance Theory. Through brief, targeted analysis of the past, Imbalance and Block Patterns are deleted and replaced with tools to develop Success, Prevention and Excellence Patterns.

Pattern Search: Objective and selective analysis of our past and present in order to arrive at a clear understanding of the Patterns we possess By understanding the roots behind them and the

Programers involved in creating them, we can make a clear choice of their purpose in our lives, and whether to save or delete them.

Power Balance Initiation: The process of deleting adopted, old programs, creating Self Programs, thereby gaining independence of thought and action.

Power Balance Theory: A philosophical and multidimensional approach to achieving Excellence as individuals, in societies, and humanity as a whole. The techniques and method for creation of Power Balance and Excellence is the science of Pattern Change Programing.

Power Balance Program: A natural inherent state of being where an individual is in harmony with all inner patterns of Self and the environment. A balance between the innate dimensions that coexist within each individual creating harmony and power balance within self and with others, inner peace, creativity and excellence.

Power Chaos Theory: The theory that order stems from chaos, thus order must welcome chaos as its catalyst and precursor.

Prevention Program: Patterns that can be programed that will prevent crisis stemming from Power Blocks and Power Imbalances from developing. These can be programed both in childhood and adulthood.

Programs: Paths modeled and taught by significant influences in our lives. Examples include: Power Imbalance Program, External Focus Program and Power Balance Program.

Programers: Individuals, institutions, organizations or any entity that has significant influence in shaping individuals life patterns. i.e. parents, teachers, role models, societal leaders.

Programing: The process of inputting thoughts, emotions, ideas, values and beliefs consciously or unconsciously into an individual which creates life patterns. These can be either Imbalance and Block Patterns or Power Balance and Excellence Patterns.

Psycho-Universal Spirituality: A non-selective compassion for all that exist in the universe, spiritual principles and patterns of guidance chosen by deductive reasoning and scientific analysis of right or wrong, and recognition of the collective universal wisdom and nurturance available to us, all.

Roozeh: A physical fast, helping individuals overcome addictions.

Societal Power Balance: A state of civil evolution where equal regard is given to all persons and equal knowledge and opportunity are available to all.

Sokoot: A mental fast, where an individual engages in periods of silence, healing emotional and mental addictions.

Toxic Patterns: Create toxicity within the individual and society. Examples include Patterns of Hatred, Prejudice, and Rigidity.

Universal Law. The Universal Paternal and Maternal Power Balance of Wisdom and Nurturance within and around us.

Universal Mind-Body -Spirit Prayer: Hymns to our inner soul, inner Self, inner music in silence while creating movements that stem from our inherent balance connected to the Universal Parental Power around us.

Universal Parental Power: Union between the Universal Paternal Power of Wisdom and Universal Maternal Power of Nurturance.

Universal Pendulum Theory: The idea that the entire universe is in a constant natural process of swinging from life to death, dark to light and hot to cold. This swing unfolds universal laws governing all living things and provides us with the universal knowledge of the truth necessary to heal ourselves.

Universal Self: An individual free of self-limiting discrimination and toxic programing, and at one with the inherent goodness, nurturance and wisdom of the universe.

Universal Spirituality (Patterns of humanity): non-selective compassion and connection one feels for the universe, including the environment, people and the spirits flowing among us.

To Our Children
Creators of Tomorrow

This is my legacy that I leave to my children,
Shaun and Ellie,
whose inherent inner wisdom
and clarity has created nurturance
and abundance of compassion
within me,
not only for them, but for my Self,
and for the entire race of humanity.
The meaning of life, has become clear
only by the Power Balance,
of our existence
of our togetherness,
and of our separateness,
of our sameness,
and of our differentness.
I have experienced life,
on both sides
of the Universal Pendulum,
through their vision.
I see my children
within me, beside me,
and most often,
beyond me,
in my ever-changing
Patterns, that are
Programed towards the
ever-growing mission
to clean the air
from toxins of all nature
so that all our children
can breathe, comfortably,
in an environment of
peace, progression,
and Universal Harmony.

1995 Book Release List
Rose Assier Parvin

Rose Assier Parvin
A Reformed Western Psychotherapist

BOOK ORDER BY MAIL
Send your order to:

BOOK ORDER BY PHONE OR FAX
(714) 723-5748

UNIVERSAL PUBLISHING COMPANY PO BOX 15424, NEWPORT BEACH, CA 92659

Please send me _____ copy(s) of:

Bk#1	Pattern Change Programing: Creating Your Own Destiny (Hardcover, 768 pages.)	$70
Bk#2	Answer to Humanity: Reclaiming Individual Power and Dignity	$29
Bk#3	Power Balance Therapy: An Evo-Revolutionary Psychology of Being	$15
Bk#4	Programing Excellence: Individual Power Balance	$15
Bk#5	Humanity Held Hostage: The Day America Cried	$15
Bk#6	Preventive Family Therapy	$15
Bk#7	Beyond Patterns	$15
Bk#8	Self-Programer: the path of living, loving, healing and excelling	$15
Bk#9	Pattern Changes	$15

Videotapes_____ for Bk# _____ ask for brochure

I am enclosing $ _____________

Audiotapes_____ for Bk# _____ ask for brochure

Total $ _____________

Free copy of "SELF-PROGRAMER" monthly newsletter with my purchase _____.

NAME ____

ADDRESS ____

CITY _____________________ STATE _____________ ZIP _____________

CHECK _____ VISA _____ MASTERCARD _____ # _____________________

SIGNATURE _____________________ EXP. DATE _____________